84
Ribbons

84
Ribbons

Paddy Eger

Tendril Press
AURORA, COLORADO

Reach for
your goals!

[signature]

Published by Tendril Press™
www.tendrilpress.com
PO 441110
Aurora, CO 80044
303.696.9227

ISBN 978-0-9858933-2-3

Library of Congress Control Number: 2013943617

10 9 8 7 6 5 4 3 2 First Publishing: 2014

Author Photo by: Yuen Lui
www.YuenLuiStudio.com
Lynnwood, WA
425.771.3423

Cover Photo by shutterstock.com:

Art Direction, Book Design and Cover Design
© 2008. All Rights Reserved by
A. J. Images Inc. Business Design & Publishing Center
www.AJImagesinc.com — 303•696•9227
Info@AJImagesInc.com

To all who love ballet.
May it fill your heart and soul with joy

Dance is the hidden language of the soul.

— Martha Graham

 $\mathscr{M}$ arta circled the narrow corridor outside the Olympic Hotel's Grand Ballroom. She shook out her hands and adjusted her leotard again, pulling the leg bands out and letting them snap against her tights. After ten years of lessons, recitals, and training, today's audition would decide her future.

The ballroom door opened. A slender man dressed in black leaned out. "Hello, girls and boys. I'm Damien Black. Hand me your audition paperwork and pin on the number I give you. We'll begin shortly."

Marta pinned on number seventeen, her age. A bit of good luck? If you believed such a thing. Today would be the final test. She'd received no call backs or invitations to join the ballet companies from earlier auditions. Feedback would have helped, but they only sent rejection letters.

Miss Holland, her dance teacher, worked with her before and after each audition, helping her iron out small problems with lengthening her arm extensions and improving her timing. Now audition season ended. Ballet companies moved forward to settle into new seasons. She'd given each audition her best. Today provided one last chance.

Five minutes passed before Damien Black opened the door and signaled the dancers into the ballroom. "Form a line," he said.

Judges sat at two long tables. As the lines formed, they began pointing to dancers, whispering to each other and writing on the audition applications.

Marta stood in fifth position and finger-combed her curly brown bangs, pressing them against her forehead. Her heartbeat hammered in her ears as she portioned out a performance smile and swallowed hard to calm herself.

She glanced to either side. Every dancer remained statue still. She lifted her rib cage and tightened her back muscles to control her twitching. How could the judges possibly write so much before any dancing began?

After they lowered their pens, a petite, wrinkled woman rose from the table. Her red lipstick clashed with her pink blouse and her blue eyeliner. She leaned heavily on a carved wooden cane as she spoke. "I am Madame Cosper, director of the Intermountain Ballet Company. With me are Damien Black, ballet master, along with Mrs. Scott and Mrs. Zachary, distinguished ballet patrons."

Madame Cosper's harsh voice, narrow face, and odd outfit matched the directors at her previous auditions. All taught with such intensity, so unlike her dance teacher back home who smiled all the time. At least Damien Black acted friendly enough.

Madame Cosper thrust her chin forward and squinted. "Today's audition will assess seven elements including basic style, floor exercise form, your ability to quickly learn choreography, rhythmic sense, interpretation of the *Sleeping Beauty* waltz as a group performance *and* as a solo, in addition to your prepared solo." She made an abrupt turn to point her cane like a sword. "You, number six. Get rid of that gum!"

A low chuckle spread through the assembled dancers as the gum chewer deposited his wad in a nearby trash can and returned to the line.

"Quick, quick!" Madame's voice reminded Marta of a drill sergeant. "Spread out. Six people to a *barre*. We don't have all day!"

Marta wiped her damp hands on her leotard before she took hold of the cold metal *barre*. She shook out both legs and stood ready to begin. Why, after years of dancing, did she continue to feel nervous?

"Let's begin. First position, and one, two, three, and four."

The pianist, seated to one side of the room, shifted from background music to *barre* exercise music in 4/4 time. Marta kept her free arm curved, pulled her spine straight, and tucked in her derrière as she lowered into a first position *demi-plié* and rose. She repeated her movement, this time dropping into a *grand plié* before she rose onto *pointe*, held her *relevé* four counts, then lowered her body to a neutral stance. Next, she moved to a *plié* in second position.

"Number three, you're dropping your arm," Madame said. "You, boy number ten, tuck your shirt into your tights. Ack! Sloppy. Pay attention, boys and girls. Remember, *barre* exercises are part of your evaluation."

Miss Holland had taught Marta that the trick at auditions meant dancing well without standing out. After all, *corps de ballet* dancers performed as background until they earned solos. Even so, Madame Cosper expected perfection.

After *barre* exercises, the hopefuls moved to floor exercises. Marta stood between two blondes with perfect ballet bodies, perfect arms, and perfect hair. She fingered her curly mop and sucked in her bottom lip as she watched and listened to Madame's directions. Previous ballet company judges appreciated her flowing arms, lyrical head movements, and precise footwork. Would that be enough to compensate for her difficulty remembering long sequences of choreography?

Half an hour later, while the dancers rested in fifth position, Madame paced and explained the group audition piece. "We'll teach you a waltz from *Sleeping Beauty*, a portion of our fall program. You'll dance it three

times: the first two as rehearsals, the third we'll score as your group performance evaluation."

Madame walked through the steps, moving her hands to demonstrate
foot movements like Miss Holland and other instructors did. She barked
the combinations over and over as the hopefuls executed the steps.

After twenty minutes of practicing she said, "Stop. We'll begin your
two rehearsals now." She nodded to the pianist.

Marta's insides tingled. She touched her mom's necklace that hung
on a silver chain beneath the neck of her leotard imaging her mother's
presence. As the music began, she took a refreshing breath and glided
into the waltz.

Balancé, balancé, relevé, dip, *bourreé* left, *boureé* right, repeat, repeat. The crescendos and orchestrated hesitations pulled Marta into the
music. She executed each step, adding elongated flourishes to show her
ability to finish each move before beginning the next.

Madame clapped to emphasize the beat. She mouthed the steps, then
marked an agitated beat with her cane against the wooden floor.

"Stay on the count, boys and girls. Lift higher, extend your arms."

When the second rehearsal ended, the dancers leaned forward, pant-
ing and resting with their hands on their knees.

"Adequate. I see little evidence of happiness. This is a waltz. Show
your joy. Finish every move before you begin the next."

Well, at least I did *that* right, Marta thought.

"Now, begin the scored waltz."

Marta adjusted her leotard and began, completing each combination
of steps. For the turns, she focused on a spot above the judges' heads,
lifted her rib cage, and whirled around and around, elevating her arms
to improve her balance. As the piece ended, she bowed and held the
pose. Thank heavens she'd avoided crashing into the guy who threw his
arms around like a fish out of water. He was all over the dance space,

causing a number of near misses. No one needed or wanted that kind of attention.

"Mediocre at best." Madame scowled as she paced before the judges' table. "It's a quarter after eleven. Return by a quarter of one, sharp. We've allotted each of you ten minutes for performing this dance and your solo. We'll post your audition times on the door. Mark the beginning for your solo music distinctly. Leave it in the box by this door with your audition number clearly printed on the top. Dismissed." Madame pounded her cane one last time, then pointed its black-cushioned tip toward the exit.

Like Marta, every dancer wore a sheen of sweat. She wondered if any of them shared her concern of remembering the performance piece after so few rehearsals. She began a silent walk through, marking the location of each step and the position of her arms.

"You! Number seventeen," Madame Cosper said. "What are you doing?"

"Walking through the waltz, Madame".

"Move along. The judges need to meet without your snooping."

"Yes, Madame." Marta scooted out of the room in time to see dancers dressed in street clothes heading out the door in clutches of two or three. Traces of laughter lingered as the exit slid closed. A few mothers dressed in tailored suits herded their daughters and sons toward the hotel's formal dining room. Ugh. How could anyone eat during auditions?

Marta stowed her ballet shoes and slipped a flowered jumper over her leotard. She exited the hotel and headed downtown, treating herself to a quick window shopping tour along Seattle's posh Fifth Avenue.

The August sun soothed her damp, tired body as she strolled north along the gently sloping street. She remembered the waltz movements and hummed the music as she passed two theaters: the Music Box and the Coliseum. She completed a simple turn as she stopped to read the coming events posters.

Since the age of ten, she'd hoped to be a prima ballerina with a prestigious ballet company like Ballet Russe or Sadler Wells. She saw herself performing in Seattle, dancing perfectly with flowing arms and effortless turns. Her partner's skills would showcase their ability to dance in unison. Together they'd be honored with half a dozen bows before she received a bouquet of purple roses.

The street noise brought her back to where she'd stopped. She walked on. Window dressers worked on mannequins, removing the flowered tops, colorful swimsuits, and big beach hats like she'd seen in the summer issue of *Seventeen*. Autumn plaids, fitted wool jackets, and brown penny loafers lay nearby. Breezy summer fashions of 1957, like her carefree life, changed before her eyes. Next month she'd either be dancing for a ballet company or looking for a job. Both prospects scared her.

Back in the ballroom hallway, Marta placed her sheet music in the designated box and read the notice attached to the door: *Stay quiet. Do not leave as the order may change. Be prepared to dance five minutes before your assigned time.*

Her name appeared fourth. Perfect! She'd ride the ferry home in time to go to the dance studio and share her audition with her mom and Miss Holland.

She paced the hall but kept watch as dancers entered the ballroom. She listened as their music started and stopped. As each dancer exited, none glanced sideways or spoke to the others. A handful of hovering parents wandered the hallways, trailing dancers, asking, "Well?"

A twinge of sadness settled in. Sign-up week at the dance studio back home kept her mom too busy to come to Seattle. Previously she'd driven Marta to and from auditions. They'd discuss the judging and make predictions on the outcome. So far they'd been wrong. Marta had not been offered a position. Maybe going alone was best. Wearing her necklace, loaned for this occasion, kept her mom close but gave Marta a chance to take charge of herself.

The hall clock read one-thirty. Ten minutes before her audition began. Marta straightened her practice skirt and completed her warm-ups. She mentally danced her selection one last time and took deep breaths to quiet the gathering butterflies.

Damien Black opened the door. "Mr. Dankin? Miss Sel, Sel-birth?"

Marta smiled and stepped forward with the other dancer. Her turn began in minutes. Why had he called two names?

He ushered Mr. Dankin into the ballroom and stepped into the hall. "We've changed the dance order," Damien said as he scanned the list. "You'll be last."

Her insides dropped like an elevator moving from the top floor in the Bon Marche to the bargain basement. She gritted her teeth and nodded; her skin warmed like she'd stepped into a furnace. Now she'd be wandering the hall for more than three hours. She wanted to scream. Instead, she dropped a dime in the pay phone and dialed.

"Good afternoon, Holland Dance Studio. This is Elle."

"Hi, Mom."

"What's wrong, honey?"

Marta explained the change of schedule while attempting to stay calm.

"You know what they say; save the best for last."

"I hope you're right."

"Keep your spirits up," Her mom said. "You're a talented dancer."

"Thanks, Mom. I'd better get back. See you at home."

The hour hand crawled around the clock as one by one dancers entered and exited the ballroom. She stretched, replayed the dances in her head, and paced the corridor.

At a quarter of five the music inside the ballroom stopped once again. She swallowed hard, retied her black practice skirt, and fingered the trickle of sweat above each ear. The ballroom door opened. Could the exiting dancer hear her heart pounding like a snare drum?

Damien scanned his clipboard. "Miss Sel-birth?

Marta followed him into the ballroom. Light flooded one section of the polished floor. The judges watched her stop to rosin her *pointe* shoes.

"This is Miss Sel-birth," Damien said. "After the group waltz she'll dance "The Sugar Plum" from Tchaikovsky's *Nutcracker*." He turned to Marta. "When you're ready, signal the pianist."

Marta moved past the judges to stage right. She positioned herself, nodded to the pianist, and waited for her musical cue.

The waltz music rushed through her, filling her with energy. She moved from one side of the room to the other, letting the music overtake her thinking. Each step automatically blended into the next. Her arms remembered every position and nuance.

During her dozen dizzying *pirouettes*, she slipped once, but covered the slip with a tiny hop. As she ended the selection, she held her pose for five seconds, then straightened to fifth position and watched the judges mark her evaluation form. The pianist sat quietly, waiting to play her individual piece. Back at the Bremerton studio, she'd walk in circles to relax; during an audition, such actions underscored an unprofessional dancer.

Madame squinted and set down her pen. A scowl ran from her brow to her chin in one long crease that sideswiped her nose. She spoke to Damien, then both resumed writing.

"You may begin your personal selection," Damien said.

Marta moved to stage left. When the *Nutcracker* music began, she became the sugar plum fairy, gliding through each measure. As her solo neared the end, she adjusted her tension and took a deep breath. Her *relevé* to *pointe* prepared her to hop forward, using her flowing arms to distract her audience of judges from the strain of bearing her body weight on the tip of one *pointe* shoe.

When the pianist played the last chord, Marta held her ending pose, again for five seconds, while she slowed her breathing through semi-closed lips. After curtsying, she straightened, collected her music from the pianist, and stood before the judges.

Minutes passed. She relaxed, moving from exhilaration to total fatigue. Madame's face wore a stony glare of displeasure; maybe she preferred the alternate choreography with head whipping *fouetté* turns. As the other judges finished writing, they shared impersonal smiles with Marta.

Damien's head popped up. "Did you take all your training in Bremerton?"

"Yes."

"What traditional ballet solos and ensemble pieces have you danced?"

"I've danced "The Sugar Plum," as well as many *Nutcracker* character dances. I've also performed several sections from *Sleeping Beauty* and *Swan Lake*, including the cygnets."

"Ah, yes, the swans. Any others?" he asked.

Marta's mind went blank. "Ah, didn't I write them on my form?"

"No."

Madame Cosper tapped her pen while staring at Marta.

"Let's see. I did a solo from *La Sylphides* and … Miss Holland created a solo for the music of *Clair de Lune*."

"Show us," Madame said.

"I didn't bring the music for either one."

Madame nodded to the pianist. He began playing *Clair de Lune*.

Marta walked to one side and posed. The pianist nodded and began again.

The beginning *relevé* to *pointe* followed by a *développé* transitioned into *bourees* diagonally across the room. Marta lowered to fifth position and swept her arms overhead like a blossoming flower. After another relevé to *pointe,* she extended her right leg and left arm to an *arabesque,* which she held four counts.

Madame stood abruptly. "That's enough."

The judges looked at Marta, conferred, wrote, then looked toward Madame. This unexpected solo surprised Marta. No other auditions asked for additional dances. What could it mean?

Madame leaned on her cane. "Why do you want to join *our* company?"

Marta's butterflies sank. She stared at the wall behind the judges while she organized her thoughts, wondering what Madame wanted to hear.

"Miss Sel-birth?"

Marta stretched tall and made eye contact with Damien, then Madame Cosper. "Last year I saw your Christmas tour in Bremerton, I mean in Seattle, I mean Spokane. I enjoyed the program. The dancers were so precise. I'm precise. I know I'd fit in."

While the judges resumed writing, Marta held herself in fifth position with her fingers intertwined behind her back. The warmth of embarrassment tingled through her body. What a dumb answer! Blah, blah. She sounded like a talking wind-up doll.

Damien stood. "Thank you, Miss Sel-birth. We'll contact you with our decision within ten days. Sel-*birth?* Is that right?"

"Almost. It's pronounced 'sell-brith.' Thank you for the audition." She curtsied and exited. In the empty hallway she closed her eyes and sagged against a wall, replaying her audition, trying to decide if it had been a success or a mess.

The sunlight through the hall window cast late afternoon shadows as she entered the restroom to change into street clothes. Passing the mirror, she stopped. Who was she? A dancer who'd never stepped inside of the exclusive Cornish Arts School; a girl who took lessons twice week from an unknown instructor, not twice day from a famous retired dancer. Hopefully her performance today was enough.

She replayed each part of her audition. Did other dancers feel as let down as she did right now, or did they rush around bragging? How many had slipped or flubbed a turn? How did they answer the judges' questions? Had others been asked to perform an additional dance? No matter. She'd know her fate within the next ten days.

She fumbled through her purse and checked the ferry schedule. Drat! She'd miss the six o'clock ferry to Bremerton if she didn't hurry. She ran down the steep sidewalks, over to Marion, and across the trestle, dodging strolling pedestrians. She raced to the ticket booth, down the ramp, and over the grating to board the ferry just as the deckhands threw off the heavy lines.

When the ferry lurched from its moorings at Coleman Dock, she grabbed a support pole to steady herself. Once she felt the familiar jitter of the ferry, she walked to the stairway.

Marta loved everything about the ferry *Kalakala*. The shiny silver body with round windows dated back to World War II. It poked along the waterways like a silver slug and annoyed people in a hurry to travel between Seattle and Bremerton.

At the top of the wide staircase, she bypassed the circular cafeteria counter with its checkerboard tile floors and headed for the overstuffed vinyl seats along the edges. She preferred to ride backward, watching the twists of Rich's Passage framed in the big, round windows. Staying awake became a challenge tonight.

Marta yawned as she stepped off the ferry and followed the snaking line of passengers up the ramp and out of the terminal. She trudged past the YMCA, inhaling the familiar scent of chlorine from the community pool. Her wait on First Street lasted ten minutes, which was more than long enough to stand in front of taverns, tattoo parlors, and pawn shops.

The bus headed north through town and west toward Callow. When she reached Fifteenth, she got off and walked down the hill to her street, Rhododendron. Her parents' house with the postage stamp-size front yard welcomed her. August's dusky sunset light glanced off the large side yard of fruit trees and the grape arbor. She smelled the freshly mown grass and watched the sprinkler trace a full circle on the lawn. If she'd had more energy, she'd have stood in the cool water, letting it wash away her tiredness.

Her mom opened the front door. The music of Mozart flowed across the yard. Her mom smiled, reaching down to pet Bubbles, the cat, now stretched across the sidewalk. "Long day, huh? How did it go, honey?"

Marta hugged her mom, then picked up the cat. "Okay, even though I had to wait forever."

"Wish I could have been there," her mom said. "Tell me every detail."

After dinner, her mom set a bowl of garden-fresh strawberries on the table and sat down to enclose Marta's hands in her own. "Honey, you've always done your best. Give them their ten days. They're missing a dedicated dancer if they don't select you."

Marta watched her mom move around the kitchen. They shared many features: same height, same slender build, and same curly brown hair, but her mom wore hers shorter, shaped closer to her face. At thirty-five, her mom looked more like her sister than her mother.

A shudder ran down Marta's spine as she thought of Madame Cosper's stern face. "Madame Cosper tapped her cane constantly as we danced. It's annoying. I'm probably better off not making her company. You won't be able to get rid of me as soon as you'd like."

"Marta! What a thing to say. You think I want to get rid of you?"

"I know you love me, Mom, and I can stay here as long as I want, but--"

"I want you to get that position if that is what you want. Deep down, however, I don't want to lose you this soon. Since your father died, you've been my support. Plus, you love the music he loved. That's like keeping a piece of him close by."

A lump clogged Marta's throat. Her mom turned away with her head down.

"What's wrong?" Marta asked.

Her mom inhaled a ragged breath, turned back, and smiled. "Nothing. I love you, and I know that whatever happens you'll be fine. We'll be fine."

§

After her mom went to bed, Marta paced the small house, then took a hot bath. As she towel-dried her hair, she rummaged through her dad's records, smiled, and put *Clair de Lune* on the turntable. She lowered the volume on the stereo and grabbed the afghan off the back of her dad's leatherette rocker.

Miss Holland created that dance just for her after learning it was one of Marta's dad's favorite selections. She settled into the chair and rocked. The music pulled at her like moonlight tugging the tide. She closed her eyes and let herself drift off to sleep, knowing that her mom, and her dad, would be proud of her no matter what happened.

The following week Marta ambled home from her tutoring session with Mrs. Richard. Over the past two years, they'd worked to ensure she'd graduate from high school. Algebra and science bored her and were not useful to a dancer. But high school demanded she sit in class and learn formulas and facts if she wanted to graduate. And, graduation was a family requirement she planned to honor. She'd be the first.

During late spring, Marta completed a blur of ballet company audition forms with Mrs. Richard's help. Today they'd filled out store clerk applications, just in case she ended up working at Woolworth, PayLess Drugs, Bremer's, or Barr's Hat Shoppe. She'd miss Mrs. Richard's support, but the time had come to move on.

"Did I get any mail?" Marta asked as she dropped her supplies on the kitchen table. Expecting the reply, "No mail," that she'd heard each day since the audition, she disappeared into her room to change clothes.

Back in the kitchen, she washed her hands and reached for a hand towel. "What's for dinner?" No answer. She turned to ask again. Her mom dangled a large envelope at eye level.

Marta read the return address: Intermountain Ballet Company. Her stomach did a flip flop. "Did you open it?"

"Of course not. This is your mail."

Marta's knees turned to mush. "Open it for me."

"Come on, honey. Be brave."

Marta hesitated, then snatched the envelope and held it against her chest. Her hands shook and her body pulsed, ready to explode. She closed her eyes, took a deep breath, and ripped open the envelope.

The packet of papers stuck to her sweaty fingers. She waved them back and forth like a thick paper fan, then stopped and read the cover letter to herself.

Tears clouded Marta's eyes. She read the letter again.

The Intermountain Ballet Company has completed its auditions for 1957. We are happy to inform you that you've been selected....

Marta took a deep breath and wiped her eyes. She walked into the living room and back to the kitchen, staring at the letter. A smile played across her lips as she made a slow turn, then jumped up and down. "They want me, they want me! Mom, they want me!"

Marta whooped and hollered and jumped and cried before she fell into her mom's arms. They held each other so tightly they blended into one.

"I'm proud of you, honey. You deserve this. What does the letter say?"

Marta paced the kitchen as she read the details of her new life aloud. The dance company wanted Marta in Billings in two weeks. She'd need a large suitcase for touring, half a dozen practice leotards and tights, and six pairs of *pointe* shoes to begin the year. The company would pay for one night's lodging in Billings, but she'd need to find her own place to live and provide her own transportation to and around Billings.

Every few minutes she stopped, did a few ballet turns, then resumed pacing and reading. "I wish Dad could be here to know that I made it."

"He knows. The whole street heard you. Why not heaven as well?"

Marta kissed the papers and threw them in the air. "I did it, didn't I?"

The papers fluttered across the floor. As she retrieved them, she noticed a strange stillness inside herself. The butterflies she expected to be clamoring to escape her chest stayed quiet. A calmness spread through her, slowing her breathing as it moved into her arms. She'd done it. Her dream for a career as a professional dancer began in a few days.

The packet also contained a one-page biography of Madame Cosper and Damien Black, a map of Billings, and housing contacts. The enclosed ballet company brochure read:

The Intermountain Ballet Company
proudly presents...
1957-1958 Performances

October 4-20
Classic Sampler Excerpts from
Sleeping Beauty and Coppelia and select solos

November 28–December 10
Regional Nutcracker Tour

December 13-24: Nutcracker in Billings

February 6-23: Giselle

April 3-20: Serenade

May 30–June 8
A Tribute to American Composers
(selections TBA)

"Look at this, Mom. I'll be dancing many of my favorite ballets this year."

Her mom took the brochure and nodded. "It's a wonderful program. Miss Holland will be excited to see this. I wish you were dancing closer to home so she could watch you dance."

"Me, too. Will you be able to come to Billings?"

"I'll try. I can't promise, but I'll try."

Her mom picked up the biography page. "Hm-m. You'll want to read this. Both Madame and Damien have impressive backgrounds. Madame danced as a principal for the New York City Ballet, and Damien's choreographed all over the country. They've been in Billings for close to ten years."

Bubbles jumped into Marta's lap and settled into a purring ball as Marta scanned the brochure. "Madame looked beautiful as a dancer. Now she looks tired. Maybe she's friendlier when she's directing her company."

"One thing's for sure--you're on your way to collecting those eighty-four ribbons. Even more. When you chose to save your *pointe* ribbons, I feared you'd be setting an impossible goal, but now--"

"Now it's possible." Marta danced around the kitchen, circled her mom, then twirled down the hall and into her bedroom.

She took down her wooden cigar box of ribbons and sat on her bed. Every time she opened the lid, she felt a tingle of excitement. She ran her fingers through the pink satin ribbons and smiled. Twenty ribbons so far.

Savings the ribbons began when she received her first *pointe* shoes. Miss Holland told the class about Maria Tallchief, a famous ballerina. A reporter wrote that Maria wore out hundreds of *pointe* shoes during the first dozen years of her career. Then and there, Marta decided that she was going to save the ribbons from every pair of *pointe* shoes she wore out. "I'm going to be a ballet dancer like Maria Tallchief," she confided to Miss Holland. "And, when I collect eighty-four ribbons, I'll be ready for my first professional solo."

"Why eighty-four ribbons, Marta?" Miss Holland asked.

"If I work hard, I'll perform lots. That means I'll wear out several pairs of shoes every year. After I dance in the corps for a year or two, I'll save dozens of ribbons, so I'll earn a solo. I counted. I think eighty-four ribbons is about right."

She found a magazine photo of Maria Tallchief and hung it on her bedroom wall. Evenings as she got ready for bed, she copied the pose Maria held. Each day as she prepared for ballet class, she touched the photo for luck. After five years, the touching had faded the photo to a mere shadow. But now her life as a dancer was beginning. Was eighty-four a reasonable number of ribbons? It had been a childish idea, but just maybe it was accurate. She put the photo in the ribbons box and set it aside to take with her to Billings.

Marta left home Thursday afternoon, August twenty-ninth, with two medium-sized suitcases checked through to Billings. She carried her small white shoulder purse and a vanity case. The hat and gloves she left home wearing had already been tucked into her bag. She hoped young Montana women didn't stick to "the rules" during hot summer days.

The calmness from the day she received the invitation had lasted only a day. Jitters took over regardless of what she did to ease them away. Now she squeezed and released her mom's hand every few seconds. "I hope I can do this. Wish you were coming with me."

"Oh, honey. I wish I could. But your greeter will meet you and help you get settled. I'd just be in the way. Now stop worrying. You'll be fine. Your friends last night thought you'd be a star before long."

"Friends are good for that."

Marta's mom brushed away imaginary lint, a sure sign she'd cry any minute. "You have enough money? Remember to eat. And call me as soon as you arrive."

"I promise."

They stood side by side waiting for her bus to be announced. Her mom held her hand the way a parent holds onto a young child about to cross a busy street. They both startled when the loudspeaker blasted through the Greyhound depot. "Now boarding for North Bend, Ellensburg, Moses Lake, Ritzville, and Spokane."

Marta grabbed her mom. They hugged with arms tangled in arms and heads tucked tightly against each other's shoulders.

"What if I'm not ready Mom?"

"You can do anything you set your mind to; why would this be different?"

"I feel funny inside. First I'm scared, then I want to laugh, and then I think I'm going to throw up."

"Remember to breathe once in a while." Her mom shook her head and let out a slow sigh. "Marta, I love you so. I can't tell you how much I'll miss you."

"All aboard for North Bend, Ellensburg, Moses Lake, Ritzville, and Spokane. Last call, last call."

Marta boarded the idling bus and slid into an empty seat next to a window. When everyone had settled, the driver closed the door and the bus pulled away. Marta waved until they rounded a corner and her mom disappeared from view. Twenty-four hours ahead she'd be searching for a place to live in a town with no friends or familiar faces. Time to be brave and independent. Time to bury her fears. Time to take charge of her own life.

She placed her hand in the pocket of her shirtwaist dress and fingered the small leather pouch. It held the last stones her dad had polished, connecting her to the time she spent in the garage helping him tumble rocks. When she first bagged them, she'd felt a finality, an ending of knowing her dad. Now, they'd be a lasting connection, a talisman to carry on all her travels.

The bus traveled east from Tacoma, leaving the Puget Sound basin behind. Evergreen forests gave way to crags of granite where stubby alpine trees twisted and stretched sideways.

Across the Cascade Mountains, farmlands surrounded the roadway with long stretches of green fields similar to Gran's Wenatchee farm. At the dozens of stops, Marta got off to stretch and execute a few *pliés*. The fresh air at the stops exaggerated the stale, gassy smell of the interior of the bus and the heavy scent of unwashed travelers.

In Spokane she changed buses. For the rest of the trip, she sat hemmed in by a plump, elderly woman who pulled out an unending supply of snacks and knitting. The woman rambled from one conversation to another, leaving no gaps in her comments for Marta to speak.

The swaying bus made Marta's stomach queasy. She set aside her *Seventeen* magazine and closed her eyes. First thing she'd do with her first paycheck would be to start saving for a ticket home, by train.

All night, the bus twisted through the Rockies, following its headlights along deserted roads. In the early morning, Marta's head jerked off her purse she'd used as a pillow against the window. She stretched her torso from side to side to loosen the kinks. Outside, brown prairie grasslands and scrub brush slid past in a blur. Her seat companion snored on.

The bus meandered through the tiny towns of Drummond, Deer Lodge, and Opportunity, making brief stops in each before descending into a wide valley. The bus slowed and turned off the highway. Sun streamed through the gritty window, blinding her view of the town. "Billings," announced the driver. "All travelers going beyond Billings check inside the depot for connections."

People rustled in their seats, collecting their belongings. Her seatmate moved slower than syrup. So far she'd not attempted to retrieve her over-sized bag from the shelf overhead.

While Marta waited for her seatmate to pack up, she reorganized her questions for the greeter. She needed to locate her overnight accommodations and the ballet company, find housing in town, and learn to navigate Billings. Her hands began to tremble as she thought about all she had to do. Thank heavens for the greeter.

Marta stepped off the bus and into intense midday heat that hit her like an oven on broil. She began to sweat. Her mouth felt dry as a cotton ball. She moved to the side of the bus with the other passengers, watching the driver unpack the baggage compartment.

Bag after bag formed a pile beside the bus. People grabbed their bags and walked away. Now the pavement was empty. The driver closed the baggage compartment and walked toward the depot.

Marta looked around. "Excuse me, sir. Are there more bags stored on the other side?"

"No, Miss. That's all I had. If yours isn't here, it must not have made a transfer along the way. Check inside at baggage claim."

Marta closed her eyes and let out a calming breath. Okay. It would work out. She'd ask her greeter what to do when she called her, after she got a drink of water.

The drinking fountain dribbled water; she couldn't get a sip. She moved to the pay phone booth to call the greeter.

Her dime slid into the coin slot and dropped down inside the telephone. After she heard a dial tone, she placed her finger in the first slot and pulled it to the small, curved metal stop. She listened to the clicks as the dial rotated back to its starting position before she stuck her finger in the next slot. Number by number she waited as the dial clicked back to its original position.

The phone rang and rang. No answer. She gave up and moved to the baggage counter. A tired worker hefted a large box to the counter where a shaggy-haired man signed for it and walked away. The worker turned his attention to Marta. "Help you?"

After she filled out her information, the attendant handed Marta two missing baggage claim tickets and disappeared through a dingy door. She stared at the tickets, too depressed to move. There'd be no chance of changing out of her wrinkled, smelly traveling clothes now.

She called the greeter again. Still no answer. Next she called the ballet company. The man she spoke with said the ballet office was closed for meetings until Tuesday morning.

She retrieved her overworked dime and placed a call to her mom.

"Mom? I'm in Billings. The greeter hasn't come, my bags are lost, the dance company office is closed until Tuesday, and I'm so thirsty I could drink cold coffee."

"Don't fret, Marta. I'll mail out *pointe* shoes and dance clothes right away. In the meantime keep calling your greeter. Maybe the person had an emergency."

"Okay, Mom. I love you."

Marta gave up on phoning the greeter and exited the depot. The Montana heat blasted her again. Her head ached from the bus trip, and her stomach growled from lack of food. Thirst became a focus, but she pushed it away. She'd wait and use the inn fountain so she'd have money for meals with enough left over to buy clothes and shoes before her first day.

At the curb she checked the map. The inn looked to be a couple of blocks north along Twenty-seventh Street. Thank heavens downtown Billings streets lay flat as a pancake.

Downtown appeared larger than Bremerton, but smaller than Seattle or Tacoma. Block after block of three and five story buildings hovered over small businesses. The pavement sizzled with heat. Marta took advantage of the recessed entries to look at merchandise as she cooled down. Clothing shops, jewelers, a dry cleaner, a department store, two cafes, and a drug store filled in spaces between hotels and office buildings. Across Twenty-seventh she spotted a five and dime, a bank, and a pet shop.

She continued through town, heading toward a long, high wall of rock. At the Rimview Inn she went directly to the drinking fountain in the foyer and took in a dozen swallows of tepid water. At the check-in counter she paid for an extra night to allow time to find a place to live, then dragged herself up a flight of stairs, briefly glad she didn't have extra bags in tow.

The room smelled antiseptic and looked spartan. Marta flopped on the orange bedspread and faded into a dreamless sleep. She woke to darkness. Her stomach growled and grumbled as she headed to the reception desk.

After a few minutes a plump woman with brown hair and a warm smile appeared from the back room. "Hello. May I help you?"

"Hi. Is there a cafe nearby where I can get something to eat?"

The woman sized her up. "If you're twenty-one you can go in the bar."

"I'm not. I'm seventeen."

"Well then, I'll order you a sandwich to eat out here." The woman called the sandwich order into the bar, then turned back to Marta. "Are you in Billings for long?"

"I hope so. I'm joining the local ballet company."

"That's exciting." The woman's eyebrows raised, and a wide smile brightened her face. "Do you wear those fluffy short dresses?"

"Sometimes. Have you been to a ballet?"

"Not yet," the woman said. "Every year I plan to go. I like the music, so I'd probably like the dancing."

Marta smiled. "I hope you will come this year."

A thick ham sandwich with a fat dill pickle, a pile of potato chips, and a bottle of Coke arrived on the counter. Marta started to protest.

"I know you didn't order the Coke; I added that. The chips and the pickle come with our sandwiches."

Marta opened her purse and drew out her wallet.

The woman waved her hand at Marta. "Put your money away. I'll come see you dance one of these days. I'd be proud to say that I bought you dinner."

"Thanks," Marta said. She took her food to one of the faded overstuffed lobby chairs and devoured half of the sandwich and the pickle before taking a few sips of the Coke. The uneaten half sandwich and the chips she wrapped in a paper napkin and slipped into her pocket. She sat back and drank the rest of the Coke, feeling the bubbles erupt in her mouth and nose. Tomorrow she'd return to her usual much smaller and healthier meal portions.

Marta found the pay phone in a small alcove off the lobby and called the greeter again. Still no answer. Next she called her Mom, collect.

"Hi, darling. Feeling calmer?"

Marta paused. "A little. I crashed when I got to the hotel. I didn't sleep very well with the bus twisting and turning. We made so many stops between Tacoma and Billings that I lost count."

"Well, at least you're rested now. How's the inn? Is your greeter helpful?"

"It's an old inn. Reminds me of the beach lodge at Kalaloch." Marta paused, expelling a slow breath. "I haven't reached the greeter. It's strange not knowing anyone or where anything is located."

"It will all work out; you'll see."

Marta ran her fingers up and down the metal phone cord. "Did you do anything like this when you were my age?"

"No. When I left high school, I married your dad. We were busy working and saving money for a house. Then you came along. You were my adventure, and my blessing."

Marta smiled to herself. "I won't disappoint you."

"You could never disappoint me, honey. Now, get some rest. Call me whenever; remember it's cheaper after nine. Laugh when things get too crazy; it helps."

After her mother hung up, Marta listened to the dial tone drone on and on before she hung up, feeling a break in connection to her mom. She roamed the lobby, waiting to thank the night clerk for the food. When she didn't appear, Marta returned to her room and went to bed.

ๆ

Morning sunlight slipped in along the side of the window shade, warming Marta's back. The clock registered six o'clock. She stood, stretched, and peered out the window. Not a person or an evergreen tree in sight.

She curled up on the bed for a moment. When she next scanned the clock, it read nine-thirty. She sat up, shaking her head to clear away the sleep. Outside she heard cars and trucks rumbling along the avenue and voices moving along the sidewalks. Saturday looked to be a busy day in town. She'd better get moving. Too much needed to be done for her to sleep late.

She showered and rolled her worn clothes in the damp towel to soften the wrinkles. After she ate the leftover half sandwich and chips, she hurried down the stairs and out onto the sidewalk. She stood under the entry awning, attempting to orient herself to the town. The map the ballet company sent looked like chicken scratches. It didn't make sense. She stepped back inside the inn to check the telephone book for a better map.

The woman from last night spoke when she saw Marta. "Good Morning! Nice day isn't it?"

"Yes. Thanks for last night's food. That sandwich tasted great. I was starving."

"Nothing like a little food to make you feel better." The woman eyed Marta's rumpled handful of papers. "New task today?"

"I need to find a ballet shop and a place to live," Marta said, "but this map is useless."

The night clerk stepped from behind the check-in counter. "Let me have a look-see. I've lived here seven years. My name is Trudy, and you're Marta, right?"

"Yes, I am."

Trudy scanned the list. "The dance shop is down the block. We can start there. You have a wide variety of apartments and rooms to consider. Here are my suggestions." She circled places she considered acceptable, handed the list back to Marta, and picked up her purse and lunch bag. "Let's get going. It will take a couple of hours to visit all of them. I need to be home by twelve-thirty. I assume you'll accept a ride?"

"I'd love a ride," Marta said, "but I can't pay you much."

"Pish, posh, Marta. I know how it feels to be new in a strange town."

Trudy's car interior was super-heated from the early morning sun. Marta's blouse stuck to her back. The hot air burned her throat. Trudy started the car. "They say today will be a scorcher. Already is."

The Dance Shoppe sign said, "Closed until September 6." Way too late to help Marta.

Trudy drove Marta around the city looking for housing. The first apartment complex sign said, "No Vacancy." The second turned out to be too expensive. Marta ruled out the third, fourth, and fifth because they were dingy or too far out of town for walking to the ballet company.

At a quarter to twelve, they stopped at the Belvern Boarding House on the east side of Yellowstone Avenue. Its freshly painted exterior and overflowing planter boxes invited a second look. A man in bib overalls pushed a rotary mower in the side yard, tossing up the scent of dry grass. Marta approached the front door.

"There's no one home right now," the man shouted. "Aggie gets home about five o'clock. Come back then."

"Thanks, I will."

When she climbed back in the car, Trudy started the engine. "I have a friend who knows Aggie. She's got a great reputation. If she has a room, take it."

Trudy drove Marta back to the inn and left with a wave. The smell of cinnamon, hot dough, and chocolate chip cookies floated out the door of the nearby bakery. Marta stepped inside and bought an inexpensive cheese bun for her dinner. She took it back to the inn and sat eating it in one of the foyer's cushy chairs while she planned her next move.

Marta placed several calls. No other shops in town carried dance-wear. They all suggested calling the Intermountain Ballet Company. She already knew that wouldn't work.

At a quarter to six, Marta rang the Belvern boarding house doorbell. As she waited, she brushed back her damp hair and finger-pressed her wrinkled clothes.

A chunky woman about Marta's height came to the screen door. She wore a pinstriped summer dress covered by a white apron. "Yes?" she said, as she wiped her hands on a kitchen towel.

"Hi. My name is Marta Selbryth. I came about the room. Is it still available?"

"Yes. Please, come in." The woman opened the screen door. "I'm Mrs. Belvern. Two rooms are available. Follow me."

The upstairs room above the entry hall smelled of lemon furniture polish. The room faced the street and the side yard. A faint breeze fluttered the white lace curtains, creating wavy patterns on the hardwood floor.

Marta surveyed the furnishings: a bleached maple bed, two mismatched dressers, and a rocking chair, all well-used. One of the blue and white flowered wallpaper walls had a small sink with a mirror. The closet appeared spacious for such an old home. Although the room was twice the size of her bedroom back home, it felt cozy.

Mrs. Belvern pointed toward the hall. "The shared baths are next door. You'd need to work out a schedule with the other upstairs tenants."

Marta entered the bathroom. The large room split into two spaces each with locking doors. One room had a claw foot bathtub, a sink, a toilet, and a mirror. The other was similar but with a small shower. The linen closet in the entry area had four shelves. Two held personal items; one held a pile of towels, extra toilet paper, and tissues; the last shelf was empty.

"Each tenant has a personal shelf," Mrs. Belvern said. "Extra towels and supplies are stocked here as well. You'll need to launder any towels you use. The wash machine is in the furnace room in the basement. Check the schedule for available tenant wash times. You'll need to purchase your own laundry detergent once you settle in. Clotheslines are available out back and in the furnace room."

Mrs. Belvern pointed to a phone hanging on the wall in a tiny alcove. "Upstairs tenants make local or collect calls from here. Incoming calls ring up here as well as downstairs. I prefer they be answered downstairs when possible."

Marta nodded.

The second room, on the main floor, looked north onto a large backyard where neighboring houses and fruit trees blocked direct sunlight. With flocked forest green wallpaper, dark maple furniture, and one tall sash window, the room felt too dark for Marta's taste.

"Two boarders share the bath next door. There's a small closet to store personal items. Boarding house guests also use this bath, so I provide a basket of hand towels intended for their use."

"Are the rooms the same price?" Marta asked.

"Yes, seventy-five dollars a month, which includes breakfast as well as weekday and Sunday suppers."

"I'd like to rent the upstairs room," Marta said. "I like the view of the street and having a breeze. Could I move in tomorrow, Mrs. Belvern?"

"Certainly," the landlady said. "That gives me time to dust and check things over." She extended her hand to Marta. "Welcome, Marta. Call me Mrs. B." She gestured toward the street. "I'm sorry I don't have parking spaces."

"I don't have a car. That's why I need to be in town. How far is the bus depot from here? My bags are lost. This morning they said to expect them tomorrow."

"Oh my. That's unfortunate. You can walk there, but it's quite a distance. But, in this heat, how about I meet you there at noon tomorrow? We'll pick up your bags and get you here in nothing flat. Take my phone number in case you think of any questions."

"Thanks, Mrs. B. Getting help with the bags would be great."

The sidewalk sizzled as hot as stove burners as Marta retraced her route back to the Rimview Inn. Her sandals stuck to her feet and sweat coated her body, but she congratulated herself on finding a room. When she got her bags tomorrow, she'd be set.

Marta took a cool shower and wrapped herself in the two small bath towels provided by the inn. She rinsed out her clothes and hung them over the shower rod to dry while she stretched out on the orange bedspread. She awoke near sunset. Her clothes felt damp to her touch, but she put them on so she could walk through town in hopes of catching a breeze.

The huge mercury thermometer on the bank wall read eighty-five degrees well after eight, much warmer than the warmest days back home. She stopped in a small park to sit in the shade of a droopy willow and eat the remains of a second cheese bun she'd purchased earlier.

A thought startled her: she was totally alone. She had no one to talk to, no one to laugh with, and no one to tell her everything would be okay. But this chance to dance was what she wanted, and that meant handling her own life day after day. She stood, straightened, and looked around. She *could* do this.

When she returned to her room, she thumbed through the *Seventeen* magazine her mom had tucked in the toiletries case. At nine-thirty she called home collect to report her day's progress: the heat bothered her, she'd not found a place to buy dance clothes, yes she ate, and best of all, she loved the boarding house room she'd found.

"Did your bags arrive?"

"I hope they'll be here tomorrow. Mrs. Belvern will help me collect them. I have two dressers, so send my extra box. And, Mom, there's even a rocking chair."

"Great," her mom said. "Sounds like you've found a good place to live."

"Only two problems left: I'm melting, and my clothes stink."

Marta woke when her leg jerked her awake. She lay in bed, in the dark, clutching the thin sheet that covered her. The recurring dream of falling had followed her to Billings. This time she danced on the rock wall behind the inn. Wheat stalks poked out of her hair. She wore *pointe* shoes and a sheer flowing skirt with a border of apples and cinnamon rolls. Circling and dancing, she'd approached the edge of the cliff and lost her balance. She shuddered, then took several deep breaths. Would the dream of falling ever go away?

On her way to the bus depot the next morning, she took a parallel street, passing the Fox Theatre. Tall glass cases flanked the doors with posters of coming events including performances by the Intermountain Ballet Company. The doors were locked, but she peeked inside and saw the ornate foyer of a real performance hall. No more picking splinters from her *pointe* shoes from performing on a decrepit junior high stage like back home. Maybe the theatre even had dressing rooms and those little lights around the mirrors like in the movies. That would be impressive.

The Greyhound depot echoed its emptiness as she entered. Her toiletries case stuck to her hand as she set it on the cement floor to rummage through her purse for her claim tickets.

The attendant shook his head. "Sorry. They didn't arrive. Write down your phone number. I'll call when they show up."

Marta wrote down the number and exited the bus depot. That meant she had nothing appropriate to wear tomorrow, her first day at the ballet company. Hopefully Madame Cosper would understand.

Marta stood in the shade of the building as Mrs. B. drove up. They both smiled as Mrs. B. exited her car and opened the trunk. Marta put in her case and explained about her errant bags.

"That's too bad. Let's get out of this heat," Mrs. B. said. "I thought we'd drive past the Intermountain Ballet building and follow the shortest route from there to my boarding house. Then I'm ready for a cool drink before Sunday supper."

After conversation and a refreshing lemonade, Marta showered and redressed in her stinky clothes. She sat and rocked until dinnertime when she descended the stairs, stopping on the landing to check her hair in the large wood-framed mirror. She crossed the entry hall, following the sound of conversation to her left. Jitters, usually reserved for dancing, raced through her. She shook out her hands as she approached the dining room.

Mrs. B.'s eyes glowed with a smile as she encircled Marta's clammy fingers in her hand. "Welcome, Marta. Your place is at the far side of the table."

The starched tablecloth, linen napkins, and flowered china plates reminded her of holiday meals at Gran's. A low bouquet of sunflowers and orange nasturtiums graced the middle of the table, surrounded by bowls of food: cold chicken, fresh green beans, a fruit salad, and dinner rolls.

Marta felt eyes track her as she rounded the table. The man seated next to her stood and pulled out her chair. "Thanks," she said.

Mrs. B. waited for Marta to sit before she spoke. "Friends, I want you to meet Marta Selbryth, the newest dancer for the Intermountain. Let me introduce your fellow boarders, Marta. You met James, he held your chair."

"Hello, Miss," James said before tucking his grizzled chin down to his chest.

"James has lived upstairs for two years. He works at the oil refinery where I'm a secretary."

"Next is Carol. She's a student at Eastern Montana and also lives upstairs."

Carol nodded, then straightened her silverware before she went back to a studied picking at her cotton tank top and fluffing her short black hair.

"On my right is Martin. Everyone calls him Shorty. He's an engineer at Copper Creek Mining out west of town."

Shorty stood, extending a grime-encrusted hand across the table to Marta. "Miss."

Marta considered the boarders: two old men and a snooty student. They didn't fit into her dream of being independent and living alone. But, since she could barely afford the boarding house rent, she'd need to make it work for now.

Conversation about the heat accompanied the meal. Bowls of food circled the table. Marta ate small portions. With tomorrow as her first day dancing, being bloated wouldn't be a good idea.

"Eat up everyone. I don't want a bunch of leftovers," Mrs. B. said.

Shorty laughed. "I've got a great leftovers story. Last year about this time, a dog ran into one of the shallow mine shafts we were working and hid. We knew he was there because he howled something fierce when we left each day. Started noticin' if we left our lunch boxes out, they'd be scratched up and opened. Come to find out, he ate our leftovers before we took our lunch boxes home at the end of the shift.

"We tried to coax him out, but he stayed there and howled away. Finally we got a piece of steak and dragged it out of the mine. He followed that meat right to the entrance and never came back."

Mrs. B. smiled. "Guess I could send leftovers to the mine if you leave too many."

Everyone but Carol laughed. The men didn't need another plea to eat up. They obliged her request, taking second and third helpings.

With the dishes cleared, James and Shorty commandeered the table for a game of cards. Carol disappeared. Marta wandered around the common room, checking out the bookshelves and furnishings, then walked into the kitchen.

A large farmer's table filled the center and held piles of dishes, pots and pans, and kitchen canisters. Cabinets lined the walls, encircling two refrigerators, a double sink, and a long tile counter. Windows with chintz curtains flanked the back door. Mrs. B. stood at the sink, her back toward Marta.

"May I help you, Mrs. Belvern?"

Mrs. B. turned and smiled. "You most certainly may. I've put the leftovers away and the dirty dishes are stacked. Now for the fun." She opened a kitchen drawer and pulled out a flour sack towel. "Use this, or would you rather wash?"

"Drying is fine," Marta said. "That's my job at home."

Marta and Mrs. B. worked through the pile of dishes. Marta enjoyed holding the hot, slick dishes and wiping them dry. More than that, she enjoyed the continuous flow of conversation.

"Good," Mrs. B. said. "That's done until tomorrow night. Thanks for your help. You know, Marta, if you want to work in the kitchen, I'll lower your rent."

"Really? That would help. I'll have dance expenses, but I don't know how much until I get started. I can bake for you when I have time. It relaxes me and helps clear my mind."

"Believe me, fresh baked goods are appreciated by my boarders. Let me know if you need anything special."

Why had she volunteered? At home her mom had to coax her to help. When would she find the time? Plus she seldom ate sweets.

"Is there anything I can do to help you settle in?" Mrs. B. said.

"I'd like to find a bike to ride to the ballet company, and I need to wash my clothes."

"Both are easy to solve." Mrs. B. took Marta into her garage where a green bike rested in a corner. "It isn't pretty, and the tires need a little air, but use it as long as you like."

Later, Marta borrowed an over-sized housecoat from Mrs. B., then washed her handful of clothes in the laundry room sink and hung them on the backyard line. Next, she took a long shower and borrowed a giant, fluffy towel to dry off. Before she went to bed, Marta decided to "move in" by arranging the photo of her parents and her pouch of stones on the dresser near the bed. She tossed the stuffed version of her cat, Bubbles, beside her pillow. Last, she adjusted the rocking chair to where the breeze crossed the room and sat down to enjoy her first evening in her new home.

As dusk changed to dark, the distant hills looming behind the roof across the street faded to black sentinels. Not as magnificent as the Olympic Mountains back home, but they broke up the expansive Montana sky.

$\mathscr{S}$weat ran down Marta's sides as she stopped pedaling and leaned the bike against a metal railing. The mile ride felt more like ten in the midday heat. Add in her nervousness about becoming a *real* dancer, and she was soaking wet.

A simple wooden sign hung from two chains above the door of the two-story, wood frame building. It read, *The Intermountain Ballet Company*. She quivered with the same anticipation as during auditions. At one-thirty today she'd begin her career as a professional dancer.

She saw a bronze plaque to the right of the front door and walked up the four wide steps to read it.

Davis Button Factory

Founded in 1866 by Jerome Davis

He made every shape and size buttons

as long as they were round and white.

She guessed it was a joke. Only partly funny. Didn't look like a factory now. Up close it looked old and in need of paint. Not nearly as appealing as the photo on the subscription brochure they'd sent her or from her quick look as she drove past it yesterday.

She wiped her sweaty palms on her skirt, smoothed back her ponytail, and inhaled. Here goes, she thought.

The heavy oak doors opened to a second set of doors. In the dark entry, narrow rectangles of sunlight filtered in through high windows. The place echoed its silence. No music. No smell of sweat and rosin. No voices. She retraced her way to the entry steps.

Outside, she unfolded the letter and read the details: one-thirty, today, September 2, and this building. She reentered the quietness and stepped further in, approaching a closet-sized room off to her right. A man sat inside with his feet propped up on a small desk and a newspaper spread across his belly.

"Excuse me," she said. Her voice echoed through the cavernous space.

The paper lowered, revealing a gray-haired man with one long eyebrow that stretched above both eyes. "Whaddaya want?"

"I'm sorry to interrupt. I'm supposed to be here at one-thirty and--"

The man checked his watch, then stared at Marta. "You're early." And with that, he returned to reading the newspaper.

Marta waited until she realized he wasn't about to speak again. She returned outside and sat on the front steps. Was the letter a horrible joke?

Young people approached along the sidewalk but disappeared before they reached her. She pulled out the letter again. Yes, it said today at one-thirty. Nothing made sense.

A slim young man wearing shorts and a t-shirt climbed the steps at a diagonal, stopped, and walked back to where Marta sat. "Need help?"

"I have an appointment for one-thirty. I'm joining the ballet company."

"Follow me," he said. "We use the side entrance. My name's Jer."

"Hi. I'm Marta."

They walked along the sidewalk to a bright green door. Inside, a long hall held the residual smell of rosin. Photos of costumed dancers lined the walls. Marta slowed to scan them.

The young man stepped into the men's dressing room and pointed down the hall. "Better hurry. Women's room is at the end, and practice starts in a few minutes."

As she approached the women's dressing room, she adjusted her ponytail, exhaled, and stepped through the doorway. Two long rows of locker bays with benches in between filled the space. More than a dozen young women stood partially dressed. The room hushed when they spotted her.

Madame Cosper thumped into the dressing room. "All right, girls. Let's get started. New girls continue to use the back row."

Marta blinked in surprise. *Continue* to use the back row? Had they arrived earlier? What's going on? Marta tried to think of what to say as Madame stopped beside her.

Madame Cosper's make-up caked around her hairline, and her blue eye shadow trailed off onto her cheeks. She leaned forward on her cane. "Where have you been? Practices started days ago."

"I, ah…My letter said to arrive today. I, the greeter didn't meet me."

"That's the old letter. We don't have greeters this year. You should have called and checked. No matter now. Get changed."

Madame's verbal slap startled Marta. This wasn't starting out as she had hoped. "I have no dance clothes."

"Why not?"

"The bus company lost them."

Twitters circled the dressing room.

Madame struck her cane against a nearby bench. Marta jumped. "Borrow clothes or go home. Come early tomorrow and buy what you need from the dance mistress. You *must* dress professionally even if you are only in the corps."

"Yes, Madame." Marta dipped her head like a scolded child. No welcome, no we're glad you're here, nothing but a chastising in front of the other dancers.

Madame exited the room with her chin high, like a dancer exiting the performance stage.

"Borrow my extras," said a voice next to Marta.

Marta turned.

"I've extra clothes and ballet slippers, but no extra pointe shoes." The girl who spoke had long, thick brown hair and hazel eyes. "I'm Lynne Meadows," she said.

"Hi. I'm Marta."

The girls nodded and smiled to each other. The other dancers closed their lockers and trailed out of the room.

"Too bad about not getting the correct information and about your bags. Keep these as long as you need them."

"Thanks."

Marta's hands trembled as she changed into Lynne's donations. "The last thing I need is Madame mad at me from the first day."

"Yeah, She's a piece of work, all right." Lynne checked the wall clock. "Hurry. Only two minutes until practice resumes."

Marta followed Lynne into the rehearsal hall. At the doorway she paused to evaluate the space. The spartan room had a long wall of mirrors, a tall stool, an upright piano, and high, narrow windows where hot sunlight streamed in. Wooden barres lined two walls. The wooden floors gleamed, polished to a high luster. Miss Holland would have loved this huge space instead of her smaller room with a cement floor covered with linoleum.

Dancer whispers continued until Damien Black, the man from her audition, entered. Dancers straightened and gave him their complete attention.

"Good afternoon, boys and girls. Let's get started, shall we?" He nodded toward Marta. "I see everyone has arrived. Good."

Marta felt heat move up her face as dancers focused on her before moving to a *barre* and standing in first position. Marta waited to see where Lynne stood. No sense standing at the wrong *barre* and being sent elsewhere. Dancers were picky about their spaces. Someday she'd have a space reserved by her position, just not soon.

A cane-wielding Madame Cosper entered and moved with an irregular gait toward the stool and leaned against the seat. Silence filled the room floor to ceiling and wall to wall. "Ready, begin," she said.

The pianist kept his eyes on Madame Cosper, following her clapped tempo, playing the exercise music from memory. Another surprise. Back home Miss Holland used records; she didn't have the luxury of a pianist.

"One, two, three, and four, backs straight, arms soft. Pull your *derrières* under… tight-er, tight-er. Keep the beat, two, three, four."

Marta felt a tap on her leg. She stopped and turned. Madame pointed to her left foot. "Your ankle is rolling over. Fix it."

Marta nodded and adjusted. From the corner of her eye, she watched Madame circle the room and use her cane to tap offending arms, legs, backs, and heads. The thought of that cane tapping her again made Marta shudder. Criticism meant you were noticed; better than being ignored, maybe.

After warm-ups and floor exercises, Damien led them through the *Sleeping Beauty* waltz. Thank heavens she remembered most of the choreography from her audition. Unfortunately, she danced off the beat. The more nervous she became, the more mistakes she made. Fingers, hands, arms, head angle, back, leg positions, room positions, tempo, choreography, and music cues. So much to think about. Every time she turned the wrong way and bumped into dancers, Madame glowered and shook her head. Marta shook off her frustration and took a deep breath. Maybe smaller movements were called for until she caught up.

The atmosphere in the dressing room relaxed when the afternoon rehearsals ended at four-thirty. Principal women dancers kept to themselves. Even in the dressing room they had first rights to lockers and showers. Corps dancers chattered about plans for the rest of the day while awaiting their turns to shower.

Marta skipped a shower and slipped her skirt on over the borrowed clothing and headed for her bike before Madame returned.

"Marta! Wait up." A voice stopped her. She turned to see Lynne hurry her direction.

"Thanks again for the rescue," Marta said. "I'll get clothes and shoes tomorrow."

"No problem. Are you as tired as I am? I've been here days longer than you, and I still get cramps and feel like I can't keep up."

"Wish I'd been here earlier. I can't believe my letter. On top of being exhausted, today totally embarrassed me. Does Madame always tap her cane to correct your body positions?"

"Yeah. Don't let her get to you," Lynne said. "Damien does most of our practices. He's okay." Lynne pointed to a beat up blue 1939 Ford in the parking lot. "I'm heading out. Do you want a ride?"

Marta looked at the car. The right fender had several dents and the hood ornament leaned to one side. A good washing wouldn't hurt either.

Lynne laughed. "I know. It's a disaster. It looks worse than it drives."

"Thanks, I'd love a ride, but I need to pedal myself home. Maybe another time."

"OK. See you tomorrow. Nine sharp. Happy pedaling." Lynne climbed into her car and chugged down the street.

Marta headed home on the bike. Home to the boarding house, for now. When she saved enough money, she'd look for an apartment and then a cheap car. They'd allow her to become totally independent.

The smell of pot roast reached Marta as she parked the bike around back. She needed to find the energy to stay awake for the next couple of hours to eat and be sociable with the boarders. But first, a shower.

On her way to dinner, she stopped on the landing to check her damp hair. It looked kinda scraggly, but then it always looked that way after a shower.

Mrs. B. stood in the archway wearing a red checked apron over a powder blue dress. "Good evening, Marta. You're right on time. How was your first day?"

"Okay, but I'm exhausted," she said as she walked around the table of seated boarders. James pulled back Marta's chair as she approached. She smiled, "Thanks, James. But you don't need to do this every night."

"Ah, yes I do," he said. "My momma said to seat a lady properly is the gentlemanly thing to do, Miss Marta,"

All the boarders except Carol laughed as the ritual of the chair began.

Dinner in the boarding house looked formal, but in reality the hour invited casual conversation. A well-set table of a striped linen tablecloth with matching napkins and garden flowers in a bowl appeared to be Mrs. B.'s standard. They took second place to the ample array of food: pot roast, mashed potatoes, corn on the cob, a green salad, and choco-late cake. Marta shuddered at the sight of so much heavy food. She took a small portion of beef, no potatoes and no corn, ate her salad without dressing, and avoided the cake.

The boarders encouraged her to share her day. She in turn listened to their stories. Carol remained silent with a look of disinterest affixed to her face. Why does she live here if she's that detached? Must be like me, Marta thought, unable to afford anything else.

Shorty and James claimed the dining table for cards. Carol disap-peared upstairs as Marta cleared the table, then scraped and piled the plates next to the sink. The peacefulness in the kitchen helped her unwind.

The clock read seven-thirty by the time she climbed the stairs to her room. Did she have energy to stay up a little while? No; she'd almost gone face down in her plate. Why did her letter have the wrong date? And why did Madame expect *her* to call and check? She *had* called once she reached Billings. The man said the ballet company offices were closed. Tomorrow she needed to be artful, on tempo, and well-rested. All the more reason to go to bed early.

The Baby Ben bedside alarm clock clanged. Marta punched down the "off" button. She stretched and massaged the knots and stiffness in her legs and arms. Through the floor vent she heard Mrs. B. rattling dishes.

The smell of bacon curled up through the vent as well. She gagged. What a disgusting smell. How could anyone eat fried fat for breakfast? Thoughts of skipping breakfast crossed her mind, but Mrs. B. would be disappointed if Marta didn't eat as a member of her big happy family. Marta covered her head with her pillow to block out the kitchen smells as she struggled to come fully awake.

Right on schedule, Marta parked the bike by the side entrance and found the ballet mistress. She purchased the needed clothing and shoes, then caught up to Lynne stretching at the *barre* in the large practice room alongside other dancers.

"Hey, Marta," Lynne said. "How are your muscles?"

"The bike ride loosened them some, but I'm still stiff. It will be tough to become a graceful muse for Madame."

"I worry about you and that bike. You do know it snows here from November to March? You should get a car."

Marta shook her head. "Can't. No money. Besides, we got our first car last spring, so I've never driven in snow."

Madame entered the practice room and tapped her cane. "Time to begin, boys and girls."

Marta took a cleansing breath and focused straight ahead. Okay, Madame Cosper, you can't find fault with my appearance. Today I'll make my dancing flawless as well.

Madame and Damien set a fast pace. Today the mazurkas in *Coppélia* were introduced, practiced, and expected to be committed to memory. Next, they returned to the choreography for *Sleeping Beauty*.

The section of the waltz she'd learned for the audition took definite shape as lines moved to circles and circles to lines. Over and over, again and again, the corps moved around the soloists, creating depth and background.

Marta bumped into dancers as she struggled to learn the newer choreography. They frowned and pushed her out of their space. Maybe Lynne would help her catch up after hours. Madame certainly didn't show any sign of assisting her.

The morning practice lasted forever; eating toast and tea didn't provide sufficient energy to dance. She'd need to add peanut butter or cheese to her toast. At lunch she'd eat protein, if she could stomach it.

Marta sat in the Bison Café with Lynne and Jer, the young man from her first day. Bartley, the other new corps girl, came along. She stood several inches taller and appeared thinner than Marta. She wore her golden hair in a high bun and glided like a beauty queen whenever she moved. From the looks of her street clothes and shoes, she could afford the latest styles.

"Well, ladies, how do you like the corps?" Jer asked.

Lynne shrugged. "The girls are okay. Some of the guys think they are hot stuff. They keep asking me out. Not going to happen."

Bartley smiled. "That red headed guy always tries to stand next to you. You'd make a cute couple."

"Right." Lynne rolled her eyes. "I like college men. They have more to talk about."

Jer stopped chewing his burger and looked up. "Are you saying we're dumb or something?"

"No, just focused on yourselves."

"At least I eat real food." He pointed to Marta and Bartley, who had side salads with chicken slivers sprinkled over the top. "Is that all you girls are eating, rabbit food and baby portions of chicken? You need energy to survive Madame."

Marta watched Bartley fork up another bite. "This works for me," Bartley said.

"Me too," Marta said.

Lynne finished her tuna sandwich. "Eat your cow and leave them be, Jer. If they don't eat, they'll pay the price before today ends. I, on the other hand, will be lively and energetic." She slurped the last of her milkshake. "Guys are all alike. They eat anything and everything. I'm lucky as well. I'll burn off this lunch in no time."

Marta picked at her salad and drank a second glass of water. Bartley smiled and pushed away her half eaten salad. She grabbed her purse and walked to the cashier to pay for her meal.

"I guess she's ready to leave," Jer said.

With Madame overseeing the soloists and taking care of the operation of the company, afternoon rehearsals were pleasant. Damien's style allowed Marta to focus on the choreography rather than worrying about the meaning of Madame's frown line that deepened whenever she looked toward Marta.

The four new dancers stood in the back row. Patrice Royal, the aqua-eyed principal dancer, stood center front, a place reserved by experience, talent, and hard work. Marta scanned the row of demi-soloists. They were lean and skillful, not even breathing hard after long sections of choreography. How many years did it take them to gain so much stamina and work their way to the front row?

She surveyed the other corps members, standing one row ahead of her. Too many dancers to surpass to become a principal dancer any time soon.

In an hour's time, sweat dripped off every dancer, spreading droplets across the shiny floor. Opening the doors and windows didn't relieve the humidity. While the troupe rested, Karl, the guard and maintenance man, mopped. His grimace reminded her of her first encounter with him. Didn't anyone but Lynne smile around here?

Rehearsals ended early today for costume fittings. The costume shop ran the width of the building and covered half the upstairs. Stepping inside provided a visual feast. Rows of clothing racks held a variety of costumes: a rainbow of long gowns and tutus, tunics, vests, capes, jackets, and aprons. Bolts of blue cotton, red velvet, and misty silk lay on tables; niches overflowed with feathers, bodice forms, beads, and trim. Marta wished she could touch the fabrics to feel their luscious textures. Her mom would be thrilled if she could work with this array of fine fabrics.

Two assistants sat at long tables sewing and repairing while others hand-cleaned and pressed costumes. This would impress Miss Holland. She got excited when the costumes she ordered from various dance wear companies reached her on time. Most required massive adjustments before recitals--another task for Marta's mom.

When her turn arrived, Marta stepped onto a small raised platform. Rose Vagus, the costume mistress, recorded her measurements. Marta used the time to scrutinize her own body in the massive mirror: thin nose, high cheekbones, thin neck, and breasts small enough that she'd not need to bind herself for costume bodices. Now, if she could drop a few pounds, everything would be perfect.

"There, that's it," Rose said. "Buy a hair piece to fill in where your hair is thin. Don't gain or lose any weight; we only take your measurements once a year. And don't go fixing things yourself. We do all the repairs, understand?"

"Yes, mistress." In high school Marta had taken in her own costume to prevent her mom from noticing her increasing thinness. Many days her mom squinted, trying to figure out what was different, but Marta didn't volunteer any information.

As she exited the room, she passed Lynne, who sat on a folding chair reading *Photoplay* magazine as she waited for her turn. They exchanged smiles.

"Lynne Meadows," called a voice from inside the costume shop. Lynne stood, tossed down the dog-eared magazine, and stepped into the costume shop.

Marta slowed as she passed Bartley. They looked totally different. Bartley's golden hair lay flat against her head in a perfect bun; few hairs escaped. Marta's brown hair kinked different directions, springing from her bun whenever she sweat, usually all day during rehearsals. Bartley's sleek copper skin glowed. Marta's fair skin and freckles washed her out.

Bartley smiled. Marta hesitated. "May I ask about your name?"

"Everyone does," Bartley said. "It's my mother's family name. Dates back a hundred years. Since I have no brothers, I'm the first girl to get stuck with it."

"Hm-m. I kind of like it," Marta said. "Sounds dramatic; a good name for a principal dancer."

"True, but you should see all the mail I get for Mr. Bartley Timmons."

Marta returned to the practice room downstairs. Did Marta Selbryth sound like a good name for a principal dancer? She hoped so. But first, she needed to perform her way out of the back row.

She stood at the *barre* practicing her *port de bras*, reaching back further and further to challenge her flexibility. From upside down, she saw Patrice enter the room. What was the protocol when a principal dancer entered a room? Ignore her? Leave the room? Pretend she didn't see her? Too late for any of those.

Patrice crossed her arms and smiled. "You have a nice extension."

Marta reached tall and viewed Patrice through the mirror. "Thanks."

As soon as she spoke, she regretted her comment. What a stupid thing to say. But what should she have said?

Lynne walked in as Patrice exited. "What did she want?"

"She said I had a nice extension."

"What do you know, she speaks to corps dancers. Watch out for her. Jer says she doesn't like many people, especially dancers who threaten her role as princess of all things."

"I'm no competition. I'm barely keeping up. These practices make all my past ones look like kinder class."

Lynne laughed. "Don't be too sure. We made the cut. Who knows, maybe one day we'll both be a princess of all things, if Madame stops correcting us and gives us the chance. Did you hear her mention my turnout, again?"

Marta stretched over the *barre*. "Does she mention everyone the same?"

"No. Marguerite only gets compliments. I wonder why she's special. I'll ask Jer. He seems to know everything."

Marta wondered as well. Madame seemed disinclined to mentor the new dancers. Would she let them audition as understudies this year? Doubtful.

In a moment of frustration and tiredness, Marta felt a tiny rebellion rise inside her. She limped around the room, imitating Madame, pointing an imaginary cane toward Lynne. "You there, Lynne. Keep your mouth quiet and get back to work. You're only a corps girl."

Lynne stood statue still, not laughing or cracking a smile as Marta continued.

"Keep your chin up! Up, up!"

Marta saw Lynne's face turn chalky white as she tossed a small motion of her head toward the door and moved her eyes that way as well. Marta turned.

Madame stood in the doorway. Her eyebrows met above her nose as her face twisted into an angry glare.

Marta's feet felt glued in place. A blast of fear exploded through her body.

Madame shook her head slowly, lifted her chin, and thumped away.

Tick, tick, tick. Only the sound of the second hand on the clock interrupted the silence in the room. Marta couldn't move or breathe.

Lynne stepped to the hall doorway and peered out. "She's gone."

Tears filled Marta's eyes as she attempted to breathe normally. "I may be gone as well."

Marta sat in her room and rocked, watching the day fade to dusk, then dark. Her body ached more from crying than dancing. Madame's angry face arose whenever she closed her eyes.

A gentle tap on the door startled her. "Who's there?"

"It's Mrs. B. I brought a pot of peppermint tea and dry toast. Shall I leave it here in the hall?"

"Just a minute." Marta ran her fingers through her hair and snugged the ties of her borrowed housecoat before opening the door.

Mrs. B. smiled. "I'm sorry you're not feeling well. Can I get you anything else?"

Marta shook her head. "I have a confession. I'm not really sick. I couldn't face dinner tonight. I got in trouble today, and I don't know what to do to fix things."

"Do you want to talk about it?" Mrs. B. said.

"Maybe. But I don't know what good talking will do." Tears welled up. She wiped them away. "Can you stay for a minute?"

"Of course." Mrs. B. entered and placed the tray on the dresser by the window. She moved to sit in the rocking chair and folded her hands. "How can I help?"

Marta paced her room then sat on the edge of the bed. "I made a terrible mistake. I mimicked Madame and she saw me. Now I'm afraid she'll send me home."

"Hm-m. That sounds serious. You don't seem like a person who'd intentionally hurt someone's feelings."

"I'm not. I mean, I was tired and frustrated. I missed several rehearsals, and it's hard to catch up. Madame glares at me and isn't helping me and... I don't know."

"So it's her fault that you got in trouble?"

Marta startled and stopped pacing. Is that how she sounded? That she was blaming Madame for her rudeness? "No. It's my fault. I--I'm frustrated and embarrassed and scared that she'll send me home."

Marta resumed her barefoot pacing. The only sound in the room was the creaking of the rockers as Mrs. B. kept the chair moving back and forth.

"I wish I could go back and undo what I did," Marta said.

"At times we all do, dear, but we can't. So, what are you planning to do now?"

"I don't know yet."

Mrs. B. stood and patted Marta's shoulder as she reached for the door handle. "In my experience, an apology is always a good place to start. Whatever you decide to do, you need to figure it out as soon as possible."

Marta stared at the closing door. Mrs. B. was right. But what do you say to someone like Madame who dislikes you, someone who controls your future?

The clock hands moved in slow motion. All night Marta alternately paced, rocked, and stared out the window. She replayed the situation with Madame again and again. Why had she mimicked her? Because

Madame scowled at her and didn't appear to approve of her? Or was she frustrated with herself for making so many mistakes? For not being as good as the other dancers? She was trying to learn the choreography as fast as possible, but her best didn't seem good enough—for Madame or for herself. How badly did she want to be part of the company? Badly. Somehow she needed to make a significant change, and fast.

As the pre-dawn sky lightened, she knew what she wanted and need-ed to do. Apologize. She splashed her face with cold water and combed her hair. Except for losing her Dad, facing Madame could well be one of the hardest things she'd do in her life.

Breakfast sounds, voices, and clattering breakfast dishes traveled up through the floor vent. She knew she couldn't eat or sit at the table and act as if nothing had happened, so she slipped out the back door and pedaled into town.

The cool morning air and the quiet streets encouraged her to keep pedaling. She moved through town, past the train depot, toward the re-fineries. Up to now her mom helped her work through decisions. This time she was on her own.

Mom always said to keep things simple. Marta decided her next step. She'd go in, apologize, and hope to be forgiven. She'd not bring up her frustrations or make excuses; she'd be contrite and just say "sorry."

Marta stopped pedaling, got her bearings, and headed to the ballet company building. After she parked the bike, she drew in several deep breaths and shook out her hands and arms.

Exhaustion weighed her down as she climbed the stairs to Madame's office. Light escaped from under the closed office door. Marta shook out her hands again, took a deep breath, and knocked.

"Who is it?" Madame's voice sounded tense and formal.

Marta cleared her throat. "It's Marta Selbryth."

No reply.

She waited. Silence. Should she knock again? As she raised her hand to knock, she heard the thump of Madame's cane against the wooden floor. The door opened wide in one quick motion.

Madame Cosper stood before her with one hand on her cane and one on the door handle. "Yes?"

Marta dipped her head, curtsied, then pulled herself tall to face Madame. She took a quiet, deep breath. "I've come to apologize."

Madame stared at her. She started to speak, stopped, and moved back to sit at her desk before motioning Marta to enter. Everything about Madame was composed: her makeup, her hair, her clothes. Marta felt like a disheveled child with trembling knees as she stepped into the office.

Damien sat at a desk near the door. He eyed her with studied calmness. Now she needed to face both of them. Her heart raced as she adjusted her shoulders and curtsied toward Damien.

Madame played with her rings as she eyed Marta, who stood with her hands clasped behind her back. "Well?"

"I apologize for my actions yesterday. I acted rude and disrespectful. I hope you will forgive me. I--"

Madame raised her hand to stop Marta. She looked from Marta to Damien. "We've discussed your actions. Horrible rudeness. We cannot tolerate such behavior from professional dancers."

"I know. And I am sincerely sorry for what I did," Marta said.

Madame pointed her finger at Marta. "We've expended time and money selecting you to join the company. You arrived days late, unprepared, and not dressed as a dancer. Perhaps this is a joke to you."

"No, it's not a joke. I understand. But Madame, I came on time from what the letter said. I expected the greeter would help me, but I'm alone, and I'm trying to get caught up. I'm a good dancer, but this is hard and..."

"Life is hard; ballet is harder. You need to take responsibility for your actions. All your actions."

Marta lowered her face. Her heartbeat thumped in her head and her palms sweat. How could she make Madame and Damien understand? Her dream hung from a gossamer thread.

"Damien and I have *never* experienced behavior like this," Madame Cosper said. "Personally, I feel you should leave. I don't think you're strong enough for the company."

A shock wave jolted Marta. So, just like that. Her career was over. What would she tell her mom and Miss Holland?

Damien stood and walked to the side of Madame's desk. "I, however, think we need you. You have good musicality and potential to develop into a strong dancer. If you work hard, we can uncover it. Right, Anna?"

Madame looked down and ran her hands over her desktop.

"Anna?"

Madame looked up. Her lips tightened. "It's too late in the season to audition another dancer. But, if you pull another stunt, you'll be dismissed. Do you understand?"

"Yes, Madame." A sigh escaped Marta's lips as she cleared her throat. "Thank you." She tightened her elbows against her sides to steady herself.

Damien opened the office door. "Now, Miss Selbryth, you need to leave and get ready for today. Rehearsal begins in twenty minutes."

Madame stood and leaned forward. "We'll be watching your every move. Do you understand?"

"Yes, Madame."

Marta backed out of the office. As she descended the stairs, she wiped her eyes on her sleeve and tried to collect herself before she vibrated into dozens of pieces and crumbled to the floor.

The hallway to the dressing room lengthened before her. She hurried into a bathroom stall, locked the door, and sat on the closed toilet seat. With her head resting in her hands, she willed her body to stop shaking.

A faint knock sounded on the stall door.

"Occupied."

"Marta, it's me," Lynne said. "Are you okay?"

"Peachy."

"What happened?"

"They gave me a second chance."

Marta stood at the *barre* waiting for the warm-up music to begin. Damien led the morning, paying Marta no obvious extra attention, but she sensed his scrutiny. Her movements felt wooden; the lift for every *relevé* came from muscles she doubted would support her. If she wasn't dealing with her tiredness and almost losing her position, she'd be exhilarated by the fragile strength that blossomed inside her, allowing her to dance even though she should collapse from lack of sleep and food. Maybe this was how it felt to be an adult.

Damien stopped the morning early. "Nice work, everyone. We have meetings with the trustees the rest of the morning. Return at two-thirty sharp. No rehearsals Friday, but Monday we'll complete the *Sleeping Beauty* excerpts from acts one and two. Dismissed."

Lynne and Marta turned uptown, away from the restaurants the dancers patronized. For the next hour they walked through town and talked. They ate lunch seated in a booth at the back of the B & B Café. Marta kept up a running conversation. "And, she said she doesn't think I'm ready. I don't know if I'll make it or not."

Lynne pushed her empty plate away before she spoke. "Stop all your sad little me, Marta. It's over. You apologized. I know it's too soon for you to laugh about it, but you *were* funny."

"I doubt I'll ever laugh about it."

Lynne checked her watch and plucked her purse from the seat of the booth. "Time to get back. Damien says we need you. Hang on to that. Soon we'll be too busy for Madame to remember what you did."

Back in the dressing room, Bartley stood adjusting her leotard as Marta and Lynne entered. "Where did you two go? I waited outside for you."

"Lynne and I needed to talk, so we went for a walk. I almost made a mess of my career yesterday when we were practicing together."

Marta explained the incident and her discussion with Madame and Damien. "You've probably never done anything stupid."

"Right." Bartley shook her head and laughed. "Like the time I made the fly curtains crash during a performance. Four people got caught up in them. They fell like dominoes. I hid in the dressing room until everyone left the theater. The janitor finally kicked me out."

"But mine wasn't an accident. I insulted Madame."

"A mistake's a mistake," Bartley said. "You're not the only one who's got issues with Madame. We're all in this together."

"Exactly," Lynne said. "Let's make a pact. Let's become the three ballet musketeers: what's your problem is my problem."

Bartley smiled. "I'd like that."

"Me too," Marta said.

The girls joined their hands in a tower of crossed palms. A wave of contentment relaxed Marta's tense shoulders and uncramped her frustration. Gaining two new friends sounded like a sure way to move forward.

At the end of the day, Bartley left for a relative's birthday dinner while Lynne stayed with Marta to practice the newest section of the dance. Sweat streaked the backs and sides of their leotards. They rested, leaning over their legs, hands pressed against their knees.

"I wish we could get in here on weekends," Marta said. "I'm having trouble after the second entrance."

Lynne stretched side to side. "You worry too much. Just count out the beats and we'll work on it until it makes sense."

Karl stuck his face into the practice room; his gnarled hand covered the light switch. "Time to close up. You two get going."

"Okay, Karl," Lynne said. "Give us five minutes, okay?"

"No sir-ree. Leave right now. 'Cuz, if I give you five, you'll want ten, and then you'll want twenty. Pretty soon I'll be here all night waiting for you two."

"Yes sir." Lynne saluted Karl. "We're gone. Come on, Marta, let's get a shower."

Karl pointed his finger at Lynne's face. "No-o-o, no! You two head out the door now or I'll have to tell Miz Cowper."

They grabbed their street clothes and headed out the door with Karl close behind. As he closed the dancer's entry door, the lock clicked and the night light came on.

"Thanks, Karl!" Lynne said. "We're locked out to get dressed on the street." She stepped into her skirt and slid her ballet shoes into her dance bag. "I'd like to be there when he calls her 'Miz Cow-per.' She'll have a cow over that. Come on. Stash your bike in my trunk. I'll drive you home."

Over the long weekend, Marta tried to erase her encounter with Madame and Damien. Friday she slept in, then baked bread, cookies, and rolls. Over dinner cleanup she shared the outcome of talking to Madame with Mrs. B.

"That's good, dear. How do you feel?"

"Relieved. It will take her time to forgive me, but I have all year to prove myself."

Saturday, Marta filled a Mason jar with garden flowers for her room and washed out her lone set of clothes. On a walk to town, she bought underwear, a blouse and skirt, two bath towels, Lifebuoy soap, and eighteen inches of black ribbon for her ponytail. Sunday she wrote a note to Gran, took a long nap, and went to see the matinée of *Tammy and the Bachelor* with Lynne and Bartley. Nothing released her from thinking about her encounter with Madame for long. Somehow she needed to be more like Lynne, get beyond thinking about it and begin proving she could change.

৽

After Monday rehearsals, Marta came home to find her lost luggage and the boxes from her mom piled in the entry hall. Seeing the return address created a homesickness she didn't expect. As she unpacked *pointe* shoes and her dance clothing, she also lifted out family photos, her sewing box, fall clothes, shoes, the quilt Gran made, and a small diary. She opened the diary and read the first page:

> Dear Marta,
>
> The house is too quiet with you gone. Bubbles wanders around crying, looking for you. I'm almost as bad; I can't get used to your being away.
>
> I shipped a few extra things. I'll wait for your calls each Sunday. I love you and I know you're doing a fabulous job.
>
> XOXOX Mom

Right. A fabulous job of almost losing her position. Marta brushed her hand over the cover of the diary and sighed as she tucked it into a bedside drawer. She had lots to write, but not yet.

The sewing box felt heavy. Inside she found wooden embroidery hoops, a box of sequins, scraps of velvet, a length of mauve chiffon, twists of glittery yarns, and a dozen new spools of thread. Marta stroked the fabrics. Her mom knew she'd need projects to keep her hands busy. Being in charge of herself took as much energy as dancing; being alone evenings took more.

Marta stowed her clothes and carried the empty suitcases and boxes to the basement. She placed the photos on her dresser by the window, folded the quilt over the back of the rocking chair, and sat down to rock before going to bed. Since the time she could climb into her dad's chair, she'd loved to rock. Year after year, she solved problems in his chair. Today had been a roller coaster of emotions but she'd survived her apology, gotten her luggage from home, and sealed a friendship with Lynne and Bartley. Maybe this chair provided the same comfort, the same effect as her dad's. She closed her eyes and rocked.

At a quarter to five, the music stopped and the practice room emptied. Marta stretched side to side and swiveled her ankles. She longed to remove her *pointe* shoes, but if she planned to stay and practice, she needed to keep them on a little longer. She distracted herself from the pain by humming today's music as she moved through the choreography.

Having the entire room to herself energized her. She moved through a dozen *changements, pas de bourees,* and *balancés.* On and on she danced. The *Sleeping Beauty* choreography helped her brush aside the pain in her feet.

She focused on her dad and how he loved the ballet. He'd have come to every performance and grabbed a front row seat, if he'd lived. And her mom. She loved ballet and dancing enough to work six days a week at Miss Holland's studio for the past nine years so Marta could have free lessons.

The mirror reflected back her improving footwork. Her arm extensions looked more natural. Madame and Damien would surely notice. Soon they'd no longer doubt her ability and dedication. Her family could be proud of her as well.

As she finished, the tension in her shoulders melted away, leaving her battered feet as her only problem. She sat down on the practice room floor to remove her pointe shoes and pick the lamb's wool from her open blisters. Pain flared as she exposed the raw, red circles on each toe. Time to start soaking her feet each night in Epsom salts and hot water.

Lynne stuck her head in the room. She'd already changed into street clothes and held her keys in one hand and her sweaty workout clothes in the other. "Eww. Your toes look as hideous as mine feel. The guys are lucky they don't wear torture shoes."

"I agree. Are you in a hurry?"

"Kinda. My aunt has company coming. I promised to help her get ready. See you tomorrow."

Lynne disappeared down the hall, leaving Marta no chance for a much-desired ride home.

∾

As Marta pedaled west, the straps of her leather sandals pressed into her skin. She stopped, unbuckled her sandals, and hung them over the handle bars. The rough pedals dug into her bare feet, but she focused on her evening: shower, dinner, soak her feet, and fall into bed—hopefully in that order.

With a shower and dinner completed, Marta lay motionless on her bed, letting her body sink into foggy thoughts of the day's practice. She'd survived Madame's regimen, but each day brought one difficult expectation after another. "Keep the pace, watch your arms, head up, don't crowd the principal dancers." Would the commands and the scrutiny of the corps dancers ever end? She pushed herself to standing and spread a bath towel on the rug beside her bed.

She returned from the kitchen with a tea kettle of hot water and a tin basin that she placed on the towel. She sprinkled in Epsom salts and trailed her fingers through the milky water until it cleared. Then she sat on the edge of her bed and held her breath as she dipped her feet into the steamy water.

Relief and pain hit simultaneously. Broken blisters flared like liquid fire when the water rippled across them. Lynne and Bartley were probably doing the same thing in their apartments. Sacrificing her feet was a small price to pay if it meant continuing to dance as a professional.

She let her thoughts drift to imagining her mom fixing dinner for one: a salad from her vegetable garden, baking powder biscuits, and fresh blackberries. Her mouth watered as she visualized her mom's low calorie cooking. Mrs. B. created great meals, but her dinners catered to hungry men: roasts, mashed potatoes, gravy, corn or peas, and pie or cake every night.

Dancing demanded proper food. Every dancer discovered a way to handle food issues. Lynne and Jer ate like hungry bears. Bartley never craved food or looked tired. Marta took small portions, ate half, and pushed the rest around her plate.

Marta considered her weekday schedule. It started at dawn and continued until she pedaled home, showered, ate dinner, and helped Mrs. B. Then she sat alone in her room or flopped across her bed. She loved the music, the dances, Damien's calm directions, her new friends, and her new ballet home. But when she had free time, loneliness flooded her brain. She remained too tired to plan a sewing project. Maybe over the weekend she could make the time to embroider a scarf or something.

Friday afternoon Marta stood in line behind Lynne and Bartley waiting to collect one hundred-thirty dollars, her two-week paycheck. She had enough money for rent, her own stash of food, and shopping for small touches to make her room homey. Next payday she'd open a checking and savings account and begin to repay her mom. Sending money home would be a nice change.

"Hey, Marta. Are you going with us tomorrow?" Lynne asked. "Should be fun, right, Bartley?"

"Right," Bartley said. "Cowboys on horses and weird rock formations. Whoopee for us."

Marta shrugged. "Not Saturday. But maybe Sunday."

"Got a hot date?" Lynne said.

Marta laughed. "Only with my comfy bed"

Mrs. B. hung up the damp flour sack towels and put on her rings as Marta put away the last dinner bowls. "I overheard you tell Shorty and James that you'd like to be able to practice on weekends. I have an idea that won't cost you a penny."

Mrs. B. led Marta to the basement and flipped on the light in the storage room. They navigated through the tenant suitcases and boxes, passing assorted piles of household supplies, as well as an array of dust-covered objects.

The musty smelling space opened up to an area the size of a small practice room at the ballet company. A small, dingy window let in light and a view of the flower bed next to the back steps.

Mrs. B. pulled hanging strings that turned on two ceiling lights. "What do you think? Would this work for you?"

Marta walked a slow circle around the room. "Wow. It's a great space."

"I knew you'd see its potential. Needs a little cleaning and rearranging, but it's yours if you want. Feel free to use whatever you find."

"Really?" Marta did a quick inventory: a large mirror, a coat rack, kitchen chairs, cardboard boxes, a table, a dress form, trunks, and empty picture frames.

"We can restack the luggage in the alcove. Practice whenever you wish. The room is below the common areas so you won't need to worry about disturbing anyone."

"It's perfect. It's...thank you."

Together they restacked the renters' boxes and suitcases before Mrs. B. returned upstairs. Marta hummed as she cleaned away cobwebs and swept the floor. She salvaged several items, setting them aside until she decided how she'd used them. Only the window refused to yield to her energetic work; years of paint layers sealed it shut.

After breakfast the next morning, she rummaged through the fabric bin Mrs. B. set out. She hand-stitched her yard of rose colored chiffon from her mom to a strip of gray satin to hang at the window. Then she draped scarf-sized yardage over the dress form and moved the headless companion to a corner. She sat on the floor and tore calico and gingham into strips to wrap the empty frames, creating wall art. Lastly, she repaired the desilvered mirror with kitchen tin foil taped to the back.

She wrestled with the wobbly chair, then pushed it aside and started *pliés* to the music in her head. Next paycheck she'd scout out a record player and buy long play classical records, or perhaps her mom would send a few of Dad's.

That afternoon she practiced her corps dances numerous times before heading to the kitchen to bake bread. As she set the dough to rise, a calmness settled in. The basement improved her mood like a giant hug. Billings and the boarding house felt more like home every day.

For Saturday dinner, Marta went to her portion of a shelf in the boarders' refrigerator and took out her bread. She swirled on creamy peanut butter, moving her knife from top to bottom and edge to edge before adding a dollop of Mrs. B.'s raspberry jam. She folded the bread in half without cutting it and took a small bite as she grabbed an apple from the basket on the worktable and headed down the stairs to the basement.

"What are you doing?"

Marta stopped and looked up. Carol leaned over the entry railing. Her black hair fell forward over her face; her eyes and nose looked like a white mask floating in the dusky light.

"You're not supposed to go down there unless you're washing clothes. And I don't see any clothes."

"Mrs. B. is letting me use part of the basement as a practice space."

"Hm-mp. So you say. Just don't interfere with my guests and my privacy." Carol turned away, then turned back. "And keep your music turned down."

Marta stayed in the stairway listening to Carol's feet slap noisily against each step until she reached the upstairs landing. When the carpet silenced her movements, Marta shook her head. Good riddance, Carol, she thought as she reached for the storage room door.

"Marta?" Shorty called down the steps. "Whatcha doin'?"

"Hi, Shorty. "I'm going to practice."

"Is it okay if I come watch?"

She laughed. "I'd rather you not, but come down and see how I cleaned up the space."

Shorty clumped down the steps and held the battered basement door open for Marta. He scanned the room and nodded. "This is real nice, Marta. Did you fix it up yourself?"

"Yep. It's old stuff. Mrs. B. said to use whatever I found down here. Now I'm working out how to make a *barre*."

Shorty scratched his graying stubble. "What do you need?"

"Something like a broom handle to attach to the wall."

"Hold on," he said. "I saw an old broom on the back porch that looked kinda ragged. Bet that would work. Be back in a minute."

Marta sat on the floor nibbling her sandwich and wiping away the jam that gathered in the corners of her mouth. Shorty returned with a neatly cut broom handle and two shelf brackets. His wide smile displayed his crooked teeth. "How's this, Marta?"

Marta ran her hand along the handle and laughed. "You've massacred Mrs. B.'s broom."

"Yep. She even handed me the saw."

They mounted the broomstick *barre* waist high on the wall and stood back to admire their work.

Marta handed Shorty the tools and nodded with approval. "This looks great! Thanks."

"My pleasure, Miss Marta. Maybe someday I'll see you dance."

"When I have records and a player, I'll invite you down, and I'll dance for you. How'd that be?"

"Sounds great," Shorty said.

"Is there any way we can pry the window open?" Marta asked.

Shorty ran his hand along the bottom edge of the window and scrunched up his mouth. "Not sure. Might take a chisel or crow bar. I'll talk with Mrs. B. For now I guess I'd better let you practice."

"Thanks, Shorty. I appreciate your help."

Sunday morning Marta stood on the front porch, waiting to join Lynne and Bartley for the day. Lynne drove them out along the Yellowstone River, stopping at two roadside parks where they walked the trails. Then they took the county roads through miles of rolling hills where late blooming wild flowers swayed in the breeze, creating a sea of pastels.

In the cowboy town of Hardin they bought ice cream and wandered through the trading post, trying on western hats and boots. At dusk they ended their adventures at Lynne's place near Lake Elmo.

Lynne lived in an apartment above her aunt's garage. Its one room furnishings consisted of two overstuffed brown chairs, a twin bed with a nine-patch quilt, two dressers, and a round maple dining table with two chairs. A bulky television stood near the table; its wooden box took up a space large enough for another dresser. A metal unit housed the sink, a counter, a small refrigerator, and a two-burner stove all in one.

Lynne hung her purse on a hook inside the door. "Well, what do you think? Not bad for twenty dollars a month. Anyone want a beer?"

"Beer?" Bartley said. "What are you doing with beer? Madame would kill you."

"She'll never know unless you tell her. The neighbor brings over a couple when he comes to visit. Beer tastes good on a hot day. From the looks on your faces, I guess it's no to beers and yes to root beer instead."

Lynne opened bottles of root beer, handed them out, then flopped across her bed with a bag of potato chips. "When did you two know you wanted to be dancers?"

Bartley sat in one overstuffed chair with her legs over the armrest. "When I was three. I told my mother I wanted ballet lessons and a wand. Wasn't that silly?" She shook out her ponytail, letting her hair trail down her back.

"Did you get both?" Marta said as she sat at the table.

"Of course. I'm my father's angel. I still get whatever I want. Back then he installed a *barre* in the pool house and hired a ballet teacher to come to the house twice a week. I felt like a princess."

Lynne tossed the open bag of potato chips to Bartley. "Sounds like your family had lots of money. Did you go to public school or private?"

"Private boarding school. What about you, Lynne?"

"Born and raised in project houses," Lynne said. "Public school and YMCA dance classes until I turned nine. Then I got a scholarship to a dance school. I quit high school at fifteen to work and pay for advanced ballet lessons, and here I am, on my way to becoming a ballerina."

"Yep. Here you are," Bartley said. "Did your parents pamper you, Marta?"

"I guess. We listened to ballet music from when I was a baby. I started lessons when I was five. My dad never saw me dance in *pointe* shoes."

"Why not?" Lynne said.

"He died when I was seven. He fell through a railing at work. I miss him and hearing the sound of his voice when he'd come home from work each night."

Marta walked to the window and looked out, seeing nothing in particular. What was it her dad always said? Something about never really leaving home? Why couldn't she remember?

When she turned back, Lynne and Bartley were staring at her in silence. She smiled. "Let's focus on our dancing and being best friends, okay?"

෨

Bartley drove Marta back to her boarding house and headed to her place to help with a party for visiting dignitaries. As Marta entered the boarding house, she inhaled the aroma of Sunday dinner, now long finished. James and Shorty sat playing cards. Mrs. B. walked in from the kitchen, carrying a vase filled with an assortment of garden flowers. "Did you and your friends have a nice day?"

"We did. We forgot about dancing for a few hours."

"Did you find a record player or any records yet?" Shorty asked.

"Not yet."

"Shorty told me about your practice space," James said.

"It's great. Come and see it."

Both men followed Marta to the basement. As she opened the door, she wondered if they'd begrudge her having a special privilege in being allowed to use the space. Maybe they'd have liked it for a shop or a place to make a game room. She need not have worried.

The wobbly chair leg had been wired back into position. A small, well used record player sat on the leveled card table, and four long play albums rested against an apple crate. Marta looked from one face to the next. "Where did all this come from?"

"James and I fixed the chair 'n the table," Shorty said. "I had the player, and James gave you the records. We hope you like it. We don't mean to interfere."

Tears flooded Marta's eyes as she scanned the room. "You two are wonderful. Thank you." She stepped to the table and fingered the record player, then smiled at the two gentlemen elves. "I'll need to plan a performance, won't I?"

Both men laughed.

"We promise we'll not come down unless you invite us," James said.

"Tell her about the window," Shorty said.

"We unstuck the window. Used a crowbar to break the paint free. Then we put a new lock on the top." James unlocked, opened, closed, and relocked the window. "Now you'll have fresh air whenever you want."

"Thank you, James; thank you Shorty. Everything is perfect."

The men backed out of the room. Marta trailed her hand along the record player and checked the album titles: *The Overture of 1812, Beethoven's Concerto in D, Christmas at Carnegie Hall,* and *Tchaikovsky's Nutcracker Suite.* She placed the *Nutcracker* record on the turntable and gently lowered the needle onto the first ring. Then she sat on the floor, feeling the music flow through her.

Images of her recital performances drifted through her mind: the sugar plum fairy, the waltzes, the quirky Chinese doll dance. She loved every dance. Soon she'd learn more of the choreography and perform the dances as a professional. Life looked good.

On her way upstairs to her room, she crossed through the kitchen and knocked on Mrs. B.'s door. When the door opened, Mrs. B.'s face wore a wide smile. "Did the men surprise you?"

"Yes. It's a wonderful surprise," Marta said. Her lips quivered; she rubbed her mouth to control the tears that threatened to overcome her.

"I didn't think you'd be mad, that's why I let them go ahead and work down there. They've been waiting for you to return." Mrs. B. touched Marta's arm. "Would you care to join me for a cup of tea? I'm suddenly thirsty."

They sat at a small table in the bay window of the common room. The only sounds were spoons scraping inside porcelain cups.

"So, Marta, you have a studio back home?"

"That's what I called it, but it was just our garage. We didn't have a car, so we hung a mirror in it, and my dad gave me his old record player and several classical records." Marta stared out the window, then looked back at Mrs. B. "Now, you've given me a space too. Thank you. It's like being home."

The two women sat in peaceful silence watching the shadows deepen. Mrs. B. set her cup back onto the tray and stood. "Thank you for sitting here with me. A cup of tea is such a pleasant way to end the weekend. But now I must get ready for work tomorrow. Night, Marta"

"Night, Mrs. B." Marta put her cup on the tray and lingered in the common room until it was time to place her Sunday call to her mom. Tonight she had lots to share.

*B*y the end of September, practices for the fall performances and Marta's energy were both winding down. Her turns hadn't smoothed out, so Lynne offered to work with her after rehearsals.

Marta listened for Lynne's count: "...three, four, begin." She stared at the cascade of red ribbons purposely mounted above eye level in the far corner and did a *relevé* to *pointe*. Like the other dancers, she used the ribbons to focus her direction and body position for turns. She began spinning across the room doing quick *chaîné* turns, linking corner to corner with tight steps, her arms opening and closing near waist-high to complete and balance her circling.

At the corner she stepped out of her turns, staggered, and grabbed the floor by forcing her toes flat to prevent herself from falling over. "I can't do one more *chaîné*; not one. Let's move on."

"Okay. Those looked better. Now, your *pirouettes*. Remember to lift your nose and your spine."

Marta executed a *plié*, then a quick *relevé* to *pointe,* and began her turns to the right, spotting a small wall crack above the center of the practice room mirror.

"You're dropping your chin," Lynne said.

After a dozen turns, Marta stopped and repeated *pirouettes* on her left side.

"Those look great, Miss Lefty, but, you're tipping a bit. Maybe spot higher, or maybe you need to stop and eat."

Marta stopped and panted. "Both might help. Thanks for staying to help me. I'll take a ride tonight if you're offering."

They turned off the light in the small practice room and walked toward the dressing room. As they approached the large rehearsal room, agitated voices tumbled into the hallway. One was a male voice they didn't recognize, but the other belonged to Madame Cosper.

"Don't talk to me that way, Herbert," Madame said. "I'm the director. Who do you think you are, making judgments about my priorities?"

"I'm the money that keeps this dance company in the black," the male voice said. "You're the one who sends it into the red. That's who I am."

"I am trying to create a first class troupe. We have our strongest dancers in years, but they're dancing in thread bare costumes. New costumes would showcase the troupe, especially when we travel. The committee won't release money unless you urge them. Please, Herbert."

"There is no money to release, Anna. You'll have to make do with what you have to attract additional benefactors. Now, I must go. Good night."

"Herbert, please. Stay. Talk to me." Her voice changed to something softer, pleading. "Don't go."

"Diane is waiting for me. We have a social engagement."

"I've missed you, Herbert."

The room went silent. Marta looked at Lynne; both girls backed away and slipped into the practice room, waiting for Madame and Herbert to leave.

Booted footsteps moved toward the front door. That door opened and clicked shut. Madame's cane thumped closer. Marta and Lynne dashed to the dressing room.

"Take off your practice clothes," Lynne said, "and get your hair wet. Pretend you got out of the shower. Hurry!"

They scurried out of their practice clothes, splashed water on their heads, and started re-dressing in street clothes as Madame entered the dressing area.

"Oh! Why are you two still here?"

"We worked on turns in the small practice room," Lynne said. "Heading out now. Good night, Madame."

Madame stepped aside. "Wait!" She thumped her cane.

Both girls froze mid-stride.

"Exit through the front door. And don't make a habit of staying late. I don't have time to check for you two every night."

"Yes, Madame," Marta said. "Good night."

On the street, Lynne chuckled. "Hm-m-m. Sounds like they're more than benefactor and company director. And did you hear her say she had the strongest dancers in years?"

"Too bad she doesn't share her appreciation with us," Marta said. "Do you think the company is running out of money?"

"I doubt it if Madame is asking for new costumes. Maybe Bartley knows. Let's remember to ask her...or Jer."

"What made you think of pretending we'd been in the shower?" Marta asked when they were in the car. "You were so careful about what you said."

"Marta, I have four older brothers. I had to be devious to listen in on their conversations. I hid in closets or behind curtains. It's paying off now. Do you think Diane knows her Herbert is visiting Madame?"

"You aren't going to tell anyone, are you?" Marta said.

Lynne pursed her lips and smiled. "Only if I need to."

୬

Marta yawned as she trudged up the boarding house stairs to her room. Every part of her body ached, even her hair. As she reached the top of the stairs, Mrs. B. called to her.

"Marta? Coming to dinner?"

"Not tonight. See you in the morning."

Marta crashed face down across her bed without removing her jacket. A soft knock on the door roused her. "Who is it?"

"Mrs. B. May I speak with you?"

Marta opened her door.

Mrs. B. scanned Marta from toe to head. "Marta, dear, I'm worried about you. You're skipping dinners, and you look exhausted."

Marta yawned. "I'm okay. When I'm this tired I can't eat."

"What did you do back home? I can't imagine your mother let you skip meals."

"Fruit cocktail and ginger ale were all I could get down," Marta said. "You're a great cook, but when I'm this tired food isn't appealing."

"Say no more. This is your home now. You should have what you need. I have ginger ale in the pantry, and I'll stock fruit cocktail. Join us when you feel up to it. I know Shorty and James enjoy eating your portions, but they miss talking with you."

"Thanks for understanding. I'll be down to do dishes in a minute."

"Nonsense. If you don't eat, there's no need."

Marta yawned again. "Okay. Once this first show comes together, I'll be back to normal." She started to take off her coat, then stopped, afraid Mrs. B. would scrutinize her thinness the way her mom did back home. "Night, Mrs. B."

The following Saturday morning, Lynne and Marta drove to Bartley's apartment. Lynne shifted gears as they chugged south over the Yellowstone River, past a lake, and up a winding road. They turned in at the

Bar TT Ranch sign where the hard-packed dirt road wandered through a stand of cottonwoods. They followed Bartley's directions and turned left at the fork in the road. Bartley sat in a lawn chair on a brick patio in front of a small brick house.

Lynne turned off the engine and shouted, "You call this an apartment?"

"Well, it kinda is. I mean, it's..."

"This is a whole house!"

"Bartley's being modest," Marta said.

"Grab your stuff and come in," Bartley said. "I'll explain."

The house had two bedrooms, a spacious kitchen, a carpeted living room, a laundry room, two bathrooms, and a garage. A screened patio at the back of the house abutted a split rail fence. "My parents grew up with the owners. Once they discovered I'd be moving to Billings, they wouldn't take no for an answer."

Lynne flopped down in a small Danish modern chair. "Do you at least pay rent like the rest of us?"

"Of course. The bad part is that they don't want people coming and going. I had to promise that I wouldn't have friends over or have parties. Don't tell the others, especially Jer. He's a true chatterbox."

"If it's a secret, why invite us?" Marta said.

"I wanted you to see where I live. Maybe I can get you invited to one of their fancy parties. So far these past weeks I've met a handful of senators and an old time movie star. Everything is hush, hush. Guests fly in to the private runway on the other side of the ranch. The staff's not allowed to discuss anything about the ranch when they're in town."

Lynne stood and walked around the living room. "Sounds snooty, don't you think?"

"You're right, but it's all business, even the parties. I should get my own place, but for my parents' sake I stay. They're all friends of Madame and several of the ballet's benefactors."

"Really?" Lynne said. "Is that how you got your position?"

"Of course not. I earned my position just like you did. For the audition I misspelled my last name so they wouldn't recognize my family name. Then I corrected it after I was selected."

"Tricky," Lynne said. "I like that."

The girls' conversation moved to the latest movies, popular movie stars, and their favorite music. At lunchtime Bartley set the table and brought out two salads, cold cuts, and two pitchers of drinks.

"Did you fix all this?" Lynne asked.

"Most of it, but the cook in the main house brought over the cold cuts. I can cook, you know."

While they ate, they discussed their fellow corps dancers. "What do you think of Jer?" asked Bartley.

"He's cute," Lynne said, "but I don't date dancers."

"He helped me the day I arrived," Marta said. "He's the only guy that smiles and says hello. And he goes to lunch with us. Hope his girlfriend doesn't mind."

"Somehow he gets all the latest gossip," Lynne said. "He said Patrice might get engaged this fall. And Marguerite has a connection to Madame."

Bartley laughed. "I know. She's the daughter of one of the major benefactors. That's why Madame thinks she's so special. She is a strong dancer, but—"

"But nothing," Lynne said. "She needs to earn those compliments."

Marta listened to the conversation, preferring to stay out of anything about the company. Practices with Madame felt less contentious lately. She didn't want to give Madame any excuse, even gossip, to dismiss her.

After the girls cleaned up the dishes, they walked around the property. At the duck pond they took off their shoes and waded in. They ended their day by invading Marta's basement practice room and convincing her to bake molasses cookies.

That evening, like every evening, Marta sat and rocked. The upcoming week they'd complete rehearsals. Her first performance as a professional dancer moved closer and closer.

*M*onday morning Marta hurried into the dressing room to change. Madame Cosper stood watching the clock and the female dancers as they prepared for the day. "Good morning, Madame," Marta said as she curtsied and lowered her eyes.

Madame ignored her and moved to where Patrice stood tying her *pointe* shoe ribbons and smoothing her practice skirt. "Good morning, Patrice. I see you're ready early." Madame thrust her chin high and turned toward Marta. "I wish everyone shared your dedication."

Marta's face heated as though sunburned. She studied the ties of her dance skirt, wondering where the criticism came from after a week of being out of Madame's sights. Looking up, she met the eyes of several corps dancers who relaxed as Madame's focus moved away from any of their inadequacies.

Madame clapped twice and shouted, "Hurry along! We're taking an informal group photo for the local paper in the large practice room." She thumped her cane once and walked away, smoothing her wispy gray chignon.

The reporter grouped the principal dancers standing beside Madame with the corps standing and kneeling on the edges. A photographer took four shots, thanked them, packed his gear, and left.

Marta took her place at the *barre* and rotated her neck to loosen her tight muscles. She swept her arm smoothly to the side, then over her head. She tilted her head forward to look out from under her raised arm at an imagined audience.

"Hi."

Marta startled at the sound of the reporter's voice.

"May I talk with you for the article?" She relaxed. He wasn't talking to her, though she wondered who he had cornered. Then she felt a tap on her shoulder.

"Excuse me, Miss. I'm Steve Mason. May I ask you a few questions for my article?"

She turned toward the reporter. He smiled. She smiled in return and smoothed her hair, then her practice skirt. "I guess. But I've only recently joined the company. You should talk with a dancer who's been here longer."

"No, you'll do fine, believe me," he said. Was he flirting? "I'd like to interview someone new. Let me clear it with Mrs. Cosper. She wanted to know who I'd be interviewing."

"She prefers to be called *Madame* Cosper. She'll say I can't talk right now; we're beginning rehearsals."

The reporter didn't move away. "How about later then? I have until six to turn in my article."

Marta glanced around the practice room, buying time to decide what to say next. When she looked back, he smiled. He was cute and looked harmless enough. She liked his intense blue eyes and the way he brushed aside his floppy blond hair. "We finish around four. I can meet you out front at a quarter after."

"Great," he said. "Thanks." He stowed his pad and pencil in his jacket pocket and headed out the door. Looking back, he nodded in her direction before disappearing.

Marta saw Madame follow his exit then turn to glare at her. Not good. Plus, the reporter hadn't stopped to ask permission from Madame.

After rehearsals, Madame stood in the dressing room doorway. "I need a word with you, Marta."

"Yes, Madame." Marta curtsied.

"What did that reporter want?"

"An interview. Didn't he talk with you?"

"No, and don't bother to stay. I want him to interview Patrice. She's principal dancer and can share more details about the company." Madame stared at Marta until she lowered her gaze.

"Yes, Madame, but he needs to turn in his story by six o'clock tonight."

Madame frowned and shouted across the dressing room, "Where's Patrice?"

A voice answered, "She left with Rose to select fabrics."

Madame scowled as she turned back to Marta. "Very well. I guess you'll do. Tell him about the *entire* company, not just yourself." She brushed past Marta as she left the dressing room.

As Marta changed clothes, a tingle of excitement moved through her. The reporter had a cute smile. His exuberance reminded her of Leo, her neighbor back home. Could be fun to talk to someone who wasn't a dancer, over the age of thirty, or Carol.

Marta sat on the steps waiting for the reporter, watching traffic move along the street. Thank heavens she'd listened to discussions at the dancers' meeting last week. In addition to talking about injuries and choreography, they'd touched on Madame's history and past company programs. She'd give Mr. Mason a quick tour and be done in time for dinner at the boarding house.

He pulled to the curb in an older black car. As he walked toward her, she stood and brushed the wrinkles from her flowered cotton skirt. She entwined her fingers behind her back, then crossed her arms in front, then put her hands behind her back again.

"Hi. Thanks for meeting me, Miss Marta Selbryth."

"How do you know my name, Mr. Mason?"

"Call me Steve." He reached his hand forward. "A reporter never reveals his sources."

His firm grip gave off comfortable heat. Marta looked toward her toes as a sudden awkwardness crept through her. When she looked up, he smiled and gestured toward his car. "Ready for that Schlitz?"

"What's that?" she said.

"Schlitz is a beer. Or, would you rather have a glass of wine?"

"Neither. I'm seventeen. Let's do a quick tour of the dance company, okay?"

"Sure," he said as he checked his watch. "We'll need to hurry so I can make deadline."

Steve opened his notebook as they rounded the building to the dancers' door. As Marta pulled the door open, she jumped back. Madame stood in the hallway.

"Madame Cosper!" Marta said. "I…We were…"

Madame ignored Marta and granted Steve one of her rare smiles. "I have a few minutes I can spare to speak with you. Your name again?" she asked.

"Steve Mason, *Mountain Sentinel*, Ma'am. Miss Selbryth planned to give me a quick tour before my deadline. Susan Zane, the arts editor, will call next week for an in depth interview with you."

"I see." Madame lifted her chin and smoothed back her hair. "Very well, then. Finish before Karl locks up at five."

"Yes, Madame." Marta curtsied, then led the way. Madame followed them down the hall. At the stairway, she turned upstairs. Marta kept walking. She stopped at the corner and pointed to the new poster. "This is our new season. It's an exciting year of dances."

Steve nodded and jotted notes in his notebook. He leaned close and whispered, "Is she always that friendly?"

"Madame?"

He held his finger to his lips and whispered, "Don't answer that."

Marta covered her mouth to hide her smile. Steve noticed more than she anticipated. It wouldn't do for Madame to think she'd spoken ill of her or the company. "Let's go upstairs."

"How many new dancers this year?"

"There are four of us: three girls and one boy."

"Why don't you call them women and men?"

Marta stopped abruptly at the top of the stairs. "I don't know. That's what they always call us."

Steve made a note. "Interesting. If my college instructor called us girls and boys, we'd feel insulted."

Marta had no response as she hurried on to the costume shop. "This is where our company stores its costumes. She took down a white tutu with a hand-beaded bodice. "This costs about four hundred dollars."

"That tiny thing? That's what I paid for my first car. What size is it anyway?"

"It's many sizes. From zero up to an eight. Seamstresses adjust costumes to the size of the dancer wearing it."

"Zero is a size?"

Marta laughed. "Let's go downstairs."

As they walked though the practice rooms, she talked about the principal dancers, the music selections, and the soloists for the fall performance.

"What solos do you have?" he asked.

"I'm in the *corps de ballet*. I'll audition as an understudy, but it often takes years to earn a solo."

"That's too bad, but it's the same in the newspaper business. Gotta intern and prove yourself before people take you seriously and turn you loose."

"Hm-m. I never thought of it that way. Is there anything else you'd like to see?"

"You agreeing to have dinner with me." He closed his notebook, crossed his arms, and leaned against the wall. His smile held her attention, encouraging her to smile.

Marta turned away to hide her fluster. He was a charming guy, tall and lean and easy to talk with. Must have a ton of girlfriends. "Let me think about that."

At the end of the long the hallway, Steve pointed to the cubbies filled with *pointe* shoes. "Why are there so many shoes?"

"Each of us will go through as many as six pairs of *pointe* shoes during a week of performances, plus several pairs a month during rehearsals. We use the shoes until they start to break down."

"Break down?"

"Let me show you." Marta handed him one of her shoes. "This is new."

Steve turned the shoe over and ran his hand along the pink satin top, the ribbons, and the toe. He flexed the shoe, then handed it back to Marta. Next, she handed him a scuffed shoe. His fingers crushed the toe. He flexed the arch back and forth.

"Feel the difference?" Marta asked.

"Yeah, I do."

"The stiffened toe of *pointe* shoes is called the box. Once it gets soft, it's tossed. Broken shoes aren't safe."

"Why keep these broken shoes then?" Steve handed back the shoe and scribbled notes.

"I forgot to toss them." She put her hand on his arm. "Don't print that."

He nodded but kept writing. "Sounds unsafe and expensive. Good thing the company buys your shoes."

"Who told you that? We buy our own."

"Pricey, isn't it?" he said.

"Steve, please don't write about the shoes. That's not anything people need to know." If he printed anything about broken shoes, Madame would be embarrassed and send her packing.

"Consider it our little secret, Marta." He closed his notebook and checked his watch. "We'd better hurry. I have one last question: how tall are you?"

Marta straightened and lifted her chin. "I'm five feet tall, and don't ask my weight. A free cup or glass of anything isn't worth enough for me to share that."

Steve held open the dancer's door for Marta to exit ahead of him. "If you can wait a few minutes, I'll file my story. Then I'd like to treat you to tea or dinner or whatever."

"You don't need to do that."

"I'd like to, Marta. After all, I took up your time."

Steve opened the car door for Marta, then circled to the driver's side and climbed in. His car reminded her of the neighbor's fastback, except it was black instead of red.

"This is a nice car," Marta said.

"Thanks. I'd like to get a new car, maybe a Thunderbird. That's a cool car. But first I need to finish school and get a job. What kind of car do you drive?"

"I don't have one."

"How do you get around?"

"I walk, ride a bike, or get lifts from my friends."

"You're not the average person, are you? Most people our age can't wait to buy a car."

"Hm-m. Maybe so," she said. "But a car costs more money than I've saved, so I'll do without for now."

✌

The newspaper offices occupied a three-story building east of Twenty-seventh. While Steve typed the story, Marta sat at an empty desk and scanned the rows of gray metal desks in the cigarette smoke-filled room. A handful of people sat working at the desks; their fingers clattering across the typewriter keys sounded like snare drummers beating out a tattoo.

Through the haze she saw a man with a rumpled shirt and a loosened tie sitting in a glass enclosure. Every few minutes Steve looked up from typing to check the time, smile at Marta, and glance at the man in the box.

The newspaper office wasn't the exciting place she imagined. The man in the glass box glowered like Madame. She shivered. Maybe she and Steve experienced similar situations: snarly bosses, unrealistic deadlines, and superhuman performance expectations. At least the ballet company building provided adequate space, good lighting, and breathable air.

Steve finished, removed his story from the typewriter, and headed for the glass office. The man read it and nodded. Steve returned with a wide smile. "It passed. Let's eat. I'm starving."

Marta pointed toward the glass office. "Is that grumpy man your boss?"

"Yeah. And my dad."

"Oh, I'm...he looked serious, all business and—"

"That's okay. He's tough, but if I prove myself, I'll be assigned more hard news stories."

"What do you mean by hard news stories?"

"You know, real news instead of fluff pieces."

"You consider ballet fluff?"

"Well, er, kind of. You must admit it isn't hard news like covering a war or changing economics."

"Ballet and its music have lasted for hundreds of years. It's important to our lives. It brings more happiness than war."

"True, but it's not headline news, Marta."

Marta shrugged and looked down to her feet. She didn't want to argue about the value of ballet even though it had become her focus. How could she explain how she felt to someone who clearly didn't understand its importance?

Steve fidgeted and scratched his ear. "Let's pretend we didn't start this conversation. Let's grab a little dinner, okay?"

They crossed the street to The Granary. The crowded restaurant had knotty pine walls above the vinyl-covered banquette seating. Waitresses dressed in square dance style dresses carried heavy trays of food as if they weighed nothing. Marta could stand for hours and smile when she danced, but the constant smell of rich food would be a challenge she'd fail.

After they were seated and had ordered, Steve slid close to Marta. "This used to be a granary and part of the college back when it was an agriculture school. Lots of students work here."

"Did you ever work here?"

"No, my dad's kept me busy at the paper since I was a little kid. I've done everything from delivering papers to sweeping the floor to loading the morning paper onto our trucks. Writing for the paper is the best job, so far."

Marta nodded. She understood how interests grew to careers. "I feel the same way about ballet. From the time I was a little girl I wanted everything ballet in my life: classes, the music, paper dolls, and the costumes. Being a professional dancer is my dream come true."

"Sounds like we both have found something we love to do," Steve said.

❧

Marta watched their waitress set down their food. For several minutes she and Steve ate in silence. Steve offered her some of his potato chips, but she shook her head.

"How's your salad?"

"Good. And your burger?"

"Excellent. So, tell me about you and your family."

"We live in Bremerton, Washington. Dad worked as an electrician in the naval shipyard. Mom works at the dance studio where I took lessons."

"Where does your dad work now?"

She stared out the window, focusing on the car lights approaching the intersection before she answered. "He died several years ago."

"I'm sorry. That must be hard on you and your mom."

"At times. What about your family?"

"I'm fortunate, I guess. My entire family on both sides lives around Billings. I can't get into much trouble since my dad's in the paper business, my uncle's a police officer, and my grandfather served as the superintendent of the school district for many years."

"You must always be on your best behavior," Marta said.

"Not really. I acted wild in high school, but now I've settled down. I'm finishing journalism classes at Rocky Mountain College this year. I'd like to work for a big time newspaper. Are you taking classes?"

"No. School's not my favorite place. Besides, ballet takes up all my time."

"How long have you danced?"

"Twelve years."

"Wow. Doubt I could stay with one job for twelve years." He scanned Marta's salad. "Do you want anything more to eat?'

"No. I never eat much after a day of rehearsals. I'm too exhausted."

"Even for dessert?"

She nodded.

"When you aren't too full or too tired, what do you like for dessert?"

"Warm chocolate chip cookies and cinnamon buns. I also love fresh picked strawberries and peaches with cream."

"All together?"

"No," she giggled. "My mom's a great cook. If I ate her baking very often I'd be fat and no one would want to watch me dance."

"I'd watch you any day, any time."

Marta looked away. His comment made her face heat up. Was she blushing? She decided she'd need to be the one watching him and what she said. "So, tell me about Billings. What's there to do on weekends?"

"Lots. I go out with friends, see movies, go to parties, and study, of course. When I have time I wander around the region or drive to our family cabin in the mountains. What do you like to do?"

"Go to the beach and throw rocks."

"Why?"

"My dad and I walked to the nearby bay a lot. We threw rocks, trying to skip them. My record is eight skips. We used the time to talk about stuff." Marta pushed her plate aside.

"What does you mom do?"

"She works afternoons and evenings at the dance studio. Then she sews dance costumes and custom clothes in her free time, plus she grows a huge vegetable garden." Marta stopped talking and cocked her head. "You ask lots of questions."

"I am a reporter. I'm curious about you." Steve pushed his plate to the side, picked up the check, and reached for his wallet.

"Even curious about fluff like sewing?"

"Yep."

On the drive to the boarding house, Marta leaned her head against the passenger window. She watched the busy streets and sidewalks morph into tidy rows of brick and wood frame houses with tidy lawns. She relaxed, enjoying being with Steve.

When he pulled up outside the boarding house, he turned off the engine and shifted to face her. "I apologize for what I said about ballet being fluff. I don't know much about it. How about you teach me?"

"If you *really* want to learn about fluff."

Steve started to defend himself then stopped with a chuckle. "Good one, Miss Fluff. When can I have my first lesson?"

"Tomorrow, after I—oh no. My bike. It's still at the ballet company."

"No problem. I can drive you to the building in the morning. What time should I come by?" He slid his arm along the back of the seat. His fingers brushed Marta's shoulder. She flinched. He moved his hand away.

"Eight-thirty, if you keep your hand off my shoulder."

"But it's a nice shoulder." Steve leaned in to kiss her.

Marta put her hands on his chest and pushed him away. "Whoa! What do you think you're doing?"

He laughed and covered her hands with his. "Should I say I'm sorry? You're a lovely woman, Marta, and...since this was our first date, I thought—"

"Date? It's an interview, not a date, so think again. Jerk!" She pulled away, fumbled to open the door, then raced into the boarding house.

She clenched and unclenched her fists as she stomped up the stairs to her room. What a dope to believe she could become friends with someone outside the world of dancers, someone with interests beyond choreography and aching feet. Tomorrow she'd be walking to practice, hoping the bike hadn't been stolen. Thanks, Steve.

Pale morning light filtered in through the curtains; Marta's clock read six. She stretched, used the shower at her reserved time, dressed, and went to set the breakfast table.

The boarders were eating when the doorbell rang. Mrs. B. answered it, saying, "Thank you." When she entered the dining area she held a small bouquet of red carnations, white daisies, and orange dahlias.

"Ah! Flowers," James said. "That's a nice way to start any morning."

"Who are those for?" Carol leaned forward expectantly.

"Marta," Mrs. B. said as she handed her the flowers.

Marta's face heated up as she accepted the bouquet. How embarrassing, but nice. She thought she knew who'd sent them, but she didn't open the attached card. Instead, she hurried to the kitchen, filled a Mason jar with water, added the flowers, and carried them to her room. After closing her door, she inhaled the sweet-spicy scent of the carnations and read the card:

> Sorry I was such a jerk.
> May I drive you in to work?
> Please give me another chance.
> Teach me all about the dance.
> Steve
> P.S. I'm waiting outside.

She peeked out her window. Steve stood leaning against his car, reading the newspaper. He didn't notice her watching him.

Now what should she do? She'd stomped away from his car last night, and he brought her flowers this morning. He must want to be friends. But did she?

She tucked the note in her dresser drawer and checked her hair in the mirror. After she gathered up her dance clothes and her sweater, she hurried down the stairs. A nervous tingle ran through her body as she opened the front door.

Steve turned as she walked down the porch steps. "Hi, Marta. Did you like the flowers?"

"They're lovely. Where did you get flowers so early in the morning?"

"My aunt owns a flower shop. I help her during holidays, so I have a key. This morning I let myself in and grabbed, I mean, I picked out a bunch of flowers and wrapped them."

"They're nice, but you *were* a jerk, Steve."

"I guess. I wanted our relationship to begin better than that."

"Relationship? It was an interview, nothing more."

"Maybe. Let's talk in the car while I drive you to your dance school. Okay?" He opened the passenger door and gestured toward it.

"It's called the ballet company," she said, "and I'll take a ride. I just hope no one stole the bike overnight."

On the ride to town, neither spoke until Steve handed Marta the newspaper. "Here, read the story. Let me know what you think."

Marta scanned the photo and story. He'd done a good job explaining costumes and the upcoming performances, as well as complimenting the company and Madame with no mention of broken *pointe* shoes. Madame should be pleased.

"Your article is great. I'm surprised; you were listening."

"I always listen to beautiful girls, I mean, women."

At the ballet company building, Steve let the car idle. "Can we start over and go out for coffee today or tomorrow?"

Marta climbed out of the car. "Maybe. Call me."

"I don't have your number, Miss Marta, dancer."

She leaned back inside the car and smiled. "You're a newspaper man; figure it out."

"Good one, Miss Fluff. I *will* call."

Marta watched his car turn left at the corner before she walked toward the building. Her smile vanished. Madame Cosper stood by the green door, leaning on her cane.

*M*adame straightened and shook her head. "So, you're still with him? Did you even discuss the dance company?"

What did Madame mean? Did she think they'd been together overnight? How could Madame jump to that conclusion?

"Well?" Madame said. "What did you tell him?"

"I showed him the rehearsal rooms and the costumes, and I told him how you started the company about ten years ago." Marta shrank into herself as she spoke. "I mentioned our future productions and—"

"What did you tell him about me?"

"That you were a prima ballerina for The New York City Ballet and—"

Madame held up the paper and shook it in Marta's face. "This interview was a bad idea."

"Madame, I… we…"

"Stop stuttering. Get inside for rehearsals. You've done enough damage for one day." Madame thumped down the hall behind her, then turned up the stairs to her office.

Marta felt dizzy from the conversation. She leaned against the wall and took deep breaths to calm herself before entering the women's dressing room.

"What's in her bonnet?"

Marta gasped and held her hand over her heart. "Lynne! Don't do that! You scared me to death."

"Jumpy, jumpy! Why's Madame agitated?" Lynne said.

"She thinks I spent the night with the reporter, and she wants to know what I told him."

"Ooh la, la. Did you spend the night? Wait!" Lynne covered her ears. "No. Don't tell me. I wouldn't have wanted him pickin' my brain, even though he's cute."

"I didn't spend the night with him," Marta said. "I needed a ride back here to get the bike." She paused. "When he tried to kiss me I—"

"Kissing?" Lynne said. "Tell me more! Seriously, if Madame learned to read, she'd know the article made us sound special."

"Madame read it. I saw it in her hand. I read the article. He did a good job. She doesn't want to admit I could do something right."

Lynne shook her head. "Looks like we're in for a long day if Madame teaches our classes."

Luckily Madame didn't appear in any classes or rehearsals.

The following Saturday morning, Marta slid into Steve's car wearing her best casual clothes. She'd tossed, debated, and then threw on her favorite outfit, the pedal pushers her mom said made her look like the *Seventeen* ad. With her hair released from her ballet bun, she felt like a normal girl going out for a normal afternoon with a normal friend.

"You look nice," Steve said. "Can I consider this a date, or what?"

"It's an 'or what,'" she said.

Steve laughed. "We're not driving to the ballet company or going on errands. What would you call it?"

"My personal guided tour of Billings."

"But I've also planned a stop for your favorite dessert: chocolate chip cookies."

"Change that to a tour with a snack." She laughed and leaned back to enjoy his driving tour of town.

Billings had the economy-minded department stores like back home: J.C. Penney and Sears. It also had two movie theaters, small shops, and numerous cafes and restaurants. But Billings occupied a small corner of the prairie while her hometown edged the saltwater of Puget Sound.

"Now to my favorite view of town," Steve said. He turned north toward the long ridge near the inn where she stayed when she'd first arrived.

At the top of the ridge, they pulled onto the shoulder of the road. Steve turned off the engine, circled around to Marta's door, and opened it. When their fingers touched, heat surged through her. Their palm to palm connection felt uncomplicated and comfortable.

Steve smiled and tightened his grip as he led her across the gravel to the edge. "The Rims is the best view around. Behind us lies a vast plain that stretches into Canada. I imagine it covered with buffalo when the explorers came through. Below and in front of us, beyond town, the Yellowstone runs to the Powder River near our border with North Dakota."

As Marta scanned back and forth, a small plane flew low and disappeared.

"Is there an airport nearby?"

"The regional airport is on the ridge, a short walk from here. Want to take a look?"

"No," Marta said. "Let's stay here and enjoy this view."

"This is where I come to think. It's peaceful and feels miles away from everything."

The ridge muted the sounds of Billings. Streets and avenues, filled with their various buildings, converged at a distant point like a perspective drawing she'd done in high school art class.

"Where's my place?" she asked.

"Off to the right. I live further west. I pass near your place every day when I go to classes or to work."

"How far away are those mountains out to the southwest?"

"The Beartooths? Less than two hours. Want to go?"

"Can't," she said. "I promised to help Mrs. Belvern. If I bake and work in the kitchen, she reduces my rent. That way I have spending money."

"Oh, I get it. Mrs. Belvern is your built-in excuse to avoid dating me."

"What? No, and we're not dating."

Steve laughed. "Well, you can't blame me for trying to change your mind."

He tightened his grasp of her hand as he raised his left hand. "You can trust me. I'm a perfect gentleman. Scout's honor."

"You're a persistent guy, aren't you? But I know you were never a scout; you're using the wrong hand."

"Oops." He grinned, then tipped his head and looked serious. "Miss Marta Selbryth, Queen of Fluff, I want you to be my friend. Let's get that chocolate chip cookie to prove I'm generous as well as trustworthy."

They sat in the tiny ice cream parlor by the window on curlicue-backed metal chairs with strawberry calico cushions. Marta nibbled her cookie while Steve inhaled a banana split. "So, tell me more about yourself," she said.

Steve set down his spoon. "Not much else to tell. I'm twenty-one and an only child."

"I'm an only child too."

"Did you like it, or did you wish you had a big brother or sister?"

"I have my Mom and my dancing. That's been enough."

"Don't you want anything else, like to go out, travel, have adventures?" He reached across the table and took her fingertips in his hands.

The electricity surged again, warming her entire body this time.

"Why don't you want to date me, Marta? Haven't I been a perfect gentlemen?"

"Not perfect, but a gentleman. It's just that dancing is hard work. I'm exhausted by evening. Then I help Mrs. B. Right now I can't handle much more."

"I get it. School is demanding as well. Classes, projects, reading for hours, and preparing for tests. Then I work for my dad's paper. But I still find time to go out."

Marta looked down at their joined hands. "I've never dated."

Steve smiled and squeezed her hands. "Promise me when you are ready to date I can be first in line? After all, I did buy you a cookie."

She laughed and pulled her hand free. "Okay. But, for now I need to get home."

At the boarding house curb, Steve reached for Marta's hand again. She looked away as though the street held an interesting vista while she debated her next move. After a few seconds, she turned to face him.

"Thanks for the tour and the cookie," she said. "You were a gentleman."

"Does that mean I get a thank you kiss?" His eyebrows lifted as he waited for her reply.

"Do you *ever* give up?"

"Not when I meet an interesting young woman." He hopped out and opened her car door. "Tomorrow at noon? Part two of the tour?"

Marta smiled, then hurried up the front steps. At the door she stopped, turned, and called back, "I'll bring snacks."

Sunday morning Marta slept in. At noon she sat in the porch swing, rocking back and forth, humming and rehearsing the corps movements in her head. Finding time to go places with Steve would be a welcome break from her dance routine. She'd complained about how her empty time dragged on. Maybe the time had come to start dating, and Steve would be a great way to begin.

A bubble of excitement jittered through her as she watched his car pull to the curb. Before she stood, he approached her, taking the porch steps two at a time and bowing. "Miss Fluff, part two of your tour is ready. May I have the pleasure of your company?"

"Yes, kind sir." She curtsied, picked up a small cloth bag of snacks, and hurried down the steps.

They headed through town, away from the Rims, along a narrow road.

The sign read Lake Josephine Park. Two dozen ducks paddled around the grey-blue water and waddled in the mud before disappearing into the cattails and grass that grew along the sloped banks.

They parked and took a trail past the cattails and through a forest of spindly willows. Marta tugged Steve's hand, urging him to walk faster. When he didn't speed up, she broke away and ran around the bend in the trail and stopped on a rise. Below and in front of her a small river shimmered in the golden sunlight. "Is this the Yellowstone?"

Steve took his time catching up to her. Before he answered he reached for her hand. "Good guess. It's the Clark Fork. Lewis and Clark named it when they came through here on their way home."

"You're a walking, talking history book, Steve."

He bowed. "At your service."

Marta picked up a twisted stick. She wrote her name in the mud and dug thin trails around Steve. "This is almost like playing in the sand at the ocean, except there are no giant waves." She threw the stick into the river and watched it bobble away.

"Anything to amuse you. So, sounds like you miss the ocean."

"I do. We live near a bay. That's nice, but going to the big, wide ocean is a three hour drive from my home. I love the roar of the waves. When

I walk along the shore, I feel their thundering pull through me. It calms my thinking."

"Marta, you surprise me every time you speak. You have an unusual view of the world."

She smiled and studied his face. "How do you view the world?"

Steve laughed. "I don't really think about it much. I take each day as it comes. If I'm going to spend time with you, I guess I need to figure that out, huh?"

"Maybe."

They climbed the grassy bank of the river to eat their snacks: peanut butter sandwiches and apple wedges. Neither spoke for several minutes as they ate and absorbed the sunshine on their faces.

"I'm lucky you interviewed me," Marta said. "It's fun getting to know Billings with you."

"What about getting to know *me* in Billings?" He stretched his arms and reached for her hand.

"Uh-h. That too, maybe," she said as she closed her eyes.

"Marta? Are you going to sleep?"

"No. Resting and thinking."

"I've a confession," he said. "The interview was no accident. When I saw you, I knew I had to meet you. You're a beautiful young woman."

"Hardly. I'm just me."

His hand squeezed hers. The silence between them stretched on.

"Thanks for coming with me today," he said. "Can you get me a ticket to the Classic Sampler? I'd like to see those costumes and pointy shoes at work."

Marta shook her head and exhaled. "Pointy shoes? Really? It's *pointe* shoes. P-o-i-n-t-e shoes."

Steve's serious look broke apart. He pointed his finger at her and started laughing. "Got you, Miss Fluff. You're not the only one who can joke around."

Marta pushed his pointing finger aside. "Are you ever serious?"

"Of course I am. But it's fun to tease you."

လ

Back in front of the boarding house, Steve turned off the engine and helped Marta out of his car. They stood a breath apart on the porch. He pushed a stray hair off her face and tipped his head. His touch, his stare, and his closeness sent a warm anticipation through her.

"I need to go," she said. "I enjoyed the weekend. Thanks, Steve."

"Any time. Want a ride tomorrow morning?"

"That would be great."

"Is it time for that first kiss yet?"

She looked away. "Yes."

He put his hands on her shoulders and continued staring at her. She backed up one step. He drew her closer as he kissed her cheek, her nose and her forehead. She smiled and stepped forward. His thumb slid under her chin and kept her face toward him.

His kiss on her lips arrived with unexpected softness. She closed her eyes and let all thoughts float away. When she opened her eyes, he smiled, then backed down the porch steps and drove away.

Marta stood on the porch for several minutes reliving the kisses. Her body felt light as a feather. Odd. Her feet refused to move. It was as if they were nailed to the porch. When the sensation evaporated, she moved to the porch swing and sat rocking until Sunday dinner. It must have been the kiss.

လ

Marta's next day of rehearsing flew by. What had changed? Nothing except her interest in Steve. Madame actually smiled her direction during the *Sleeping Beauty* waltzes.

That night Steve called the boarding house. "You'll never guess what the paper wants. We're going to write a short series about the new corps dancers at the ballet company."

"What? Why?"

I convinced my dad that it would be interesting for readers to learn about ballet through your eyes."

"But Steve, you don't know anything about ballet."

"I know. We'll be a team. I'll talk with you and learn about ballet. Then I'll write the rough copy. Susan, the arts editor, will refine it and add other information about the company. She wants to promote ballet. Isn't it great? We can work together."

"But Madame will never approve."

"She already has. We'll interview her as well. We can write our part between your shows, I mean performances. Madame Cosper asked to review the copy before it goes to press. Susan surprised me and agreed. So, what do you think?"

"I don't know. Why don't you interview the other three new dancers?"

"I will. But you'll be my primary contact. Susan thinks hearing from the new dancers may attract young people to the performing arts. As a side benefit, it will give us more time to get to know each other."

Marta sat in her room thinking about the ballet articles. She liked the idea. Maybe it would put her back into Madame's good graces. Plus, the thought of spending additional time with Steve sent a warm thrill through her.

$\mathcal{T}$he week before their first performance, the dancers moved from the company practice rooms to the Fox Theater, from spare work spaces to a velvet curtained stage with elaborate scenery. Brilliant stage lights added to the magic. Instead of a lone pianist, they danced to an entire orchestra. Now, their first performance, her first performance, began within the hour.

The ballet sampler they prepared divided into three distinct parts. Part One shared scenes from *Coppélia*. Assorted solos followed in Part Two, giving the corps dancers a chance to rest before returning to end the evening with scenes from *Sleeping Beauty* in Part Three.

That last segment worried Marta. It contained her fast change from light, festive fairy to angry, spiteful fairy, thanks to Madame's assigning her the role of Carabosse.

"Half hour," the stage manager called into the theater dressing rooms. A moment of panic froze Marta in place where she sat between Lynne and Bartley finishing her makeup. Their long table lay strewn with make-up pots, used tissues, combs, brushes, and open lipstick tubes. Dozens of small bare light bulbs lit the mirrors and whitened their faces.

Marta looked around at the other corps dancers. None returned her glances. She focused on darkening her eyebrows and adding deep blue eye shadow and true red lipstick. She smudged her lips together and touched the photo of her mom that she'd tucked along the edge of the mirror in front of her.

eye shadow and true red lipstick. She smudged her lips together and touched the photo of her mom that she'd tucked along the edge of the mirror in front of her.

None of the friends spoke. Marta assumed Lynne and Bartley had drifted away to block out their nervousness. She certainly had. Could she find a word for the fluttery feeling zigzagging through her body? It felt different than stage fright, more mellow and expectant, yet intense. Her dance performance life began in less than thirty minutes.

She slipped on her leg warmers and a thin sweater as she moved to the stage for final warm-ups led by Damien. Lynne and Bartley joined her at a portable *barre*.

"Are you guys as jumpy as I am?" Marta asked. "It's like someone poured live crickets down my throat."

"Waiting is the toughest part," Lynne said. "I feel like an imposter or a novice. Like I'm not supposed to be here." She swiveled her neck from side to side and brushed back her hair.

"We're supposed to be nervous," Bartley said. "But we'll be fine once we start dancing. We know our dances, so stop worrying."

"Right," Lynne said. "No need to worry. Forget about your tortured feet, the long hours, and the endless rehearsals. We'll show them smiles and grace in spite of all that."

All talking ended when Damien stepped forward to lead the dancers through *pliés* and stretches. Marta surveyed the stage. All the dancers had vacant faces, even the principals. They probably felt something similar to the crickets that jumped through her at breakneck speed.

"Fifteen minutes," called the stage manager. The stage crew made final adjustments, removed the *barres*, swept the floor, and rechecked the lights. The dancers stood in the wings in throbbing stillness. Wardrobe staff checked the hooks and eyes on every costume, then positioned themselves backstage to assist with quick changes.

Marta shook out her arms and legs, then dipped the toes of her *pointe* shoes in the rosin box. No one, corps dancer or principal, ever underestimated the powdered rosin's effect; slipping while dancing on stage could be disastrous.

"Orchestra to the pit," came the next reminder.

From backstage Marta heard the pit fill with musicians. Music stands and chairs scraped across the floor. "A" sounded. Audience conversations hushed.

Marta inhaled, then released a long, cleansing breath. She shook out her hands again, then wrapped her arms around her waist in silence. Her heart pounded in her ears like a bass drum.

A slow crescendo of applause began, signaling the conductor's arrival on the podium. Marta tossed her extra clothes into the basket already heaped with leg warmers, sweaters, shirts, and towels from other dancers. She pressed her hands down the sides of her lemony knee-length skirt and straightened the attached apron with its embroidered Central European motifs of arches, swirls, and flowers. All the female dancers shared that detail, creating a unifying stage presence. Male dancers carried the motif on their exaggerated sleeves and high-waisted belts.

"Places!" The corps moved on stage and posed. Jer stood nearby at the back of the stage. He smiled at her. She lifted her chin and nodded, hoping she looked calm despite the frantic jitters that shook her insides.

The narrator stepped in front of the curtain and read his lines. After a brief applause, the orchestra began the overture of *Coppélia*. Audiences around the world enjoyed the light-hearted music and story of Swanhilda, a young girl who becomes jealous over her betrothed's fascination with a life-size doll. Thousands of dancers before her had performed the same steps on hundreds of stages around the world. Now Marta was joining their number.

She took another deep breath as the curtain opened. With her back muscles taut, she lifted her chin and strolled across the stage as if she'd done it hundreds of times.

The stage lights blinded her. She took another deep breath as she posed, waiting for her musical cue, a low, slow tremolo of violins. Her dance career began with simple nods and pantomime to those standing near her as the principal dancers entered the stage, joining the others in the village square.

Coppélia opened with a waltz. Like the other corps dancers, Marta executed continuous balances, exaggerated leans toward her partner, and twirls that blurred like a sea of spinning pastel parasols. Her arms opened and closed as she circled and moved across the stage in perfect alignment with her fellow corps members. Her headpiece ribbons flapped against her face as she turned, but she ignored them by focusing on her footwork, her arms, and keeping to her prescribed locations on the stage.

After a series of slow, lyrical balancés and turns that encircled the principal dancers, Marta moved to her place on the edge of the village scenery to become a background presence before the dance ended. She breathed through her mouth while keeping a gentle smile on her lips. If the audience saw her heaving breaths, it would break the magical spell of the story.

The excerpt from Act II of Coppélia opened in the mechanical doll shop. Lynne and Bartley danced the role of two girls who accompanied Swanhilda as she spied on the lovely doll, Coppélia. Marta watched from the wings as the girls wound up Coppélia and the other dolls to dance brief solos before flopping forward as though their springs had expired. The audience rewarded them with chuckles, murmurs, and well-deserved applause.

Back on stage for the final excerpt, Marta waited at the back of the stage as Swanhilda and her betrothed danced. She joined the festive dancing as the happy couple walked off to be married. She felt a happiness of her own. So far the performance had gone off without a hitch; much better than their dress rehearsal when Madame shrieked at the corps and had them repeat their movements over and over and over again.

Bows and curtain calls followed as Part One ended. Everyone smiled through semi-closed lips before exiting to the dressing rooms where they could lean over to inhale deeply and catch their breath. Madame stood in the wings with her arms crossed and a scowl plastered on her face. That didn't bode well for their next rehearsal.

During the first intermission, stagehands cleared away the sets, leaving a blank canvas that the stage designer backlit with a profusion of pastel blues, greens, and yellows. The soloists showcased scenes from a variety of ballets: Greek gods and muses from Apollo, sylphs from La Sylphides, and comedic dances from Gala Performance.

Part Two exiled Marta and the other corps dancers to the dressing rooms to keep backstage clear. They took the opportunity to get drinks of water, change into their Sleeping Beauty costumes, and adjust their make-up to less vibrant tones.

Marta stood between her friends adjusting her hairdo while enjoying a quiet moment between dances. "I'm exhausted, but I think Coppélia went well. I did see Madame standing off stage. She looked disgusted. I don't know what bothered her."

"I didn't see any major mess ups," Lynne said. "Regardless, I can now say I've almost soloed."

"It all happened so fast, almost like I dreamed it," Bartley said as she adjusted her Sleeping Beauty headpiece. "Audiences love when the dolls get wound up. It's hard not to laugh when I'm there beside them.

Maybe Madame didn't like the tempo. It was a little slow, but that's not our fault."

"Well, I think you two did a super job," Marta said. "The audience loved it, and that's what matters."

Lynne tugged at her bodice. "Good. But what matters most to me right now is binding my breasts down to fit into this bodice. If I could breathe I'd feel better."

"My being a stick of celery has advantages," Bartley said. "For dancing, not attracting guys. Marta has the best of both worlds so far: ballet slender, yet curvy."

"Thanks, but nothing will help me dance as the witchy Carabosse."

During the second intermission, the stagehands installed the elaborate castle sets for scenes from *Sleeping Beauty*. Every corps member had breathed a sigh of relief when Madame told Marta she'd been selected as Carabosse, the forgotten fairy. The quick change for the role had the possibility of being a backstage nightmare.

But Marta accepted the challenge as a way to prove herself to Madame. The choreography involved more walking around acting menacing than it did dancing. Even though the black costume and make-up buried her appearance, it became a solo, of sorts. Performing the quick change demanded timing and assistance. Each rehearsal went without a problem. Tonight tested her nerves and skills as she changed and then stepped before a live audience.

She began the performance on stage as a guest, waltzing at the palace celebration. In her three-minute costume change, she stripped off her costume, slipped into a tattered black dress and black wig, and slapped gray make-up on her face. On cue, she entered the stage as Carabosse to frighten the King and Queen and put a curse of baby Princess Aurora.

Her feet slipped as she stepped around the fairies, but she regained her balance and continued her pantomime.

Acting menacing without being too scary demanded a delicate balance. If she scared the young children in the audience, they'd not want to return. Marta danced in circles, tempting the princess to reach for the spindle. She swept close, then moved away, using exaggerated pantomime with soft hands rather than angry ones. Princess Aurora followed; her outstretched hands grabbed the spindle. Then, as she fell into a deep sleep, Carabosse drifted off the stage.

In the wings, Marta tore off her ugly costume, scrubbed away her gray make-up with a damp towel, and scrambled into a fairy waltz gown. A dresser assisted her with the hooks while she pulled on a short wig to hide her messy hair and complete her transformation into a dainty fairy.

The *Sleeping Beauty* sampler ended as the princess awakened to the prince's kiss. The royal court invited the fairies to join the festivities as the ballet swept to a close.

The applause from the audience rang in Marta's ears. She stood tall alongside the other corps members, then joined them in a deep bow. Being part of the company sent a strength through her body, replacing her tiredness with a tingling energy. Another bow and another until the corps exited to the wings, allowing the principals to step forward to receive their bouquets and further applause.

After the final curtain, the soloists attended a special benefactors' event hosted by the ballet advisory board. Corps dancers were dismissed until rehearsals tomorrow. Marta removed her make-up with cold cream, slathering her face and neck with the cold, slippery goo. Lynne and Bartley did the same.

Lynne threw a tissue at Marta. "Well, Carabosse, did you like that quick change? Feel funny about getting naked backstage?"

Marta reached for a fresh tissue. "I was too busy changing to think about it."

"Your neck is gray mud," Lynne said. "Bet that smudged mess looked good with the fairy gown."

Marta startled. "Didn't the wig cover it?"

"Not really, but you did great, Marta," Bartley said as she passed. "Madame will notice."

"Right. She'll see the slip at the beginning and the mud, as if I could have avoided them." Marta brushed out dozens of knots from her tangled hair. Her mom's face smiled from the photo in the edge of the mirror. She imagined her mother standing beside her, watching her as she dressed to meet Steve. But that hadn't happened. Her mom was a thousand miles away.

Most patrons had headed home by the time Marta emerged. When she left the building she saw Steve pacing the front walkway of the theater. He smiled when he saw her. "Hi, Marta."

"Hi, yourself. Well, newspaper man, what did you think?"

"It was great; you were great," he said as he took her hands in his. "I liked all of it. You looked strong and beautiful."

"Really? Did you know I danced the ugly fairy in Sleeping Beauty?"

"Ah, I guess I missed that."

Marta shook her head. "Where did you sit?"

Steve stared at her. "In the third row. Didn't you see me?"

"No. The footlights blur the audience."

"Huh. Come on. Let's talk over a snack." As they walked to the small ice cream parlor, he locked fingers with her. She felt the tingle of dancing continue, now from their comfortable hand clasp

Once they were seated and had ordered, Marta leaned forward on her elbows and grinned. "So tell me your thoughts about your first ballet."

"Promise you won't get mad or anything."

Marta drew back. "You didn't come?"

He laughed. "Oh, I came, but I got locked out for the second act."

Marta crossed her arms and squinted. "How on earth did you manage that?"

"Well, you know how warm it gets in the theater. I went outside to cool down after the first act. When I walked back inside, the auditorium doors were closed. The usher refused to let me back in."

"Really?"

"Oh yes. I begged and told him I represented the paper, but he didn't care. He kept saying, 'I'm sorry sir; there is no late seating.' So I went back outside and waited for the next intermission. When the ranchers and townspeople stepped outside for a smoke, I returned to my seat. So, you see, I did see the parts you were in. I just missed the solos."

Marta laughed so hard tears formed in her eyes. "That sounds crazy."

"It was. That usher meant business. Now, could you stop laughing, please? I thought you'd see my empty seat and get mad or something. I didn't want to disappoint you. Every time I saw you dance, you looked amazing. I watched your face when you played a peasant. You looked like you belonged in that village. And when you danced in *Sleeping Beauty*, you looked beautiful. I didn't miss a second of your dancing."

"Except when I mimed the angry fairy."

"Right. But, I watched her dance. She, you, did a great job menacing the princess. And I freely admit that I enjoyed being at the ballet."

Marta toyed with the crumbs on her empty plate. "Do you still think ballet is fluff?"

"Yes, but wait. It's beautiful fluff. The kind of fluff I want to see again and again."

"But you still think it's fluff?"

"Just the music, not the dancing. All of you are stronger than most athletes I know. How do the men lift dancers and spin so easily? And how do you stand on those *pointe* shoes and still smile?"

"Practice, practice, practice."

"That's why you are always so tired, isn't it?"

Marta nodded.

Steve pulled her up. "Do you have enough energy for a drive to the lake?"

"That sounds perfect."

At Lake Josephine they parked near the shore. Steve slid his arm across the back of Marta's seat, grazing her ponytail. He alternately stared at Marta and looked out the front window

"You're different tonight," she said. "What's going on in your head?"

"Tonight was a wonderful surprise for me. I never thought about all the work you do to get ready to perform. Is it hard to keep all those dances straight?"

"No, each piece of music feels different. Are you writing a piece for the paper?"

"Naw. Just curious now that I understand ballet."

"After one evening?" Marta laughed and shook her head. "Steve, you are amazing."

"What's your next ballet?"

"The Nutcracker. I'm certain you'll know the music."

"Maybe, but you might be wrong about that." He kissed her forehead. "In the meantime, may I continue driving you to practices?"

"If you want. We'll add weekend rehearsals with the children who dance in the Christmas party scene. I don't expect you'd be around for them; you're off the hook, Mr. Fluff."

"I'll drive you as early or as late as you like on days I can get away. Can I get Nutcracker tickets now?" he said.

Marta brushed her fingers over his clean-shaven jaw, then patted his cheek. "No. Ask your friend Miss Fluff in November. She's a nice person even if she is a dan-cer."

Steve captured Marta's hand. "She's a tease, that's for sure."

"Can I have my hand back, please?"

"May I kiss you first?" he said as he traced one hand down her cheek and inched closer.

She nodded.

He kissed her cheek, then her lips before he pulled back and turned on the dome light. He handed her a small, flat package wrapped in rose-colored paper. "I found this in the used book store. I thought you'd like it. The cover says it's ballet without tears. I want you to always be happy and, well, uh, I … Open it."

She undid the wrapping and lifted out a small tattered book entitled, *The Ballet Lover's Pocket Book*. The dust cover flaked as she opened the book. "Thanks. This is wonderful, Steve." Marta turned the pages and looked at each small line drawing. When she looked back at Steve, his grin made her smile. "Did you read it?"

"I thumbed through it," he said. "The author knew a lot about ballet and costumes and scenery. She plays the guitar, so she can't be all bad. Read the inscription I added."

Marta read the words aloud. "You'll always have me as your audience of one." She closed the book and reached up with both hands, cupping Steve's face. "You know, for a cowboy, you're sweet."

"I like being called a cowboy better than Mr. Fluff."

They sat in Steve's car, holding hands at the curb by the boarding house until Marta yawned and tapped the car clock. "I need to go. I plan to sleep in 'til noon."

"May I see you or call you tomorrow?"

"Yes, but not a second before noon, promise?"

"I promise. Come on. I'll walk you to the door."

They lingered in a hug. After a quick series of kisses, Marta unlocked the front door and said good night. From the common room window she watched Steve drive away. She tucked tonight away as a perfect remembrance. Her next encounter with Madame promised to be memorable, but she doubted it would be anything but continuous criticism.

$\mathscr{D}$read day: the first rehearsal after the opening performance of the Classic Sampler. Marta took special care to appear professional as she entered the large practice room. The usual banter and chatter among the corps was missing. Instead, everyone stood in silence; the floor held a sudden interest.

Madame thumped into the room and positioned herself next to the piano. "I imagine you read the reviews. The paper was too generous. Obviously they overlooked the numerous blunders, or the reviewer, Susan Zane, needs new glasses."

Marta squirmed and looked around. No one met her glances.

"I am surprised at the lack of corps pride you displayed. After all our practices and rehearsals, you still acted like you were in pain. Your entries were ragged, your gracefulness rivaled a bunch of circus clowns."

Madame swiveled to face Marta. "And you. What were you thinking? You almost fell onto the stage as Carabosse. I've seen better mime by a five year old."

The shock of Madame's attack weakened Marta's knees. She lowered her eyes and curtsied. "I'll work harder, Madame."

Madame thumped to stand inches from Marta. "I don't want 'harder.' I want smarter with more believability."

"Yes, Madame. Of course." Marta felt tears gather in her eyes, but there was no way she'd let Madame see her cry. Not ever.

"Now, let's start at the top. We have eleven performances ahead of us, and I won't let you corps dancers make a fool of this ballet company."

Hour after hour, practice after practice, Marta worked at a feverish level to impress Madame. Every free hour at the boarding house, she rehearsed Carabosse until she exhausted her reserves, dropping into bed without eating or showering. Both took too much energy.

"Marta," Lynne said. "What's happening to you this week? You look like Carabosse before you add any make-up."

"I'm okay. I just need to find a way to reach deeper and dance her as a stronger character."

"You're doing fine. I worry you're going to collapse on stage."

Marta smiled. "It's almost over. I can make it." Though secretly she had the same fear.

Each performance Madame stood in the wings and stared at her as she exited the stage. Each performance the stares grew shorter. Had Madame given up on her, or had she reached a level of performance Madame could accept?

When the Classic Sampler performances ended in late October, Marta felt relieved. Now she could rejoin the boarding house meals and go back to spending her evenings more leisurely. She could also spend time with Steve. They could use the slower schedule to write their first shared article. The arts editor had suggested a list of the ten most famous ballets with short descriptions as their starting point.

One Saturday evening, Marta cleaned the basement practice space and set two chairs at the card table. She spent several minutes fussing with her hair before Steve arrived.

"This is cozy," Steve said as he entered the basement room.

"It works. I thought if we worked here, we'd get away from the board-ers. James and Shorty love to play cards in the evening."

Steve nodded as he set his briefcase and his portable Smith Corona typewriter on the table. "Do you type?"

Marta shrugged. "A little."

"How about you talk and I'll type."

Over the next two hours, Marta shared background ballet information and talked about her favorite ballets. Steve asked questions and recorded her answers for additional articles. Then, while he wrote, she used the time to exercise without music. When she looked toward Steve, he had stopped working to watch her. She smiled.

"Is that what you do every day?" he said.

"Pretty much. We warm all our muscles slowly so we don't tear any-thing. Usually it's done in leotards, not a skirt. Why are you asking?"

"Just curious." He stood and walked toward her and handed her the article he'd typed. "Read this rough copy aloud, please. That way I can hear if it flows."

Flows. They both used the same word for different careers. Marta cleared her throat and read:

> The world of ballet is centuries old. Many of the world's favorite ballets were choreographed during the sixty years between 1832 and 1891. Newer ballets, created between 1910 and the 1930s have also become favorites at our local Intermountain Ballet Company.
>
> Madame Cosper and one of her new dancers, Marta Selbryth, shared their favorites. Madame Cosper's top ballets include (Ask Madame for her list and comments and get her final approval for the article.)

Marta looked up. "You want me to talk to her about this?"

"No, I'll have Susan share this with Madame. I need your top ballets so Madame will know what you said. Then we'll see what happens. Keep reading."

Miss Selbryth's list includes: The Nutcracker, Coppélia, Swan Lake, Sleeping Beauty, La Sylphides, Firebird, Four Seasons, and Giselle. She said, "I've enjoyed their musical scores since I was a child. The composers create a wonderful flow of music, allowing us to present a variety of dances. Each tells a story." (add Marta's descriptions as space allows)

Intermountain Ballet Company presented excerpts from Coppélia and Sleeping Beauty in their fall season opening. Next they will present full ballets for The Nutcracker, Giselle, and Serenade. The season ends with a Tribute to America and new choreography from local ballet master, Damien Black.

Contact Fox Theater box office for tickets to future performances.

"That made what I said sound really good," Marta said as she handed the copy to Steve.

"Doin' my job." Steve put the article in his briefcase." If there's space, we can add the overview of each ballet that we've discussed. For now, we're done. How about we get something to eat?"

"Let me fix something here. Then we can sit on the porch swing and—"

"Wait. I have my own ideas about what we can do sitting in the swing."

Choreography for the Nutcracker had began even before the Classic Sampler performances ended, followed by auditions for parts. On tour and at home, guest dancers would perform Herr Drosselmeier and the Nutcracker-turned-Prince. The walk around parts of party scene members, soldiers, and children would be selected from the local dance schools and interested adults. Patrice Royal, as principal dancer, earned the choice of roles: the Snow Queen or the Sugar Plum Fairy. Corps dancers performed the Waltz of the Flowers and vied for short solos.

The demi-soloists would perform as snowflakes. That left company-wide auditions for Clara, the Chinese, Russian, Arabian, Spanish, and

Flute dances, as well as Mother Ginger. True, they were small solos and required quick changes, but the dances were coveted. All except Mother Ginger, who danced on short stilts.

Over the past sixty years, choreographers had modified and restaged the various roles to meet their needs. Damien favored recreating the 1940s version as close as possible. All the dancers had to readjust their thinking and dancing; every rehearsal became crucial. Marta, Lynne, and Bartley practiced each evening in Marta's basement studio.

The evening before auditions, the girls finished rehearsing and relaxed, seated against the basement walls with their feet stretched out in front of them. "Ah. This feels so-o good," Lynne said.

Marta laughed. "That is one of my favorite things about having the space. Of course having you here is great as well. We're like the three musketeers."

"More like the three actresses we just saw in that old musketeers movie," Lynne said. "Bartley, you're Lana Turner, the beautiful countess. Marta is June Allyson, abducted by wicked Richelieu, and I'm the queen. I look like Angela Lansbury, don't I?"

"Hardly. Would you ever want to be an actress?" Bartley asked.

"Naw. Too much work," Lynne said. "I'd have to walk and talk. In ballet I just dance."

"I think we're ready, don't you guys?" Marta said. "Wouldn't it be great if we landed the best solos?"

"Marguerite would have a cow," Lynne said. "Maybe she'll get Clara. Suits her. Have you noticed how she imitates everything Patrice does?"

"Like Patrice's footwork will rub off on her," Marta said. "I have to admit she learns the choreography quickly."

"Not as fast as Bartley. How do you do that?" Lynne said.

"I watch the movement patterns on the floor. Then I dance them and play the records every night before I go to bed."

"I can't do that," Marta said. "I need to watch and count."

Bartley stood and reached out to pull Marta to her feet. "Maybe that's why Madame watches you. Sometimes you just stand there and look disinterested. Maybe you should try moving around more while you learn new sections," Bartley said. "Then you'll look more like you're practicing."

Marta nodded. Anything would be worth a try with Madame.

As the girls turned off the basement lights and started up the stairs, Bartley stopped them. "Remember what Jer overheard. When you read your dance assignments off the board, pretend you don't care one way or the other. Madame watches, and she dreads the postings because corps members act whiny when they see their roles. Then they want to talk to her about why they weren't selected, and that takes too much of her precious time."

"Tomorrow we'll know," Marta said. "Pray that Mother Ginger goes to a community adult."

It didn't.

Madame and Damien posted their selections after the day's auditions. Marta scanned the list. She'd dance with Bartley, Lynne, and Jer as Arabian dancers. Her friends would backup two other dances. Jer became a lead soldier and backup for Fritz. Clara would be played by a local dance student, leaving Marguerite free to dance as a flute and backup for other selections.

As Marta scanned the list further, her heart dropped to her stomach. Madame assigned her the dreaded role of Mother Ginger. She'd be staying late and learning to walk on stilts. She'd wear a hoopskirt large enough to shelter a handful of wiggly children before they burst out to perform their steps and then return under the skirt.

The girls dressed and met up outside the dancers' door to discuss their roles.

"You're the chosen one, Marta." Lynne said. "You can do it." She hung her arm over Marta's shoulder as they walked to the parking area. The weight of Lynne's arm didn't compare to the weight of Marta's anxiety. Even though Madame agreed with Marta's top picks for ballets in the article and approved what was written, it didn't appear to change her opinion of Marta. Or was this a test, a challenge to see if she could take on a difficult role and succeed?

"I'm glad we're dancing the Arabian together," Marta said. "Come over and we'll practice all the character dances. That way we'll be prepared for next year's auditions."

"Why does every dance company do the *Nutcracker* every year?" Lynne said. "I mean everyone knows it. Why not try something new?"

Bartley opened her purse and took out her car keys. "It's tradition. I'll bet even Steve knows the music."

Rehearsals, costume fittings, more rehearsals. The *Nutcracker* began to solidify. They danced from early morning to late evening six days a week. The daily schedules and assignments changed hourly as dancers became injured and needed time to rest and recover. Tempers grew short, and dancers raced from one rehearsal room to another to learn additional solos and rehearse ensemble pieces. The scheduling remained so hectic the dancers carried around their schedules, afraid they'd miss a rehearsal and lose their favored part.

Marta's calves and ankles ached from the short stilts strapped to her legs. It took days of practice before she could walk on them, more days of practice with the hoopskirt, and still more when she sheltered wiggly children. One boy pinched her, another knocked her foot aside, causing her to fall face first onto the floor, injuring her pride more than her body.

One late evening, she and her friends sat on the basement studio floor resting. They'd practiced their corps dances and decided to soak their feet before they left. They seated themselves around a low-sided container of hot water. Marta sprinkled on Epsom salts, and Lynne swirled them until the water cleared. The girls dunked their feet into the container and closed their eyes in relief.

"Ah-h," Bartley said. "I can't imagine a better way to spend my time."

"I can," Lynne said as she wiggled her toes. "I've had to cancel a handful of dates because of all the added rehearsals. How about you, Marta? Is Steve hanging around?"

"He's around." Marta rubbed her bruises and abrasions. "But guys, we're only friends."

"Right. Kissing friends," Lynne said. "He's always driving you in and picking you up. Any more flowers lately?"

"No. And now he wants us to spend less time talking and more time kissing."

"Don't you want to kiss him?" Lynne said. "I mean, he's cute and kind and attentive."

Marta shrugged. "It's fine, but I'm not as excited about all the kissing. I've never dated anyone else."

"You have got to be joking," Lynne said.

Marta shook her head. "I only went to one dance in high school, and that was with my neighbor."

"Marta, it's okay. I didn't date much either," Bartley said.

"What's with you two? Lynne said. "Not dating in high school? You missed out on a lot of fun. Do you guys even know how to flirt?"

Bartley threw a towel at Lynne. "Let us figure it out ourselves, Lynne. We're big girls now, not babies who need a mommy."

"Okay," Marta said. "Time to change the subject. Tell me about your personal ritual before you dance."

"I always wear Evening in Paris perfume," Lynne said.

"So, that's what smells." Marta laughed. "How can you stand such a sweet perfume?"

"It's better than sweat. Besides, when I don't wear it, I make mistakes."

Bartley wiped her feet and started putting on her bobby socks. "My ritual is to brush my hair with the small red brush I got when I did my first recital. I also fasten my lucky barrette on the right side. I do it every performance. I don't dare change it. I know a girl who changed her ritual, and she lost her position as a soloist."

"That's crazy," Lynne said. "But maybe it's all crazy."

Marta sat silent for a moment. "I'm not sure. Sounds like something to think about. I don't have a ritual. Do you think I should make something up?"

"No. It doesn't work that way," Lynne said. "Keep doing what you're doing and take care of yourself."

After a brief stop in the kitchen to return the tea kettle, Marta climbed the stairs to her room, imaging a hot shower before she dropped into bed. As she entered the bathroom, she noticed her shelf of towels and personal bottles was empty. That was strange.

She checked her room. She hadn't taken them there. Back in the bathroom she looked in each bathing area. Her towels were on the floor in the room with the bathtub. She seldom took a bath; hadn't for at least a week.

When she picked up her towels, they were soaking wet.

The hall door opened slowly. Carol entered carrying Marta's personal bottles and proceeded to set them onto Marta's shelf.

Marta felt anger rise through her. "Carol! What are you doing?"

Carol jumped, dropping two bottles. She backed away from the shelves. "Nothing. I have every right to be here."

"Not with my personal things, you don't."

"I, ah, I found them in the hall. They aren't mine. I guessed they were yours." Carol crossed her arms.

Marta stared at Carol, waiting to see her next move. As she waited, a surge of heat rose through her body like an inferno ready to explode.

Carol turned away, picked up the dropped bottles, and lined them up on Marta's shelf. She turned to leave. Marta stepped in front of her, blocking her exit.

"How did my towels get on the floor beside the bathtub? Surely they didn't walk there."

Carol shrugged; a faint smile gathered on her lips. "The tub water splashed out. I needed something to wipe it up."

Acting out the angry Carabosse of *Sleeping Beauty* was tame compared to how Marta felt at this moment. She swept up everything from her personal shelf and the wet towels from the floor and brushed past Carol. She knew if she tried to continue the conversation she'd awaken the entire boarding house.

Marta tossed the wet towels in her sink and placed her bottles under the sink on a shelf. She stared at herself in the mirror. The face looking back frightened her. Her eyebrows reminded her of Madame's when she'd mimicked her early in the year. Add on the racing of her heart, her rapid breathing, and the tears sliding down her face, and she saw herself coming apart like the seams of a tight costume. How did Carol manage to rile her? Why did her feelings escalate the longer she thought about her?

She sat and rocked, regaining more control with each forward and backward motion. She knew she'd overreacted. Maybe she *had* worked too long and hard on the Carabosse role like Lynne said. Maybe dancing professionally created more pressure than she could handle. Maybe, maybe, maybe.

*T*hree weekends later, Marta met Steve at the curb. They were driving to the mountains. November rehearsals tested her energy; her reserves were running low. Today promised to be the perfect late autumn day of lacy clouds and a light breeze; a chance to spend time with Steve, relax, and rejuvenate.

"Mornin'. How's my favorite Miss Fluff?"

"Excited to get away," she said.

Steve hefted the picnic hamper she handed him. "What's in here, rocks?"

"No. It's filled with old pointe shoes and bad reviews."

"Touché." Steve loaded the hamper in the trunk then opened the passenger door for Marta.

The drive west through the valley passed miles of barbed wire surrounding barren fields and scruffy sagebrush. As they drove higher, stubby blue-hued evergreens lined the road. Marta rolled down the window and extended her hand to catch the chilly breeze. "Will we see snow?"

"Only in the distance. Do you ski?"

"Nope," she said. "Not allowed. Might get injured or break a leg."

"Does the company dictate how you spend your free time?"

"About some things. We sign a contract."

"Well, if you're *allowed*, I want you and your friends to come up for the long New Year's weekend. I'll invite my friends as well. We can play in the snow, eat, talk, and play cards. It will be fun."

"I'd like that."

The road passed through Bridger and Belfry; more collections of wooden buildings than towns. In the spaces in between, Marta saw a scattering of ranches with animals grazing.

"Since we have all day," he said, "we're going the long way. I'll show you where the mining towns used to be. After a handful of disasters and dropping copper ore prices, the last of the families moved away about ten years ago. Only a bunch of rusty buildings remain."

"It's beautiful the way the hills fold and open. How could they leave?"

"Money," he said. "Can't raise a family without it."

Marta shifted to thinking about her mom and how simply they lived. "It must have been hard to walk away, let your home become a pile of weathered wood."

Higher and higher they drove, each turn revealing more and more of the snowy mountains. Marta stretched. "It's beyond beautiful up here."

"Yep. Kinda like you."

Steve's compliment delighted her. She stored it away along with the smile he wore on his face when he looked her direction.

The road into the cabin wound through a forest of giant Ponderosa pines. Marta leaned out the window to see their top branches. At first sight, the cabin resembled a life-size Lincoln log construction. White chinking filled the spaces between the logs. Steep steps led to a broad porch where Adirondack chairs shared the space with a massive wood pile that lined one end of the porch.

Marta stood beside the car, inhaled deeply, and looked around. "I love this. I'm surprised you don't come up here more often."

"I know. But school, the newspaper, and my ballerina girlfriend keep me in town. Come on inside."

The cabin's interior was a large open rectangle. A river rock fireplace dominated one wall and reached to the ceiling. Tan leather couches, green overstuffed chairs, and rustic coffee tables invited the pine forest inside while providing space for a dozen people to sit and relax. Marta touched the chill on the quilts and blankets draped over the furniture.

Steve moved beside her and intertwined his fingers with hers. "Well? What do you think?"

"It's wonderful. I see why you love it."

He pulled Marta's hand and moved toward the door. "Button up your jacket. Let's head out."

The trail meandered through pine trees. Their rust-colored needles littered the ground, creating a crunch when she stepped on them. At a fork in the path, they turned left and descended a narrow trail. The sound of rushing water grew louder.

Marta hurried along the trail, around the bend, and stopped. A milky stream tumbled past, cascading over small ledges and pushing out against a wall of boulders. A filmy mist hung in the air.

A small swirling pool splashed against the bank inches from her feet. The noise of the water threatened to cover their conversation. It reminded Marta of Staircase, a series of waterfalls along her favorite hike in the Olympic Mountains back home, only this stream was wider, deeper, and louder.

"This is perfect!" Marta bent to touch the water. "And so-o cold."

Steve grabbed a limb and pulled himself up onto a huge fallen log that spanned the side pool. He walked out along the trunk and sat down. "Come on." He patted a space next to him.

She reached for his hand and clambered up the log, then eased down next to him. Their feet dangled inches above the rushing water. She looked around and inhaled the mist.

"M-m-m, this reminds me of home. I thought Montana would be flat and dusty. I'm starting to appreciate your big blue sky."

Steve nodded and closed his eyes. His usual energetic manner vanished, replaced by calmness. Another surprise to unravel.

Steve took her hand and gave it a squeeze. "I love it here. I thought you'd enjoy this after all your talk of mountains and trees and water."

They sat quietly for several minutes. Then, without warning, Steve stood and walked to the bank end of the log. He took off his shoes and socks and rolled up his jeans and stepped into the water. "Ah. It's cold all right. Let's test your stamina. Cabin tradition."

"This time of year? Are you crazy?"

"Time of year doesn't matter, Miss Fluff." He stepped out of the water and released a long breath. "It's freezing!"

She hesitated, then stood and walked the log to join him. She sat on a rock and slowly removed her shoes and bobby socks. What would Steve think when he saw her battered feet?

She avoided looking at Steve's face as she bared her blisters and abraded toes and heels. She curled her toes under a nearby rock, waiting, ready with an explanation if he asked about her mangled feet.

Steve looked at her feet, then her face, then her feet again. His smile faded. "We can wait and do this in the spring if you'd rather."

"Why wait? Don't you think I can do it?"

"I never doubt you, Marta." He took her hand as he stepped back into the water.

She held her breath as she inched into the water. "Yikes! This is freezing!" She shook her hand loose from Steve's and backed out of the water.

"Didn't know dancers were pansies about cold water," Steve said, standing in five inches of water with his arms crossed over his chest.

"I didn't know reporters lacked sense."

He laughed. "Just proving I'm no piece of fluff."

Marta bent forward and scooped up a handful of water. It splashed onto the bottom of Steve's rolled up jeans.

He waded downstream, out of her reach. "Want to play, huh?" He ran back toward her shoving waves of water at her, soaking her pedal pushers as she ran up the bank.

"Stop! I give! Stop!" she screamed.

He ran forward and grabbed her ankle and slipped, pulling her into the water, losing his grip.

Marta drifted away from the bank and into the swirling water of the pool, floundering and gulping in water. She could no longer touch the bottom of the pool. She screamed and flailed as water alternately covered and uncovered her head.

Every inch of her body ached with coldness. Her arms and legs became heavy and useless against the frigid temperature.

Steve grabbed for her as the water turned her around and tugged her toward the main stream. "Hang on!" He regained a vise grip hold on her ankle as he dragged her toward the stream bank.

Marta coughed and sputtered as she tried to breathe. Sharp-edged rocks gouged her body. Her face ached from being dashed against the rocks. She rolled onto her back and closed her eyes, willing her heart to slow its pounding and for feeling to return to her arms and legs.

"Marta. Are you okay? I'm sorry, I... Come on," he said as he pulled her to her feet. "Let's head back to the cabin and dry out."

Marta rubbed pebbles off her face and hands and rang out the edges of her drenched clothes. Her ankle burned like fire when she put full weight on it.

By the time they reached the cabin, her body shook so hard she could barely stand.

Inside, Steve grabbed a wool blanket and wrapped her up. "The propane boiler takes ten minutes to heat the shower water. Stay wrapped up while I build a fire."

Marta's teeth chattered as she nodded. Then she curled up on the floor and closed her eyes.

Steve started the fire. He lifted her to a sitting position, wrapped her in two more blankets, and circled her with his arms. "I am such a fool. I didn't think any of this would happen. I'm so sorry."

Marta didn't respond.

In the shower, the blasts of hot water running down her body removed the chill, but she couldn't stop shaking as she examined her bruises and scratches. Her ankle looked normal, but ached. What a disaster. If she closed her eyes, her panic returned, so she kept them open.

Marta dried off and put on the heavy flannel robe hanging on the back of the bathroom door. The tails of the sash hung to the floor. She limped into the main room while towel-drying her hair.

Steve's face held a question as she approached the fire. "Feel better? Guess I got carried away."

"That's putting it mildly."

"You're bleeding." He reached out to touch her face. "Are you mad at me or anything?"

"Of course I am. I'm covered with bruises and scratches. My ankle is starting to swell. Remember that contract I signed? If I can't dance I'm out, o-u-t."

"I caught you as soon as I could."

"And what if you hadn't?"

"But I did. You know I care about you and don't want you getting hurt. Let me make it up to you."

Marta closed her eyes to shut out Steve's anxious face. She grabbed up her wet clothes and held them to her chest. "Take me home, please."

"Why don't we stay until you're feeling calmer. Let's eat, talk, and play cards while our clothes and shoes dry."

"No! Take me home. I want to go home. The tour starts soon. I need to take care of my ankle. I have to be able to dance."

"Okay. I understand. I'll be right back." He vanished up the ladder to a loft and returned barefoot in torn jeans and a worn sweatshirt. He handed her a pair of socks and sat putting on a pair.

Marta put on the socks, then grabbed a dry blanket off the sofa and wrapped it around herself. When Steve stepped toward her and touched her cheek, she winced.

"I'm so sorry about this. Sure you don't want to stay and relax for a while?"

"No. Stop apologizing and take me home."

On the trip back to Billings, Marta pulled the blanket up to her neck and turned away from Steve. Her stomach growled, and she ached everywhere.

Once back inside the boarding house, she faced Steve over the picnic basket and her bag of wet clothes. "I'll get the robe and blanket back to you." She pulled in her lips to hold back her tears.

"But, Marta…"

"Can you please carry the picnic basket into the kitchen?"

Steve walked into the kitchen. When he returned to the common room, he stared at her and exhaled. "I'm sorry." He kissed her cheek, then backed away. The front door closed with a soft click.

She put away the food but saved out and ate a half sandwich while she heated water for tea. Then she limped up the stairs carrying her tea and two ice packs to her room.

The ice helped ease her ankle pain, but its coldness quickly became uncomfortable. Would she be able to dance tomorrow? She had to. Madame told everyone on Friday to "be here unless you are too sick to stand." There were no options open for not dancing tomorrow.

She moved to her mirror and scanned her injuries. Bruises and deep scratches ran from her eye to her chin. Others spread like grape jam across her forehead. Her hands and forearms were skinned, like the time she was five and skidded face first down a gravelly street. Make-up, long-sleeved leotards, and her tights would take care of most of her injuries. Maybe Madame would ignore her as usual.

Her ankle continued to pulse and ache as she climbed into bed. Even with Gran's quilt added to her covers, she shivered, remembering the water covering her head, drowning her for long moments. She should have learned to swim long, long ago. Tomorrow she'd pay a price. Hopefully not one that ended her career.

"No, no, no!" Damien paced the rehearsal room, shaking his head. "You need to flow with the tempo. Watch. I'll do the series."

He stood in the center of the large practice room. "The *Nutcracker* waltz beat is dum, dum, da, dum, dum, da, dum, dum, da, da. *Balancé, balancé,* turn your body, lift your arms, deep knee bend, and stop. You're at the ball, enjoying the party. Spread apart, fill the stage with motion… am I disturbing your conversation, Miss Meadows and Miss Selbryth?"

Marta leaned her weight onto her right foot to ease the pain from her swollen ankle. She stared at Damien, then turned to Lynne, who looked at her feet as she answered. "No, sir. I was—"

"I don't care what you were doing, Miss Meadows. I allow no side conversation during practices, especially this late into performance rehearsals. Is that clear?"

Lynne nodded, placed her hands on her hips, and looked away.

The pianist began again. The corps perked up, refining their movements and blocking pose locations for the rest of the hour.

Marta used her towel to wipe away her sweat and the make-up covering her bruises as she moved into the dressing room. Her ankle continued to throb as she sat on the bench removing her long-sleeved leotard and her tights. When she looked up, Madame stood in the doorway; her eyebrows dipped together as she approached Marta.

"What's happened to your body?"

"I fell."

Madame leaned forward on her cane, holding Marta's attention with her stare. "Dancers can't be clumsy. Covering those scratches and bruises with make-up will ruin our costumes. Do you understand?"

Marta nodded.

Madame pointed to Marta's ankle. "Why is your ankle swollen?"

"When I fell, I banged against a large boulder."

"What were you doing around boulders? You *do* remember you signed a contract?"

"Yes, Madame. I—"

"Go see our company doctor. I need to know if you can perform or if I need to leave you behind." Madame turned and walked out of the dressing room, leaving Marta encased in stares from the other dancers.

Add another strike. She'd learned to walk on the stilts and corral the children. Did Madame ask about *those* bruises or compliment her mastery of the stilts? Nope. What if the doctor told Madame to leave her behind? That would end her career.

Marta threw her towel at her locker, then sat with her head in her hands.

Lynne and Bartley leaned against the lockers watching her, but she tried to ignore them.

"What is going on?" Lynne said. "What happened to you?"

"Nothing, everything. Sorry I got you in trouble. The bruises were from falling in the stream when Steve... I'll explain later. Let's get changed."

"Whoa, Marta. What happened with Steve?" Lynne said.

"What happened with Madame?" Bartley asked.

"I said I'd tell you later. I'm sorry. I ache and I'm grouchy today."

"Really?" Lynne said. "Could have fooled me. Want to join us for a shopping trip? I need a fall sweater. Bartley's helping me pick out something stylish."

"No. I need to call the doctor and try to get in today. Hopefully he'll let me keep dancing."

Bartley sat down next to Marta. "We'll drive you to the doctor, right Lynne?"

"Of course. Then we'll get you home and packed in ice packs."

Within the hour, Marta had an ace bandage wrapped around her ankle, a prescription for pain pills, and the advice to stay off her ankle as much as possible. The doctor gave her a note for Madame explaining his diagnosis and recommendation: lots of icing and no *pointe* shoes or *relevés* for a week.

After Lynne and Bartley brought Marta's dinner to her room, they tucked her ankle in ice packs and sat on her bed keeping her company while she ate.

"Thanks for everything. Sorry you didn't get a chance to go sweater shopping," Marta said.

"Lynne can borrow one of mine for now," Bartley said. "This was more important. After all, we are the three dancing musketeers of Billings. I don't know why Madame is so furious. You could've just as easily turned your ankle walking into the company."

"True," Lynne said, "but you probably wouldn't look like you'd wrestled a bear or ran through a field of blackberry bushes." She picked up her purse and walked toward the door. "Come on, Bartley. I have a late date, so I'll need your most beguiling sweater."

After the girls left, Marta sat in the quiet, allowing herself to feel a deep ache that had nothing to do with her injury. Bartley was right; she could have gotten injured anywhere. At least she hadn't broken any bones, which meant she could continue to attend rehearsals.

Afternoons, after rehearsals, Lynne drove her home over the next week, ending any chance she might see Steve. He didn't call. That created a different hurt; he'd not really cared or he'd have checked up on her by now. So much for that relationship.

The week of resting her ankle ended. Madame and Damien watched her first full day of dancing with close scrutiny. She stayed after for their verdict.

Damien and Madame met with her in the small practice room. Damien closed the door. "Please sit down, Marta."

Madame stood beside Marta and stared down at her. "I hope you've learned your lesson."

"Yes, Madame."

Damien sat in the chair next to Marta. "How's your ankle?"

"It's fine. Dancing today felt normal. I still ice it each evening."

"Keep icing it," Damien said.

"We watched you today," Madame said, "and have decided you may join us on the tour. But, at the first sign of weakness or reduced energy, you'll be sent home. Do you understand?"

"Yes, Madame, I understand."

"Good. Now go home and pack. The bus leaves at seven sharp tomorrow morning."

Marta stood to leave. When she reached the closed door, she turned back to Madame and Damien. "Thank you."

While she wanted to cheer and celebrate, she found herself alone. Thanks to Lynne's unusual "early evening date," Marta wasn't offered a ride home. Instead, she carried a bulging bag filled with *pointe* shoes, assorted warm-up clothes, and the tour packing list as she walked her bike around the building to pedal home.

At the edge of the sidewalk, she stopped and stared. Steve's car.

Marta hung her bulky bag on the handle bars, then gripped them as though she intended to rip them free. She stood looking at Steve's car, then turned and walked back toward the building to give herself time to think.

Steve leaped from his car and followed her. "Can we talk? Please?"

"Is there anything to say?"

"Yes. How's your ankle. Did you get in trouble?"

Marta nodded and felt tears gather in the corners of her eyes. "Please go." She twisted the bike around, mounted it, and pedaled along the sidewalk and onto the street.

Steve ran after her. "Let me drive you home."

She shook her head and kept pedaling toward the boarding house.

Steve hurried back to his car and drove beside her amid honks and curses from angry drivers. "Come on, Marta. Let me drive you home."

She stopped and let her body collapse against the bike handles. "Okay."

He pulled into a parking space and loaded her bike and bag into his trunk. When she was seated in his car, she closed her eyes and tried to relax.

"Hard day at rehearsals?"

She nodded.

"Want to talk about it?"

She shook her head. Who'd want to hear about her injured ankle, her fears of missing the tour, and her exhaustion? That would only make him feel worse. He didn't want to hear about repeating one section of the dance over and over, hour after hour. Or about Madame berating her for the injuries. No one wanted to listen to that much complaining, least of all someone who didn't live and breathe the dance world.

"Okay. Well, since you didn't return my calls, I took a chance and drove here to look for you."

"Return your calls? You called?"

"Of course I did. I've called every day, after dinner."

"Mrs. B. didn't tell me."

"I spoke with a young woman and she—"

Marta sat bolt upright. "You talked to a young woman? What did she say?"

"That she'd tell you I called."

Marta felt a tension rise through her body. Carol.

"I haven't seen your bike parked outside the building lately, so I figured you had rides or weren't dancing. Either way, since you didn't return my calls, I figured you needed more time. Did I tell you how sorry I am?"

"Yes, about a dozen times."

When they reached the boarding house, Steve helped her remove her bike and bag from his trunk. "Can I call you or come over to see you tomorrow?"

"We're leaving on the Nutcracker tour tomorrow. We won't be back for fifteen days."

"Fifteen days? I've already missed a week with you, Miss Fluff. May I call you when you return?"

"I guess." Marta moved toward the back porch. "Thanks for the ride."

"Wait!"

Marta turned. Steve's face held a pleading look as he stepped toward her. "May I have one of those special dancer kisses before you disappear for two weeks?"

"Okay." She felt a warm current moving through her body as he stepped closer.

Steve kissed her forehead, her nose, and worked toward her mouth. "See you soon, Miss Fluff. I'll miss you."

He backed up, pulling her hands and arms toward him before he disappeared around the corner of the house.

Marta closed her eyes to prolong the buttery feeling from being with Steve. Her earlier moodiness evaporated. Why didn't she tell him about being afraid in the water? Maybe he would understand. She had two weeks on the tour to think about it.

Her buttery feeling shifted to butterflies as she checked off items for her touring suitcase: street clothes and warm-up clothes to last two weeks, new and worn pointe shoes, as well as a nice dress in case the corps were invited to an after function. Compared to Bartley and Lynne, her clothes looked sad, well-worn, even old. She should have gone shopping when she had the chance. Too late now. Marta closed her touring suitcase and sat on it to secure the latches. She'd be the shabby musketeer.

The trip by tour bus, like Marta's bus ride to Billings, disappointed her. They rode on a charter bus that appeared to be a retired Greyhound. The tall-backed seats were comfortable, but all the sitting and jostling sapped her energy more than any morning rehearsal.

She sat alone, behind Lynne and Bartley, joining in conversations but using the majority of the time to nap or stare out the window. It wasn't the glamour she'd hoped for. Plus she had too many empty hours to re-live how she'd left things so unfinished with Steve.

Their tour schedule repeated itself like a stuck record: grab a quick breakfast, drive to the next town mid-morning, rehearse, rest, eat a light meal, perform, then crash into bed. Next morning they'd awaken early and repeat performances or move to a new town.

Bartley threw her make-up case onto the opened rollaway bed. "To-day's rehearsal felt horrible. And, can you believe this hotel is so fouled up? How could they give half our rooms to another group?"

"No biggie," Lynne said. "It's only one night, and neither Marta nor I snore."

Bartley moved to the window. "At least it got me away from Margue-rite. You'd think she came from royalty the way she prances around and coos to Madame and Patrice."

"All I care about is a hot shower and food," Lynne said. "I could eat a large cow. Are you two ready to eat?"

Marta pulled her bags onto the bed. "No. I just want to ice my ankle and sleep. Eating dinner at three in the afternoon does crazy things to my body."

"Go ahead," Bartley said. "I want to unpack and read my *Vogue*. I'm getting behind in reading my magazines."

When Lynne left, Bartley unpacked and sat down on the rollaway bed crammed next to the window. "I wish I had her easy-going confidence. It will help her move up in the company. Do you see yourself as a principal dancer?"

"I do. But it won't happen until Madame accepts me. She really likes you, Bartley. Maybe it's because you have so much energy all day. Wish I had your stamina and could survive on as little food as you do."

Bartley smiled. "It's the way I've always done things. But, I admit, I have a little help."

"You mean those vitamins I see you taking all the time?"

Bartley pulled a bottle from her vanity case. "They're not vitamins. They're diet pills. They send me to the bathroom a lot, but I don't need to worry about my energy or appetite. Take a few."

Marta read the label on the bottle: "Curb you appetite without losing any stamina. Drop unwanted pounds. Guaranteed to keep you active all day."

"They do all that and more," Bartley said as she flipped through her magazine.

"I'd better not."

"They're as safe as taking vitamins. My mother's taken them for years."

Marta turned the bottle upside down and dropped one pill onto her palm.

"Take more than that. I take two in the morning and two before performances. The Slim-eze brand works best for me."

"But Bartley, you're already slim."

"I'd be big as a whale without these pills. Plus, they give me energy. If you need a boost, these will help."

Marta shook out four more and placed them in her vanity case. She discarded the waxed bag on the sanitized bathroom glass, filled the glass with water, and swallowed one pill.

The mattress sagged as she stretched out, closed her eyes, and started to drift away. A nap would help her prepare for tonight.

Pop! Her eyes sprang open. Could the pills do that? "Bartley, do the pills make you jittery?"

Bartley put down her magazine. "They did when I started them. I can guarantee, you'll have energy to dance, and you won't be hungry until morning."

Marta began pacing the room, forgetting her stiff ankle and her plan to ice it. Her body trembled with energy like she'd run a race. She drank several glasses of water, but the shaking persisted. Finally, she gave up, made a trip to the bathroom, and headed downstairs. As she left the hotel, she met Lynne entering.

"Hey, roomie! Thought you were tired."

"I got my second wind. Want to go for a walk?"

"Sure," Lynne said as she checked her watch. "There's a great park by the river. Lots of swings. We've got time before the bus returns."

They joked around as they walked to the park enjoying the crisp edge of the early December afternoon. Lynne ran ahead, hopped on the end swing, and started pumping. "You know, I always thought traveling would be fun. I'd see the world and dance to throngs of people with all expenses paid."

Marta rocked her swing, using the balls of her feet to create motion. Her heart raced; a jittery buzz wandered through her body. She shook her head, hoping to clear away the ringing in her ears. "You got your wish. You just didn't realize it would be on a bus in small towns with the likes of us."

Lynne pumped her swing higher. "I like our company, but I wish we had a few more days off. At least our break is coming. Almost three weeks to sleep in."

Marta stopped her swing and raised an imaginary wand toward Lynne. "I grant your every desire."

Lynne huffed a laugh. "Right. Without pay. I won't be able to do anything but sleep and beg for food. I can see it now. I'll paint my face green, put on a heavy cape, and stand in front of the ballet company building with my hand outstretched. 'Help the needy dancer buy food and *pointe* shoes.' That will net me ten cents for a cup of coffee."

The audience that evening sent the dancers back to their hotel with thunderous applause ringing in their ears. All evening Marta vibrated with energy. Her usual calmness with the children under her Mother Ginger skirt turned to frustration. She had to bite her lip to keep from sniping at them.

The fluttering from the diet pills faded away by bedtime, dropping her into a deep sleep. If she'd known about Bartley's diet pills earlier in the season, she might have spared herself some of Madame's criticism.

Holiday decorations brightened the edges of shop windows as they drove from Kalispell to Boise to Spokane. Christmas trees twinkled in every hotel reception area. The holiday spirit carried Marta home. How would her mom celebrate this year without her? How would she celebrate without her mom?

Clang, Clang, Clang.

Whap! Marta silenced the clock radio alarm with one swing of her hand. Seven-thirty. She stretched full length, then stood and walked to the hotel window.

Tiny snowflakes blew like milkweed on a windy day. Heavier snow covered the ground and the cars in the hotel parking lot. Her birthday had slipped by earlier in the week. She'd turned eighteen, officially an adult, but the tour kept her too busy to celebrate beyond buying cupcakes to share with Bartley and Lynne. Did she have cards waiting in Billings?

Today would be a great day to goof off in the snow, throw packed balls, and make snow angels. Back home she'd be holding hot cocoa, reading a magazine, and watching the snow while seated in Dad's leatherette rocker. But, if she *were* there, she'd not be a professional dancer. Choices.

When she heard a rustling of bedcovers, she turned to see Lynne sitting on the bed, scratching her head and stretching her neck and arms. "Morning, Marta. Hm,m,m. A good sleep for a change. What town is this? What day is it?"

"This is Spokane and it's Thursday, December fifth."

"How do you remember all this stuff?"

"The sign on that low building next door reads 'Spokane Plumbing,' and today's my mom's birthday."

Lynne laughed. "Ah. And all this time I thought you were clever."

Marta turned away from the window. "I am clever; you're my roommate. Besides, this is the last weekend on the road. How can you forget that?"

"Right. After Cody we'll be home. No more shin splints from lousy floors, and no more bumpy bus rides. Best of all, I can sleep in my own bed."

The girls completed their morning wake-up rituals and boarded the bus to breakfast, then to practice. Only two tour stops left, each with a workshop, a school program, and an evening performance followed by a mandatory appearance at a reception. They'd end the season with holiday performances in Billings, take a three week break, and return, ready to complete preparations for their next Billings performances: the full-length ballet, *Giselle*.

Marta sat on the bus sewing ribbons onto her newest *pointe* shoes. She bit off the thread and wrapped the ribbons around the arch of each shoe. A quick flex loosened their stiffness before she slid them into her tote and pulled out her torn pink tights. She found the tear in the heel and used her hand inside the tights to stretch out the material. One tiny stitch as a time, she worked her needle and pink thread around the hole to draw the fabric together. When she finished, she examined her work.

"Are those new tights?" Lynne asked.

"No, I just repaired them.

"Let me see." Lynne grabbed the tights and scrutinized the repair. "How do you do this? I hate trying to repair mine. Makes my brain grind."

Marta smiled. "It's restful for me. Helps pass the time on the bus."

Lynne rummaged through her bag and dragged out two pair of holey tights. "If you can repair these, I'll buy you dinner every night for the next week."

Marta took the tights and held them with two fingers. "Ugh. Do you ever wash these?"

"Not usually. It's spendy, but I usually just throw them away once they get too bad to wear."

Marta worked on Lynne's tights for the next two hours. She took rest breaks when the bus passed through small towns. Their rows of houses nestled in the snow sparkled with holiday lights reminding her of glittery, homey Christmas cards.

Home, like the wintry weather, swirled in her mind, focusing on the boarding house and, less often, on the place where she grew up. She missed her mom, but would Marta still feel at home in Bremerton after living on her own these past four months?

That triggered thoughts of Steve. She missed him. The invitation to his family's cabin over New Year's remained open. Relaxing in the mountain cabin with him and her friends made thinking about Christmas without her mother bearable.

Marta roused as the bus turned into the parking lot of the performance hall. She gathered her belongings and stood in the aisle waiting to exit the bus. Her head buzzed; she swayed and grabbed the back of a seat. Three diet pills were too many. They jumbled her thoughts. She needed to start moving and dancing to block the sounds circling inside her head.

A brisk wind swirled the snow, stealing her body heat before she entered the performance hall. Inside, preparations began: lights came on and hammers and drills echoed through the hall as a small crew of ballet company workers double-checked and secured the local theater scenery.

The pattern continued. Buildings where they practiced and performed stayed cold for at least an hour after their arrival, but rehearsals began within five minutes. Like the other dancers, she pulled on her dance clothes plus extra layers. She looked strange wearing two sweaters, her pajama bottoms, and a wool cap, but rehearsals didn't wait.

Havidson Performance Hall sported a sleek wooden stage. No shin splints today. Almost as nice as the Fox Theater in Billings and a welcome surprise.

The day's workshops and performances went well. The children hiding under the Mother Ginger skirt were the best behaved to date, giving neither Marta nor Madame reason for complaint.

When she returned to the hotel at eleven o'clock that night, she called home. "Happy birthday, Mom. How did you celebrate?"

"I went for dinner at the new Oyster Bay restaurant. The food is very good."

"Did you go with Dorothy?"

"No, a new friend, Robert. I met him at Lily's canasta party."

"So, you've started dating?"

"We've gone out a few times. Nothing special. Just cards with friends and a few dinners. But, enough about me. Tell me about the tour."

Mata rattled on about the tour, her character parts, especially Mother Ginger and how tiring the bus became day after day. She decided not to mention her renewed energy from Bartley's pills. She doubted her mother would understand.

The activities in Cody were canceled due to a blizzard that closed the mountain pass. On the drive back to Billings, the driver hunched forward to navigate the icy mountain roads. He followed the same route Marta had traveled when she arrived in August, but the snow changed the scenery. The bus headlights felt more like flashlights scoping out the route than a pair of bright headlights traveling through the black and white world just beyond the bus.

Lynne tapped Marta on the arm. "Are you awake?"

"Yeah. Daydreaming."

Lynne came around the seat and plopped down next to Marta. "I'm planning my two extra days. First I'll sleep in. Then I need to Christmas shop before rehearsals begin on the eleventh. Are you buying Steve anything?"

Marta stretched and yawned. "Yes, but I kinda fell apart after falling in the stream, so I need to explain myself. He may not want to see me."

"He'll be fine. Besides, I don't think he'd notice if you handed him a rock or the Hope diamond. That guy is ga-ga over you."

"Ga-ga? What does that mean?"

"Where have you been, under a rock? Ga-ga means he's so taken with you he blanks out when he looks at you. I'll call you so we can shop together."

"Sure."

"You don't sound sure. Stop fretting about Steve. He likes you, you like him. Leave it alone for now. Buy him a nice gift and buy me something fabulous and expensive."

"Sounds good."

"You're not listening, Marta."

The bus arrived in Billings at two in the morning. Lynne drove Marta home. Minutes later, she changed into pajamas and climbed under the covers. Light from the street lamp edged in around her curtain as she drifted into a dreamless sleep in her own bed.

When she awoke, it was snowing. She opened the curtain and sat down to rock, watching the snow accumulate on the rooftops across the street. When her eyes kept opening, she realized she'd dozed and gotten kinks in her neck, so she went back to bed and slept until noon.

Marta stood in the kitchen eating a mandarin orange from the well-stocked kitchen table. As a child she waited for Christmas for all the usual reasons, but also for the festive and seasonal red paper-wrapped mandarin oranges. She poured a glass of water and swallowed two diet pills before she went to unpack her suitcase and wash clothes.

The laundry room clotheslines remained full after her clothes were washed. Someone needed to get back down and take down their clothes. On closer inspection, the clothes belonged to a female. That meant Carol.

Marta left her own wet clothes in her laundry basket and returned to the kitchen. She assembled the ingredients for cinnamon rolls. For the

Paddy Eger

next two hours she mixed, set dough to rise, punched it down, and set it to a second rise. When she rechecked the laundry room, the lines were still full, so she took down the now-dry clothes, folded them, and set them in tidy piles on the ironing board.

She'd just rolled the last of the dough when Mrs. B. returned from work.

She smiled and patted Marta's back. "Welcome back. You've been missed. How was the tour?"

"Fine. But I'm glad to be home." Yes, she thought, this is home.

The front door opened, followed by the tromp of feet upstairs, then down stairs and down to the basement. The noisy tromps approached the kitchen.

Carol walked toward Marta. "Did you take down my clothes?"

"I did. They felt dry and—"

"Don't touch my clothes."

"Carol, I needed the lines."

Carol crossed her arms and narrowed her eyes. "You should have waited."

"I did. For several extra hours. I thought you'd appreciate their being folded for you."

"I was taking a test. You'd not know about things like that since you don't go to school."

Marta's body tightened at Carol's rebuke. "At least I have manners. Why didn't you tell me all those evenings when Steve called?"

Carol's eyes widened; she looked away. "I must have forgotten. You were out some place with friends."

"No, I wasn't. I was in my room with ice on my ankle every evening." Marta crossed her arms and lifted her chin.

"Ladies, please." Mrs. B. stepped between them. "Carol, you know the rules better than Marta. If you take a call for someone, leave them a note or talk to them as soon as possible. And as for the clothes, it was kind of Marta to fold your things."

Marta smiled.

"I also know I don't like to have others touch my clothes," Mrs. B. said. "I'll string more lines to prevent future problems."

This time it was Carol's turn to smile before she flounced away.

Marta retreated to her room. Except for encounters with Carol, the boarding house presented a welcome change from the frantic days of the tour. Perhaps Carol would travel home for the holidays and give the boarding house a rest from her grumpy demeanor.

She crossed off the tour days on the December page of her calendar. The Billings performances started in three days. Hopefully the snow wouldn't limit audience turnout. After all, this was Billings, and they were used to long weeks of snow-covered roads.

Her thoughts shifted to Steve. Should she wait a couple of days to see if he called, or should she call him? Girls did call guys these days. She walked to the phone in the alcove. As she reached for the receiver, the phone rang.

*D*isappointment. The call she answered was for Carol. Marta took a message after she checked and discovered Carol wasn't in the house. She taped it to Carol's door and headed to the bathroom scale.

The dial swung back and forth, then settled on one hundred pounds. Bartley didn't lie; she'd not gained an ounce nor felt hungry since starting the diet pills. In fact, she'd lost a few pounds.

It was the next afternoon before Steve called, asking her to join him on a drive to Lake Josephine. Their early attempts at conversation faltered. Now they sat in the car at the lake, watching the snow fall around them.

"Steve? I was about to call you. I, ah..."

"Wait, Marta. Let me start. I should never have forced you to step into that icy water. Can you forgive me?"

"It wasn't your fault. I loved the trip, but I'm suppose to be professional and take care of myself. I could have walked away, but I wanted to take your challenge. Unfortunately, I paid a price for my silliness."

"But, Marta. How can you have any fun if you're always worried about taking care of yourself. You got bruised, but you didn't break any bones."

"You didn't have to deal with Madame."

"That woman. Her demands are enough to drive a sane person crazy!"

"No. In a way I understand why she got angry. She's protecting her investment in me. She can't find a replacement this time of year and get her prepared to perform on short notice."

"And who can replace you? I certainly can't." Steve pulled her close and planted a kiss on her forehead. "Plus, we have another article to write. Maybe New Year's weekend we can slip away and work on it."

She laughed. "So, all you care about is the article? I should have guessed as much."

"No, I... You're teasing me aren't you? Come on. Let's take a walk."

Snow crunched beneath their boots. He put his arm over her shoulder and pulled her closer. "You know I've missed you, right?"

"Yes."

His arm hugged her even closer against his body. He released her and stared. "Marta, have you lost weight?" He held her gaze and reached to interlock his fingers with hers. "Your face looks thinner."

"I've been on tour for two weeks, sleeping in strange beds, living out of a suitcase, and eating at odd hours. It's been crazy. Now, let's go for a walk, okay?"

Steve pulled her along the snow-covered trail. "I care about you. A lot. You're thinner, that's all. I don't want you to get sick. I worry that you're working too hard."

"I'm fine." She broke free and walked ahead toward the cat tails that glistened like icy sheaths.

"Let's start this conversation over." He hurried to catch up to her and made a sweeping bow. "My dear Miss Fluff, you look ravishing today. May I walk with you and hold your hand?"

"Yes, as long as we avoid icy streams or talk about my health."

Steve bowed. "Whatever it takes. You're a successful ballerina and I am a lowly newspaperman. I want to be with you wherever and whenever possible."

She sauntered away, then began dancing toward the pond. When she heard no sound behind her, she stopped and turned. Steve leaned against a picnic table watching the lake. "Hey, ink boy! Why did you stop?"

His taut face surprised her. "Promise me you'll take care of yourself. I always want you to be safe and happy, and have time left over for me."

"I promise." A smile curved the edges of her mouth as she watched Steve's face. Absentmindedly, she rubbed the shivers from her shoulders.

"Are you cold?" he said.

"A little. I didn't know Billings would get so frigid."

"I can fix that." He led her back to his car and bowed. "Your chariot, fair maiden."

In town he parked in front of Dalton's Department Store. He turned off the ignition and started to get out of the car.

"What are you doing?"

"Shopping for a Montana winter coat for you." He climbed out, rounded the car, and opened her door.

"Steve, I can't. I don't get paid until next week."

He took her hands and pulled her out of the car. "You need a coat. It can be a gift or a loan. When's your birthday?"

"December first, while we were on tour."

He stopped her on the sidewalk. "What? Why didn't you tell me? We could have celebrated."

"On tour, remember? Besides, you don't need to buy things for me. I can take care of myself, thank you."

"Can't tell that from what you're wearing today." He took her elbow and steered her toward the store. "Consider this a late birthday present and an early Christmas gift. Happy Birthday and Merry Christmas, Miss Fluff."

Inside, the saleswoman persuaded her to try on a variety of coats. Marta liked a red coat as well as a pale blue one, but Steve turned them away saying they weren't warm enough.

Next, Marta tried on a long, soft gray coat. She stroked the sleeves and traced the large fabric-covered buttons and the sleek front panels.

"We'll take this one," Steve said. "We also need warm gloves or mittens, a hat, and...." He scanned the tables. "Add a scarf."

He stood back as Marta selected gray mittens, a gray slouch hat, and a red plaid scarf with fringe. He wrapped the scarf around her neck and kissed her nose. "We'll take these, and she'll wear them home."

The clerk rang up the sale. Steve wrote a check and grinned at Marta as she opened her new coat and fanned herself. "I'm melting!"

"Good. Now you'll be ready to go to the mountains for my New Year's party." He grabbed her old coat off the counter as they headed out.

At the boarding house curb, they stood against his car, Steve sheltering her from the cold December afternoon. She buried her face against his coat.

"I love my new coat. It's perfect."

"No, you're perfect."

"Hardly. I, ah, I have to tell you something. I hope you won't be mad."

"I could never be mad at you."

"The reason I got so freaky when I fell into the water, is, ah, I can't swim."

Steve pushed her back to arm's length. "What? Oh my God. Why didn't you tell me sooner? Oh, Marta, I am so sorry. You must have been frightened to death."

She nodded.

Steve drew her into a long, tight hug. Neither spoke.

"Are you mad at me?"

"Marta, how can I be mad? I felt bad when it happened, but now.... You should have told me sooner."

"I felt embarrassed. Most people around Puget Sound learn to swim when they are in school. I left early those days to go to dance class, so I missed out."

"This summer I'll teach you. It will be fun." He kissed her forehead. "But right now it's freezing and time for you to get inside." He pulled her along the sidewalk and up the steps and into the boarding house.

Suddenly she didn't want Steve to leave. "Can you stay for dinner?"

He shook his head. "Company tonight at my house. I'll call you later." He hugged her and kissed her forehead again.

The empty boarding house ensured Marta of a few hours of quiet. Perhaps a nap or at least time to sit and begin embroidering a silk scarf. The next three weeks of rehearsals and performances promised little time for relaxation. The long New Year's weekend at the cabin felt a lifetime away.

The preparations for their hometown performances progressed smoothly. Marta and the rest of the corps knew the dances by memory and danced almost without thinking about the choreography or their assigned positions on the stage. Marta performed the role of Mother Ginger, stilts and all, without losing her balance. Plus, the local children didn't pinch or push while hiding under the gigantic hoop skirt.

The fact that Madame complimented soloists but didn't speak to Marta no longer bothered her. Madame only spoke to one corps dancer, Marguerite, her pet. Dancing well held a personal importance far beyond pleasing Madame. Marta performed the choreography with few errors, took Madame's and Damien's critiques with a smile, and left it at that.

After Thursday's final rehearsal before performances began, she stood inside the front entry waiting for Steve and watching Karl, the janitor, work. Karl kept his head down as he moved his mop back and forth, creeping closer to her feet. She moved out of his way when he approached.

He stopped and leaned on the mop. "You can't stay here much longer, Miss Marta. I need to lock up at five."

"I know. My ride's coming any minute." She re-crossed the entry to keep out of his way. "How long have you worked here, Karl?"

"Who wants to know?"

"I do."

He leaned on his mop again. "Started here in nineteen forty-seven; about ten years. Why?"

"Just wondered. Have you always lived in Billings?"

"Yep. Now, enough with the questions. I need to finish up." Karl began whistling as he disappeared down the side hallway.

Marta stepped outside. When Steve drove up and slid to a stop at the curb, she hopped in. "Here," he said as he handed her a nosegay of blue pansies and an open newspaper. "The ballet review. Hot off the presses."

"Have you read it?"

"Yeah. It's good," He put his arm around her shoulder and pointed to the bottom of the article. "Listen to this: 'This year's Intermountain Ballet Company presents the *Nutcracker* with exquisite beauty and energy. The audiences will applaud the colorful costumes and the extraordinary talent of the guest artists, the principals, the corps, and the children.' Great, huh?"

Marta started to speak, but Steve took back the paper and scanned the article. "Wait. Down here it says, 'Every person who enjoys a night of music will find something to cheer about in the *Nutcracker,* from the soldiers to Mother Ginger and the dances from Arabia to the waltzing flowers.' You were mentioned, Marta. That's great, isn't it?"

"Do you know your eyebrows wiggle when you're excited?" Marta took the paper from his hands. "May I read it now?"

Steve grabbed her hands, crushing the paper. "Susan Zane enjoyed the dress rehearsal. Now, can you get me tickets for all the performances?"

"All of them? Isn't that excessive for a guy who thinks ballet is fluff?"

"I've apologized for that twenty times since September. Anyway, my friends want to see you in action, I mean, dancing. I'll stay around and drive you home afterward."

Marta straightened the paper and handed it back to Steve. "You can get tickets at the ticket booth."

"No, I can't; that's the point. The performances are sold out, and Dad forgot he'd promised me the newspaper's tickets and gave them to one of his major advertisers and his wife."

"I promised my tickets to the boarders and Mrs. B.'s friends."

"Can Lynne give me hers or sell them to me?"

"Steve! Take a breath! Lynne's using hers, but Bartley might have spares."

"Great. Make her promise to save one for me. I'll keep checking with the box office. Maybe single tickets will show up." He smiled as he started the car and pulled away from the curb.

Days before Christmas, Marta rushed up the boarding house steps with her plaid scarf flowing behind her. She removed her boots and brushed the snow off her coat and left both in the entry to avoid being late for dinner.

A tall pine tree in the common room glowed with multi-colored bubble lights, sparkly glass ornaments, and tinsel, like back home. The laughter decorating the tree two days ago as well as hearing Perry Como sing holiday songs each evening eased her holiday loneliness and the distance from her mom. With a Christmas Eve *Nutcracker* performance, going home to Bremerton remained impossible, so a phone call would have to do.

Marta dried the last of the dinner dishes and turned to Mrs. B. "I thought I'd bake Jul Kaga for Christmas. It's a Swedish bread with candied fruit."

"That would be wonderful. I'll pick up the ingredients, but do you have time?"

"I'll make the time. Jul Kaga is a family tradition I love. I'll mix it up Christmas Eve after our performance, then finish it Christmas morning."

"I'd be happy to help you."

"Thanks, but I'd like to do it myself. It's my job at home."

Marta sat in the common room watching the heated bubble lights on the Christmas tree release tiny bursts up each colored tube. She and her mom used to put up the same type of lights back home, and she loved to watch their light play off each piece of tinsel. She closed her eyes and leaned back in the overstuffed chair. How could something so beautiful cause her to ache with such loneliness?

*T*he 1957 Christmas Eve performance ended with numerous curtain calls. Bartley, Lynne, and Marta stood side by side in the back row. They exchanged smiles after each bow. Now the final curtain closed, signaling the end of the *Nutcracker* for another year.

As the stagehands dimmed the stage lights, Marta allowed tiredness to overtake her body. She walked slowly off the stage as she realized her truth: she was a professional dancer. People came to see the company perform; that included her. Madame gave her tough roles, and she'd done well dancing them. She belonged here.

Lynne and Marta removed their headpieces as they walked to the dressing room. "I can't believe it's finally over," Lynne said. "Want to come to my place to unwind?"

"No," Marta said. "All I want to do is sleep. We can save the unwind for Steve's cabin next week. I wonder if Bartley plans to come with us. So far she's avoided answering me. Where's she gone?"

"I saw her rush off before we left the stage. Did she have a plane to catch or what?"

"Beats me," Marta said. "I—" Small wrapped packages sat at their places along the dressing room tables. Marta picked up hers and turned it over in her hands.

"Guess that's a 'no' for saying Merry Christmas to her," Lynne said.

Both girls ripped open their boxes and pulled out a silver chain with three tiny ballerinas dancing together. "Three dancers," Marta said.

"Three musketeers of dancing," Lynne said as she fastened her necklace.

ఴ

The dressing room filled with noise as the corps dancers filtered in, changed out of costumes, and put on street clothes. After several minutes of hustle and bustle, it quieted as dancers disappeared down the hallway to the exit.

Lynne slapped a drum roll on the make-up table, then stood and reached for her street clothes. "I'll join you for Christmas breakfast. Then we'll visit with my aunt before we…"

Marta looked up when Lynne stopped mid-sentence. She gasped and leaped to her feet, overturning her chair. "Mom! You're here!" She rushed to hug her.

"Merry Christmas, honey. I didn't want us to be apart on Christmas or miss seeing you dance your first professional *Nutcracker*."

Marta soaked up the feel of her mother's arms around her. She slowed her breathing to match her mother's and laid her head against her shoulder, relaxing in a shelter she didn't know she'd missed. She had forfeited her traditional holiday time with her parents and relatives and traveled all the way to Billings to be with her. That made every day of hard work, of performances, of tiredness worthwhile.

"I loved watching you dance. You moved so smoothly around the stage. Each dance looked perfect, even Mother Ginger. What a challenge! Performing with young children. And the atmosphere! The sets, the costumes, the staging, listening to a symphony orchestra–it was wonderful."

"It was exciting. I'm totally exhausted, but now you're here…" Marta released her to make introductions. "Mom, I want you to meet my new best friend, Lynne."

"Nice to meet you, Lynne. Marta talks about you all the time."

"Hi," Lynne said. "Boy, you surprised her."

"Good. Mrs. B. and I started to tell her numerous times."

Marta gasped. "Mrs. B. knows?"

"Yes. We've gotten to be good friends on the phone. You ladies finish changing. I'm taking you out for a special dessert."

"Uh, Mom. Everything's closed. It's ten-thirty on Christmas Eve."

"Oh, I know a place that stays open late."

The special dessert materialized in Mrs. B.'s kitchen. They shared tins of homemade Christmas cookies while seated around the kitchen work table. Conversation circled faster than the cookies. All the while, Marta clung to her mom's arm.

"I mailed your gift, so I don't have anything for you for Christmas," Marta said.

"Honey, you are all the present I need."

"How long can you stay? Where are you staying? How did you get here?"

Mrs. B. laughed. "I don't think I've ever heard Marta this excited."

"I know. This is a different person than the one I put on the bus last August. Anyway, I took the train. I'm staying here in the empty room until the twenty-eighth."

Marta stroked her mom's arm. "I'm so glad you came. I wished for something like this, and now you're here. Christmas is perfect."

"I agree, honey. We'll have time to talk, and you'll be able to get a good rest."

"Both sound wonderful." Marta relaxed and let her thoughts drift away from the conversation. She'd danced through two of the season's five programs. Her endurance grew with each one. Soon she'd be ready to audition for solos. After all, if she didn't try she'd never get a solo or a back up position. She needed both to progress in the company.

Her mom's hand on her shoulder brought Marta back to the table conversation. They'd moved on to stories of childhood Christmas gifts. Marta closed her eyes and half listened.

Lynne's laughter startled Marta awake. She turned to see Lynne stuff two cookies in her mouth, drink the last of her cocoa, and stand. "Cool surprise, Marta. Okay. Change of plans. I'll spend the morning with my aunt and our family, then I'll head over here in the late afternoon. Thanks for the cookies. Good night everyone, and Merry Christmas."

Long after the others left, Marta and her mom sat in the common room wrapped in afghans. Marta's resurgence of energy allowed her to stay alert and share random thoughts, stories from the dance company, and her time with friends.

"Where are Bartley and Steve tonight?"

"Bartley vanished. Guess she's gone to Philadelphia. Steve left right after the ballet. He's meeting his relatives on the late train."

"You mentioned that he comes to watch you dance every night. Sounds like it's getting serious, honey."

Marta shrugged and smiled. "He'd like to be, but I'm not ready to get serious. Besides, we both have crazy schedules."

When tiredness overpowered Marta, she said good night and climbed the stairs to her room. Despite her fatigue, she picked up dirty clothes, straightened shelves, and put the room in order before her mom would see it in the morning.

She lifted her window shade half way, allowing the full moon's snowy blue light to flood her room while she sat and rocked. Christmas would be perfect now.

Morning arrived too soon. Marta stretched but stayed snuggled in her warm bedcover cave, savoring the thought of the next days with her mom.

A light tap on her door ended her lounging. "Who is it?"

"Mom. May I come in?"

She hopped up and flung the door open. "Merry Christmas, Mom. Welcome to my Montana home."

Her mom walked in looking toasty warm in a chenille robe with matching slippers. They hugged before she held Marta away from her at arm's length. "You're tired. Want to sleep a little longer?"

"No, I'm awake. I don't want to waste a minute of time with you. Is Mrs. B. up yet?" Marta stifled a yawn.

"Yes. She's busy in the kitchen."

Marta yawned again. "Good. Well, this is my room." She stretched side-to-side and executed a few *pliés*. "I got used to all the hot weather, and now it's freezing cold until the heat reaches my vents, which takes a long time."

Marta watched her survey the room. "Well, what do you think? Looks a lot like Gran's house, doesn't it?"

"It does." Her mom smiled. "I like the way you've arranged everything. It feels comfortable." She hugged Marta and moved to the door. "I need to shower and get dressed, so I'll meet you downstairs in a little while."

Marta took a quick shower and towel-dried her hair. Now, what to wear? She worked her way through her small selection of clothes. Many pieces hung looser than she remembered. She grabbed her red wool skirt, a collared blouse, and a tan cardigan. She fussed with her hair, then gave up and pulled it back into a loose ponytail, leaving ringlets trailing beside her ears.

Marta hummed as she descended the stairs. From the landing she heard the rattling of dishes and pots mingled with the aroma of baking bread. Her mom and Mrs. B. stood side by side at the kitchen work table talking in quiet voices. They both looked up when she entered.

"Good morning, ladies. Merry Christmas. Do I smell Jul Kaga baking?"

"Yes," Mrs. B. said. "Your mother finished what you started yesterday. I'm baking it with the pies. Breakfast is almost ready."

Marta put Bing Crosby's *White Christmas* on the record player and hummed as she set the table for five, placing her mom at the foot of the table. Carol's place would remain empty until classes resumed in January. Thank heavens she left for the holidays.

Shorty and James appeared minutes later, each wearing their best shirts and ties. After breakfast they rearranged the common room furniture to face the Christmas tree and the turntable where Christmas records played without interruption.

When the doorbell rang in the early evening, Marta hurried to answer it. Lynne and Steve entered, bringing in a cold breeze and arms full of gifts. Lynne stepped aside to hang her coat; Steve continued into the common room without stopping. "Merry Christmas, everyone," he said. Nice to see all of you on such a beautiful day. Must be 15 degrees. I love a cold Christmas."

Marta took the packages, allowing him space to remove his overcoat. Shorty jumped up and helped. When the commotion slowed, Marta took Steve's hand and pulled him to face her mom. "Mom, I'd like to introduce Steve Mason. Steve, this is my mom. She arrived last night."

Steve reached out his hand. "Mrs. Selbryth, I'm happy to meet you. Marta didn't tell me you were coming."

"I surprised her. I'm glad to meet you, Steve. She's told me a lot about you."

"I hope she mentioned the good stuff."

"Of course."

"We're happy you could join us," Mrs. B. said. "Shorty and James hoped you'd keep your promise to join us."

"I appreciate being asked. Sorry about last night. I had pick-up duty immediately after the Nutcracker, but the train rumbled in over an hour late."

Mrs. B. served hot drinks in holiday mugs as gifts were distributed and opened. James and Shorty passed out the latest Christmas *Ideal* magazines. Marta's mom handed out hand towels with hand-crocheted edges. Lynne passed out *Popular Mechanics* magazines to the men, sachets to the women, and a pale green scarf to Marta.

Steve gave the men each a mini-pliers in a leather case. He handed Marta's mom, Mrs. B., Lynne, and Marta each a gift box of Russell Stover holiday candy, plus a packet of flowered handkerchiefs.

Marta smiled when she saw how he'd come prepared for any eventuality.

At Marta's turn, she presented the male boarders with a new board game called Clue. For Lynne she had purchased two new pairs of pink tights and attached a note which read, "I'll teach you to mend properly."

She watched Steve unwrap her gift, a dark blue silk tie with a faint diagonal design. "It's for the ballet."

Steve replaced his holiday string tie with the gift and kissed Marta's cheek.

At a lull after the gift exchange, while Mrs. B. refilled mugs, Steve reached for Marta's hand. "Come outside? For a minute?"

Marta grabbed her coat and followed him onto the icy porch. He sat in the swing and patted the space beside him. "I have a special present for you, but I didn't want to give it to you with everyone watching." He handed her a small box wrapped in silver paper with a glittery silver bow. "I planned to give this to you last night, but...open it."

When she opened the box, her eyes widened. A small, heart-shaped stone hung from a silver chain. Its pale blueness sparkled like summer sunlight on the ocean.

"It's not your birthstone, a blue topaz, but the jeweler said white turquoise is a symbol of friendship and luck. This one reminded me of the evening sky at the cabin. I hope you like it."

Marta stared at the necklace. "Steve, it's lovely. But, you already gave me a coat. This is too much."

"No. I saw this and knew I wanted you to have it."

She closed her hand around the stone. "Thanks. I love it."

Steve looped the pendant around her neck and hooked the clasp. Then he circled around and kissed her lips. Her hands shook as she straightened the heart to hang between her collarbones.

"I'll wear it whenever I'm not dancing." She paused and kissed his cheek, wishing they could linger. "Come on." She hauled him back inside.

She showed the necklace to everyone, ending with her mom who said, "How lovely. Marta's father gave me a necklace when we first started dating. I still wear it. Marta wore it to her audition for the ballet company."

Steve sat beside Marta on the small couch. He captured her hand and squeezed it. She returned the squeezes until she moved to restart the stack of Christmas records.

Steve spoke with everyone, shifting easily from mining to current events to stories about Billings, asking each person questions, like a reporter but with obvious interest. Had he learned that in college? Marta wished she had his gift of conversation.

After dinner, Mrs. B. stood. "I have a gift for everyone to share." She removed a blanket from a huge box that had occupied a corner of the room for several days. "I hope this doesn't change things too much. Everyone needs to help unwrap it."

Shorty reached out toward Marta, offering his hand. "Come on. Help us out."

The three boarders tore off the Christmas wrapping to discover an RCA Victor television. Shorty laughed. "You said you didn't want one of these things in here. What changed your mind?"

Mrs. B. pursed her lips. "I didn't want to be the only house on the block without one. Besides, there are good news programs, plays, and music. The antenna is installed on the roof. But we need to find a place to set it up."

James got up without a word, unplugged the record player, and repositioned the narrow pine table it stood on. Shorty helped him slide the TV into the corner. They fastened on the metal rabbit-ear antenna and turned on the set to check the picture. The black and white images resembled a home movie, but instead of friends they saw the Boston Pops playing Christmas songs. The record player sat forgotten on the relocated table.

"Looks pretty good," James said. "We can still play cards while the rest of you watch the tube."

"Where did you hear it called 'the tube'?" asked Shorty.

James shrugged his shoulders. "Cuz I'm quiet don't mean I don't know things."

Lynne and Marta cleared away the last of the dishes. While Marta washed, Lynne leaned against the counter. "So, Marta, have you told Steve how you feel? It's obvious he's nuts about you."

"Sorta. It's hard to explain that I enjoy his company and all, but that I need to focus on my dancing."

"Well, he's busy with school, so I'm sure he'll understand. But guys don't like to feel like women are using them."

"I'm not using him."

"Right. He drives you everywhere, he buys you gifts, and he looks at you like a puppy dog. Did you think that maybe he's cutting corners with his job or with classes to see you?"

"No. He wouldn't do that, would he?"

"From the look on his face and the way he holds your hand, he might." Lynne grabbed a flour sack towel and began drying the plates that stood in the dish rack. Then she rejoined the group without mentioning Steve again.

Marta put the dishes away and stood staring out the kitchen window. Lynne knew lots about boyfriend stuff. When they worked on the next article, she'd make time to talk things through with Steve. That gave her a week to decide how to explain dancing and how dating Steve fit into her schedule. Could be a complicated conversation.

Later than night, Marta sat with her mom in the common room, enjoying the quiet. "This would be perfect if Dad were here. I feel like I didn't know him long enough. I mean, I remember him, but I expected he'd be around for Sunday picnics, teaching me to drive, and watching me dance."

Her mom patted Marta's hand. "It's hard, isn't it? I miss him every day."

"Did you two talk about things like his work and you staying home to raise me?"

"Of course. You have to share your thoughts when you love someone. Even when you disagree, you need to share what you are thinking. Why do you ask?"

"I'm trying to figure out how to be a grownup. It's more work than I imagined." She toyed with a loose thread on the sofa. "What do you talk about with Robert?"

"Mostly day-to-day things like work, the news, movies, and our families. We're both returning to dating after lots of years without being in a relationship, so we're keeping it simple."

Was keeping it simple when dating even possible? Marta had her doubts.

Mornings Marta and her mom ate breakfast together. After Marta practiced in the basement, they shared lunch and explored downtown Billings. One blustery afternoon, Mrs. B. and her mom sat in the common room drinking tea.

Marta busied herself making dinner rolls. As she put them in the oven and began cleaning up the work table, she heard her name mentioned. She stepped closer to the common room to listen.

"And it's wonderful that you let her use the basement. Renting a practice room would be costly."

"Marta is special to us all. We live for her baking. She adds a lightness to our mealtime conversations. You can be proud of her. Now we need to fatten her up. I'm afraid she'll blow away with the first good storm."

Marta froze in place. Eat? She ate. Her mom knew food didn't interest her when she'd danced all day. Why didn't she tell Mrs. B. that fact?

"I've worried about her staying healthy," her mom said. "She works so hard. I wonder if she ever takes vitamins."

Marta stepped into the room. "I'm fine. You two worry too much. Now that the tour is over, things at the ballet company will settle back down. We'll move back into our old routines. I'll get plenty of sleep, and you can count on Mrs. B. to keep me properly fed."

Her mom reached out and touched Marta's arm. "I'm sorry. We shouldn't have talked about you. We're just worried that's all."

"I know. But, you know how I get when I'm tired; I can't eat."

"I do. Mrs. B. says you still crave ginger ale and fruit cocktail."

Marta smiled. "Yes. I know it's strange, but it works."

"Good. Let's head to the grocery store before I leave tomorrow. We can see what looks appetizing to you."

Saturday morning they stood together on the train landing. Mom's suitcase sat next to their legs. "This time I'm the one leaving," her mom said.

"I'm glad you came on the train."

"After your bus adventure, I decided the extra money·was worth it, especially this time of year."

Marta handed her mother a flat package. "Open this now, Mom. It's a copy of the newspaper's group photo from the day I met Steve."

Her mom's hands trembled as she undid the wrapping. "Marta. It's lovely. I'll put it on my desk at the dance studio to inspire the students."

"When you get home you'll find another one waiting for you, plus a photo of me in my *Coppélia* peasant costume. If you want more, let me know."

They hugged. Marta pulled back, feeling her mom's body shake. Tears crowded her mom's eyes. "I'm sorry I'm crying. I'm just so proud of your becoming a beautiful, responsible young woman."

"Thanks. I'm glad you came. Having you here made Christmas and the *Nutcracker* special. You're the one who made all this possible, Mom. You helped me live my dream."

"I truly understand how ballet is magical for you. I can't imagine you doing anything else with your life."

Her mom boarded the train. When she appeared at a seat window, they continued their goodbyes: smiling, blowing kisses, and waving as the train slid away from the station.

Marta sat on the floor in the basement practice room, resting and imagining her mom's location as the train moved through the Rockies. Their time together had raced by. Funny though, toward the end of her stay, long quiet times became more common. Had her mom changed, or had she?

After Marta turned off the overhead light, she reached for the basement door handle. It turned in her hand. She stepped back. A hand waved around for the light switch. Click!

Marta stood face to face with Carol.

"Oh!" Carol sprang back.

Marta backed up and leaned against a support beam near the door. "Can I help you?"

Carol's face turned red as a Christmas bow. "No, I'm looking, ah, for ah, ah box."

Marta brushed past her. "Turn off the light when you're done looking."

arta and Lynne drove to Steve's cabin the evening before he and his friends were to arrive. The plan for the long New Year's weekend included snowy walks, snowshoeing, and sledding, as well as cozy fires, board games, and Charades. Marta promised they'd make the cabin "warm and inviting," if they didn't take the train to Spokane to see the Ballet Russe de Monte Carlo perform. A relaxing visit to the mountains beat out a snowy trip to the ballet.

As they drove to the cabin, Marta stewed about meeting college students. Steve had called it "great fun." Great fun? Maybe for Lynne, who found it easy to talk with strangers. Marta wanted time alone with Steve to try to explain her feelings and her goals as a dancer. She didn't want to compete for his attention with brainy college girls.

When they pulled into the gravel driveway, Lynne hit the steering wheel with her fists. "Can you believe I forgot the chicken? You start a fire while I'll go back to town. We'll unpack later. Don't get in any trouble while I'm gone."

While Lynne backed out the curved driveway, Marta climbed the steps and slid across the icy porch toward the door. Slippery. She took the cabin key from its hiding place above the entry light, unlocked the door, put the key back, and stepped inside. She inhaled the icy air and repeated aloud, "This will be fun, this will be fun. I can do this."

First things first. Bring in wood from the huge pile on the porch and start a fire. Marta stepped outside and closed the door behind her. The porch felt like an ice rink. She skidded across the wooden boards toward the wood pile. Her hand reached for the porch railing.

Crack. The railing splintered as if made of pickup sticks.

The sound confused her. Her balance shifted. She grabbed for the corner porch post, but missed. Her arms pinwheeled, seeking control.

She heard a scream, her scream, as she began to fall.

Is this how her dad died, twisting and arching like a high jumper, sailing through the air? Did he scream or fall silently?

Marta grabbed handfuls of the night sky, but she crashed onto cold, rock-strewn ground. Her outstretched chin knocked her head back with a violent punch.

When she opened her eyes, fireplace logs lay around and on top of her, crushing her like petals in a flower press. She shivered. Pain swept through her body in sickening waves. Her left ankle throbbed with a wild bass drum beat. Her left hand lay beneath her in a macabre position.

Lynne's car was nowhere in sight. Should she call out? No. The nearest cabin was down the road and around the bend. Could she stand? No. She'd need to crawl to the steps.

Piece by piece, she pushed the logs off her body, no small feat with one hand. Shifting her weight onto her right elbow, she inched along the frozen ground where the overhang drip line created a bare trail around the cabin. Her fingers stiffened from the cold.

Halfway to the front of the cabin she rested her head on the ground. The pain she experienced far outweighed her incident in the stream. That meant this fall caused serious damage. Where was Lynne?

Rocks gouged her body in a hundred places as she continued to scoot forward. At the corner she rested again. She saw the steps down the long side of the cabin; a distance three times what she'd crawled so far.

What if Lynne didn't come straight back? What if she had car trouble or stopped to flirt with a mountain man? What if a prowling coyote or cougar stalked the cabin? Marta closed her eyes.

The last section of her trek to the steps took every ounce of her energy. She'd lost the protection of the roofline and began crawling through snow. With each move forward, her right hand and right leg broke through sheets of shimmering icy crust.

She slowed. Shivers changed to a strange feeling of warmth. She craved sleep.

Marta pulled herself onto her right knee, turned, and sat on the bottom step, as exhausted as if she'd danced an entire ballet. One agonizing scoot at a time, she moved her bruised body up the steps, dragging her left leg like a foreign object tacked onto her body. At the top, she pushed against the door. Locked.

The door must have latched behind her. She stared at the entry light; she'd never be able to reach the key. She slumped against the door and cried.

Minutes slowed. Rhythmic throbbing and shivering cycled through her core. She held her injured hand against her body. It felt as cold as an ice pack. Hurry, Lynne.

"Marta? Marta?"

Shaking and shouting roused her. "Marta, what happened?"

She closed her eyes until a slap against her cheek roused her again.

"Marta. Wake up!"

Car lights blinded her, but she recognized Lynne's voice through the fog of coldness that enveloped her.

"The railing... broke... my ankle..."

"Oh, no! Oh, Marta! We're driving straight back to town."

After considerable shoving and screams of pain, Marta sat hunched over in Lynne's back seat, resting her bulbous left ankle on the back of the lowered front passenger seat. The awkward angle caused her to shelter her injured left hand against her chest. She shivered even with two blankets covering her.

Maybe her ankle wasn't broken. Could be a strain that would heal in a few days. Deep down, however, she knew that wasn't true. Heartache crushed her spirit like the fall crushed her body.

"How is it, Marta? Talk to me. Good thing you're thin and light; I'd never have been able to lift…"

Marta woke and slept as the drive to Billings stretched on. Every bump, every slip on the icy road exploded her pain. Three seconds on a porch gathering wood may have shattered her future as well as her bones.

The garish blue neon emergency sign marked the hospital driveway. Lynne stopped abruptly and rushed away. Minutes later a nurse with two orderlies and a gurney pushed out the door with Lynne following close behind.

They helped Marta wriggle from the backseat and onto the gurney. Inside, they wheeled her into an emergency room cubicle. She drifted off, dreaming about her first desires to become a *pointe* dancer.

She'd walked with her mom to the studio, whirling and twirling down the sidewalk, chattering ninety miles an hour about *pointe* shoes and tutus. She'd reached the magical age of twelve, the first year *pointe* shoes were allowed. Today Miss Holland promised to hand out the coveted pink boxes.

Marta sat on the cool tiled floor beside the other girls sewing satin ribbons onto her first *pointe* shoes. She stitched from side to side, every stitch tiny and perfect like her mom had taught her. Her excitement grew with each stitch.

She stroked the perfect pink satin shoes, then struggled to slide her toes inside. They felt too snug. Her left foot ached as she pushed it into the shoe. A hand moved her hand away.

"Marta? Marta?"

She startled and opened her eyes to scan the colorless emergency room. A blanket covered her. She lay flat on her back. Lynne stood beside her.

"Lynne? What—"

"You were grabbing for your foot. An orthopedic doctor's coming in. Once I told the emergency doc that you were a dancer, he didn't want to touch your ankle. How do you feel?"

"Awful. Every part of my body aches, and I'm thirsty." Marta moved her head from side to side, swallowing her last bit of saliva.

A doctor stepped into her white-curtained cubicle. "I'm Dr. Wycoff, the orthopedist. Let's take x-rays and see what damage has been done."

Half an hour later the doctor returned and hung the x-ray film on a backlit screen.

"Your ankle is broken," he said. "Left hand is sprained. You have a nasty head wound and multiple deep bruises, but your cuts do not require stitches. I'm admitting you. We'll clean you up tonight, then cast your ankle once the swelling decreases."

Marta's eyes filled with tears that Lynne wiped away.

Once Marta settled in her hospital room, the nurse placed a metal frame under the covers to lighten the weight of the blankets on her injured leg. She applied ice packs to Marta's ankle and gave her sips of water.

When Marta lifted her left hand, the bandage squeezed like an undersized glove. She closed her eyes and shook her head.

"I'm sorry I wanted that dumb chicken," Lynne said from a seat in the corner of the room. "I feel guilty about this. It's my fault."

Marta turned away from Lynne and focused on the blue neon emergency sign outside her window. It wavered like a ghostly image. "It wasn't your fault."

"Mrs. B. is calling your mom. Should I call Steve?"

Marta turned to face Lynne. "No. He'll not be home until after the trip to the cabin. He's helping a friend move to Bozeman then heading straight to the cabin. He'll think we went to Spokane to see the Ballet Russe." She fingered the necklace he'd given her last week. If only he knew where she'd gone and could come see her, she'd feel better.

The door opened. Mrs. B. bustled in. Her tight mouth and her furrowed brow matched her worried voice. "How are you, Marta?"

"Not great. Did you reach my mom?"

"She's on her way." Mrs. B. squeezed Marta's right hand, sharing her warmth.

Marta held her breath to keep from crying.

New Year's Eve day became an endless loop of empty, painful minutes. Her cuts burned, many of her bruises were the size of dinner plates, her leg throbbed, and she ached from lying in bed. The biology lab smell of the hospital and the squeaky footsteps of the nurses played like a bad dream. If only she could escape and go to sleep in her own bed.

Evening light filtered through the wide Venetian blind slats. As Marta adjusted her covers, a familiar staccato of steps approached her partially open door. Her mom.

She rushed to the bed and swooped down, gathering Marta in a gentle hug. "Marta, honey, how are you?"

A stream of tears slid down Marta's face. Her mom brushed them aside. "That answers my question. What did the doctor say?"

"He said I broke the scaphoid. That's a small bone on top of my foot. How did you get here?"

"I drove."

"Oh, M-mom." She started to cry again.

On New Year's Day the boarders stopped in to visit. They brought a basket of fruit, a vase of yellow roses, and a bottle of 7-Up to celebrate the new year. After they toasted using Mrs. B.'s best wine glasses, they stayed while Marta's mom recited funny stories of Marta's growing up years. The embarrassment of those events distracted her from her pain. But she worried about Steve and his friends finding the broken railing and the wood scattered near the cabin. Would he think someone had tried to break in? Would he be disappointed thinking she'd not come? What a mess.

As visiting hours ended, Marta readied herself for another restless night with the blue emergency light reflecting off the window blind. Perhaps 1958 would be a better year.

The white-uniformed nurses woke her through the night to check her blood pressure and adjust the tent over her leg. Her mom dozed in the narrow chair by the window. Marta gave up trying to sleep and counted hushed footsteps in the hall until dawn.

Lack of sleep left Marta feeling fuzzy. While she had a sponge bath, her mom disappeared and returned with a shopping bag. Marta opened the bag cautiously, then smiled as she lifted out a large blue leatherette scrapbook.

The pages revealed dance photos and recital programs across several years. "Oh, Mom! My butterfly costume and my first solo costume."

"I started this years ago. I brought it along thinking we could work on it together; take your mind off your injuries."

Doctor Wycoff entered. "Morning, Miss ..." the doctor flipped open her chart. "Miss Selbiff. Are you experiencing any pain?"

"Off and on."

The doctor checked her eyes. "Possible concussion. Let's check that foot." He slid the bedcover aside and began fingering Marta's foot and ankle.

She winced when he added pressure.

"The swelling's diminished. We'll cast it tomorrow."

"When can I put weight on it?"

"Seven weeks to add weight. Total recovery will take fifteen to twenty weeks."

"Twenty weeks?"

"It's a sensitive fracture. If we rush it, you might never walk correctly or dance again. The time will go quickly." He lowered her foot, straightened the covers, and hung her chart on the end of the bed as he left the room.

Marta lay back, inhaling ragged breaths. Twenty weeks! Five months! By then the ballet company would have danced *Giselle* and *Serenade*. Only the tribute to American composers would be left.

"Marta? Honey?" Her mom touched her shoulder.

Marta heard her and felt her touch but couldn't reply. Maybe Dr. Wycoff was wrong. What if he was right? What if she could never dance again? Should she go home and see a specialist in Seattle? Dancing was the only thing she knew how to do. She hunched her shoulders and wrapped her arms around herself to keep from shaking apart.

"Mom, why don't you take a break. Go get coffee or a snack. I need to sleep."

Her mom re-straightened the bed covers, brushed back Marta's hair, then left.

As soon as the door closed and she heard her mom's footsteps fade, Marta covered her face with a pillow and cried.

The rest of the morning Marta replayed Dr. Wycoff's timeline through her mind as a continuous nightmare. Twenty weeks without dancing would take forever. Should go home or stay? Did it matter? Maybe.

Her mom sat in a corner reading a magazine when Marta's door opened slowly. Lynne entered carrying a bouquet. "Hi, Mrs. Selbryth. Hi, Marta. How do you feel today?"

"Better."

"Good." Lynne handed a bouquet of carnations to Marta. "I hope you like red. Take a whiff. They smell good."

"I love red carnations. Thanks." Marta sniffed them. "Um-m. Put them in with the flowers from the boarders."

Lynne added them to the existing bouquet, then picked up the scrapbook. "What's this?"

"Mom brought my dance photo album for us to work on."

Lynne sat on the edge of the bed, turning pages. She laughed. "You were cute as a cat."

"That's a lion for *Carnival of the Animals*. I had a ten second solo."

Lynne flipped through the photos and stopped at a hand-written paper. "What's this? You used to write with curly cues. So girly."

Marta fingered the notebook paper. "It's the first page of my sixth grade report on ballet history. She silently read what she had written.

> *Ballet started in Italy, in the fifteenth and sixteenth centuries. At first men were the only ones allowed to dance. They put on wigs and pretended to be women.*
>
> *King Louis XIV liked to dance. When he got too fat to dance, he started a dance school. Soon women began dancing.*

"I felt so proud of myself. I brought in my new pointe shoes and a costume."

Lynne snorted a laugh. "Guess we can thank old Louis XIV for our careers."

Marta stared off in space. "I'll get fat like King Louis if I don't dance."

"Marta, stop worrying about your weight. You're thin as a rail."

Her mom looked up over the magazine she was reading. "That's right, honey," her mom said. "Why should anything change over a few months? You've never gained weight in the past when you were sick."

Marta closed the scrapbook and crossed her arms over it. "That's because I watch what I eat. I've not eaten all I wanted for years."

Lynne backed away.

"We exercise and attend classes three to four hours every morning and afternoon. You know I'd get sick if I ate a normal meal."

"Yes, but Marta, honey. When you weren't dancing you ate, didn't you?"

"Hardly. I spit food in my napkin, then threw it in the garbage when you left the room. Would you have let me eat baby-size portions?"

"Of course not!"

"Exactly."

Her mom stood and moved to look out the window.

"I had to do it for dancing, Mom. Besides, the long hours were exhausting. I'd lose my appetite anyway. We talked about that at Christmas."

Her mom remained silent with her back toward Marta. When she turned around, her face looked ashen. "When did my sweet daughter stop taking care of herself?"

"I take care of myself, but I've gotten my dream answered. I won't do anything to ruin my career as a dancer, and gaining weight might end my chances to dance. Who wants to watch a fat dancer?"

A nurse entered with a tray of food and swung the hospital table over Marta's lap. "Time for lunch."

Marta saw her mom close her eyes and shake her head. "It's up to you. To mend you need to eat. I'm going to leave you two alone. I'll be in the cafeteria."

Two? Lynne stood pressed against the wall, her eyes focused on the floor. "Oh my God, Lynne. I forgot you were here."

"That's what I figured. Sounds like you and your mom need a private discussion."

"I get so frustrated when she brings up eating."

"You don't eat much, Marta."

"Not you too?"

Lynne raised her palms toward Marta. "I won't say anything more. I'm out of here. See you tomorrow if my not-so-trusty car doesn't conk out." The door swung open and drifted closed. Marta sat alone.

The food on the tray looked hideous: orange Jell-o, bits of chicken surrounded by white flour gravy, six pale green beans, a dinner roll, and a cup of watery tea. Marta picked up her fork in her right hand. It felt so awkward, considering she never ate using that hand. She rescued the chicken from the gravy and took one bite. She shuddered as she stabbed a green bean and began chewing, lonely for her mom's company and praying she hadn't damaged her friendship with Lynne.

*A*s the nurse removed the tray, Marta's mom re-entered the room, eyeing the leftovers. She moved to the window and peeked through the blinds. "Where's Lynne?"

"She left after you did."

Her mom sat down on the chair in the corner and opened her *Life* magazine. The silence in the room hung heavy as a velvet curtain.

Marta's thoughts shifted to her dad's fall. It haunted her whenever she closed her eyes and relived her terror. She'd never asked about it, but now she needed answers.

"Mom? What do you know about how dad died?"

Her mom's head jerked up from the magazine. "Nothing more than I've told you in the past. Why?"

"I wondered if you'd kept anything from me because I was so young."

Her mom stepped to the window and used her fingers to spread the slats of the blinds apart. "I told you what I knew. He fell into the empty dry dock when a railing collapsed."

Marta shuddered, remembering the somber strangers sitting in her home as she walked in from school. "Did he suffer?"

Her mom turned to face her. "They said it happened in a flash. They'd just drained the dry dock, getting ready to repair the hull of the battle-ship. He landed on the metal floor."

"When I fell, I thought about him. I wondered if he felt any fear, if he knew he was about to die."

Her mom moved to the bed and held Marta's right hand. Her lips tightened; she blinked slowly. "I don't know. I try not to think about it."

"As I fell off the porch, I wondered if I might die."

"Oh, Marta." Her mom started crying. "I can't imagine how lonely you felt."

"I thought of you, and I knew I had to be brave."

"Come home with me, honey. Let me take care of you."

"I can't. I've thought a lot about it. If I leave, Madame Cosper may give away my position. By staying, I'll convince her I'm serious and that I plan to rejoin the company. Can you see why I can't risk leaving?"

"Yes. I know you've made a life here and--"

"That's not all true. Sure Lynne, Bartley, and Steve are important to me, but the big reason is Madame. She doubts their selecting me for the company."

"She hired you. Why do you say such a thing?"

Marta squirmed under her mom's gaze. "When I first arrived, I made a terrible mistake. I mimicked Madame, and she saw me. When I went to apologize, she told me I wasn't her first choice. Since then she's given me the roles no one wants. I've done whatever she's asked without com-plaint. If I leave, she'll think I've given up."

The next morning Marta's cast extended from her foot to below her knee. The nurse spent half an hour smoothing on layer upon layer of plaster, creating a white log heavier than her entire body. Great. Now she looked broken and helpless.

In the early afternoon, Doctor Wycoff returned. "I'm releasing you today. Keep your foot elevated, even in the wheelchair for the next week. Use a bedpan if the bathroom is narrow. Be patient. It's a delicate bone. We can't rush the healing. We'll move you to crutches as soon as possible." He scribbled notes on her chart and left.

Seven weeks. Forty-nine days. Hundreds and hundreds of hours without walking or dancing. Then over a dozen additional weeks before she'd be cleared to return to the company. What would she do with herself?

Her mom collected her belongings, promising to return as quickly as possible. Meanwhile, Marta fidgeted, waiting for her mom to return. Outside, the snow clouds hung like gray blankets over the sky. That meant that Steve and his friends might get snowed in and stay longer. She should have thought to have Lynne call his home. It could be days before he knew what had happened.

Doctor Wycoff returned, closed the door, and crossed his arms over his chest. He was as tall and thin as her image of Ichabod Crane. The overhead light reflected off his shiny head. "I'm concerned about your general health. Your blood pressure is low, and you're anemic. That's unusual for a person your age. Do you eat meat and calcium-rich foods?"

"Sometimes."

"Your dieting will slow your healing."

"I don't diet. When I dance I'm not hungry."

"Lugging around a cast takes energy. I'm waiting on the blood tests we did yesterday. Stop by my office next week. Unless I'm mistaken, you'll need iron injections."

When Dr. Wycoff left, Marta stared after him. Best not tell her mom about this complication. She didn't want to sit through her mom's I-told-you-so frown, even if she might be right.

Within an hour's time, Marta sat in the back seat of her mom's Fordor Ford. She rubbed her hand along the upholstery. "I like this car. It smells new. When did you get it?"

"Last month. Robert found it in the classifieds. He says it's well cared for considering it's close to eight years old. And the price was right. Are you comfy back there? I never sit in the back seat."

"It's fine. I can stretch out my legs. Not many people have four-door cars. What happened to our other car?"

"It needed a new engine. Robert said I should get a newer car rather than keep putting money into it."

"Do you see a lot of your Robert?"

"Yes and no. He works swing shift in the shipyard. We go to movies, play Canasta with friends, and try out restaurants together. It's been a long time since I've done that."

"It's time you had someone to take you places," Marta said.

"Yes. But, you know he'll never replace your dad."

"Hm-m. He changes things though, doesn't he?"

"That's what life is," her mom said, "a string of unexpected changes."

Marta believed that. But could she handle this latest change? Everyone expected her to act strong. She'd need to push through, even if it meant putting on a stage smile.

Lynne met them at the sidewalk in front of the boarding house holding a bouquet of yellow roses. "Welcome home."

Marta looked around. "Where's your car?"

"In the shop. They loaned me that yellow clunker parked down the street. Mine got towed to the shop two days ago. The mechanic says he can keep it going a little longer. Anyway, I'm the official corps de ballet flower committee."

"They're lovely. Did they *really* send these?"

Lynne shrugged. "Of course they did. They just don't know it yet."

Together Lynne and Marta's mom helped Marta from the car and carried her and her wheelchair up the boarding house steps to the porch. Marta bit her tongue as they jostled her. She'd need to get used to being dragged around. Time for a stage smile.

Once inside, Marta inhaled the scent of Mrs. B.'s lemon furniture polish. She hadn't noticed it since the day she arrived five months ago. Why now?

Her mom and Lynne stood watching her. "Thanks for getting me home."

"It's a good thing you're a featherweight," Lynne said, "or we'd have had to leave you on the sidewalk."

Marta smiled at Lynne's attempt at humor, then she inched the wheelchair forward. "Thank heavens the room down here is empty. Otherwise I'd be a captive upstairs."

"The captive upstairs. Great title for a steamy romance," Lynne said.

"Just what I need." Marta forced a second smile as she pushed herself along the hallway and into the wall. She took a deep breath. Her mom stepped forward, straightened the chair, and pushed her into the bedroom.

Now she remembered why she'd passed on the room last fall; scant light made it through the window. This depressing room with flocked wallpaper would be hers until she could climb the stairs.

"We brought down your bedding, clothes, and a few odds and ends," her mom said. "I'll get whatever else you want later. Right now, let's get your leg elevated. Do you want help, honey?"

"Maybe. Let me try first."

The bed faced the door. Marta inched beside it. She inhaled and tried to lift herself. Without her left hand, the simplest maneuvers remained impossible. She sank back in the wheelchair. "I'll take your help."

Her mom and Lynne lifted her and set her gently on her temporary bed in her temporary room with her not-so-temporary cast.

Lynne checked her watch and backed out the door. "I've got to go."

"Date?"

"No. Damien is holding rehearsals for the understudy and solo dances for *Giselle* before our regular rehearsals resume next week. I don't want Miss Perfect Marguerite to get any ideas. I plan to beat her out. Be a good patient. I'll stop by tonight."

"Lynne?"

She stopped at the door and turned back toward Marta.

"I didn't mean to be ungrateful back in the hospital. I felt frustrated and..."

"Forget it, Marta. I'll be back later. We can talk." Lynne waved and closed the door.

"She's a good friend." Her mom placed two pillows under Marta's leg and planted a kiss on her cheek. "Now, try to rest."

"That's about all I *can* do. Thanks for being here, Mom."

The stillness in the house allowed Marta to hear her mom's light, effortless step on the stairs. Standing, bending, walking. She'd taken these simple movements for granted, until now.

Lynne returned after dinner. "Has Madame called or come by?"

"No. Damien called before you arrived. He's sympathetic but said I'm on leave; no pay, of course. I can re-audition after my doctor releases me."

"That's good news," Lynne said. "Gives you plenty of time. Are you staying here or going home?"

"Staying. You can be my spy and keep watch over things at the company. And if I send a sample of my hand sewing with you to show to Rose, she might have work for me once my hand heals. That will keep me busy and help pay my bills."

"Good idea." Lynne stood at the mirror and applied lipstick.

"Has Bartley come back? I'm worried that we haven't heard from her."

"She called but didn't tell me much." Lynne straightened Marta's covers and sat on the side away from Marta's injured foot. "When I told her about your injury, she burst into tears and said she'd see us soon."

"Lynne, I'm sorry about how I acted in the hospital. I've been so frustrated since the accident, and then my mom started talking about eating."

"I understand, but you know she's right, don't you?"

Marta nodded. "It's hard to eat when everything is falling apart."

"It's not falling apart. It's going to be okay."

Her mom knocked and entered the room with a tray of sweet-smelling pecan bread and steaming hot tea. "Thought you ladies might like a little snack."

"Thanks, but I've gotta run." Lynne stood and put on her coat. "Got a date I rescheduled several times since before our Nutcracker tour."

"Must be special. Try not to scare this one away," Marta said.

"I only scare away the icky ones. I'll call you tomorrow."

Her mom poured two cups of tea and sat in a nearby chair. "I hope you don't mind, but I straightened a few things in your room. I love your view."

"I miss that view already. I don't plan on staying in this dungeon any longer than necessary."

"You won't be here long, especially if you follow your doctor's orders."

Marta's first bite into the moist bread melted in her mouth. She smiled until her gaze settled on the dresser mirror across the room. A ghost with sunken cheeks stared back at her. She turned away with a shiver and set down her tea.

"Ugh. I'm a mess. My hair looks awful."

Her mom retrieved a brush. "Lean forward. Let me untangle those curls."

She ran the brush through Marta's hair. Down and down, following each stroke with her hand. Marta closed her eyes and swayed with the light pull of her hair and the repeating movement of the brush.

"Lynne is always bustling away," her mom said. "Is it nervous energy, or is she looking for mister right?"

"Both, I think. She's a whirlwind, busy every minute. Her energy gives me energy. I also think she's lonely and wants a guy like Steve to spend time with her."

"You haven't heard from him yet, have you?"

"No. I don't think he knows about my fall. I'm sure he'll come over once he knows what happened."

The next afternoon, Marta sat thumbing through the scrapbook. Anything to speed up the long hours of sitting. Her mom stood, straightening the clothes she'd brought down from Marta's upstairs closet.

The front door of the boarding house opened, then slammed shut. Marta checked the clock. Too early for boarders returning from work.

Footsteps traveled from the hall to the common room and back to the hall.

Her mom opened Marta's door. "I'll check," she said and walked into the hall.

"Marta?" Steve's voice echoed through the hallway. "Are you here? Marta?"

Steve. Marta's heart raced. He'd come.

"She's in here," her mom said.

Steve hurried into the bedroom, nearly bowling over her mom. He carried a bouquet of white roses.

"I came as soon as I could." He handed the bouquet to her mom and moved to the side of the bed. He caressed Marta's hair, then eased down on the floor beside the bed. "How are you feeling?"

Marta shook her head and covered her face with her hands.

"What happened anyway?" Steve peeled her fingers away from her face, kissing each finger. "Marta?"

She told him what she remembered, filling in details that Lynne relayed to her over the past few days. Steve held her hand and watched her face as she spoke.

"I'm, I'm..." She shook her head. "I'm s-sorry about the ra-railing."

"Forget the railing. I thought you and Lynne decided not to come. I figured a hungry bear poking around broke it. You guys didn't leave a trace you'd been there."

"We hadn't unpacked the car or turned on lights yet. I thought I'd bring in wood and start a fire while Lynne drove back to the store. The door locked when I went out on the porch."

"That explains it. I wish we had phone service to the cabin. If I'd known you were injured, I'd have driven down. My friends stayed until late Sunday night, so I didn't get home to read Lynne's note until after midnight. Then I had an early class and a council hearing this afternoon. But now I'm all yours."

Marta relaxed. "It's okay. You came when you could."

"Why didn't Lynne drive up and tell me?"

"Her car's in the shop."

Steve eyed her bandaged hand and her leg. "How long will you be in a cast?"

"Seven weeks."

"That will go by fast; you'll see." Steve checked his watch. "I'm really sorry, but I can only stay a minute. I need to check in at the paper before deadline. I'll come back for a longer visit tonight and tomorrow evening, if you want." He brushed back her hair and kissed her forehead. "I'm sorry this happened. Be brave, okay?" He backed out of the room and closed the door.

She stared at the closed door. Right. More advice. First Lynne, now Steve. Why did everyone pat her on the head like an injured puppy? And why did he say he was all hers when he didn't bother to call her this morning or during the day? And then when he did come, he only stayed for a few minutes? How was that being all hers? Didn't he realize how lonely she'd be cooped up in a dusky bedroom hour after hour? Didn't he realize she missed him?

Her mom entered the room carrying a vase filled with the white roses in one hand and a bulky ice pack in the other. "Steve is so thoughtful, bringing flowers. Why did he leave in such a hurry?"

"He has a deadline."

Her mom placed the vase on the dresser and readjusted the roses. "I imagine school and work keep him busy." She fluffed the pillows under Marta's cast and placed the ice pack around her bandaged left hand. "How's that? Comfortable?"

"Yes, it's fine. I've been thinking about my bills. I'll need a job once I'm able to get around."

"Your savings will cover your rent for awhile. The hospital bills will get paid when we can pay them. The important thing is for you to mend. I'd love for you to come home to recover. But if you stay here, let your friends and Mrs. B. help you get organized."

Organized. That was her mom's priority. Organized for what? She turned away. "If my friends stop by tonight, please send them home. I can't handle any more sympathy right now."

"Sure, darling. Steve, too?"

Marta nodded and leaned against the mound of pillows behind her head. What did she want to do? Maybe she should go home. Staying here she'd be alone and lonely. But if she left, Madame would think she'd quit. Either way, she needed to deal with her lead weight stocking and find ways to cope on her own.

Over the next hour she heard voices in the hallway. Her mom sent away the boarders, as well as Lynne. Kind of a nasty trick, but she'd scream if she had to listen to one more "I'm sorry" or see Lynne's apologetic face.

Then Steve knocked and stuck in his head. "I convinced your mother I needed to see you, and she gave in. Okay if I come in for a couple of minutes?"

"I guess." Marta blinked to hold back her tears. Maybe he'd be more sympathetic now that he'd come back.

He kissed her hair and her cheek, then sat on the floor talking to her about the friends that came to the cabin, about playing in the snow and missing her. They'd started talking about their next article for the paper when the pain pills kicked in. When she woke, the room was dark and she was alone.

The loneliness hung on her like an icy cloak. She realized another feeling spreading through her: drinking juice or tea after dinner was a bad idea. She turned on the nightstand lamp, looked at the bedpan, paused, then scooted to the edge of the bed. Enough of the bedpan. Time to be independent and use the bathroom next door.

arta struggled into the wheelchair and backed up to open the door. Bang. She hit one wall. Bang; she hit another. She couldn't reach the door handle.

Her arm and back muscles ached from working the wheels. She felt the urge to use the toilet grow stronger. She closed her eyes and prepared for one more assault.

"Do you want help, Marta?" Mrs. B. stood in the doorway wearing her fluffy robe. She blinked repeatedly as if clearing away her tiredness. "That looks difficult with only one hand to push yourself."

"It is. I hope I didn't wake you up?"

"No, no. I'm up nights. Heard a noise and decided to check the house. Let me help you."

Exhaustion crushed Marta by the time she returned to bed and pulled up her bed covers. "Thanks, Mrs. B."

"I'll check on you when I'm up at night, see if you need a little help. What you need is a commode in your room. Then you won't have to navigate the hall or the bathroom as often."

"Can I empty it myself? I mean, I'd feel embarrassed having people dump it for me."

"Don't be embarrassed. If I wore that cast, you'd help me, right? Now, try to get back to sleep."

Try. Don't be embarrassed. I'm sorry. Would she ever feel accustomed to hearing those words over and over and over? For the next hour she stared into the darkness, unable to focus. Seven weeks of days and nights stretched ahead like a black ribbon of highway.

৯

Sleet tapped the windows in the common room where Marta sat holding her mom's hand. "I wish you could stay longer."

"I know. I wish I could too, but I've been here a week. January is a busy month for ordering recital costumes. Miss Holland needs to place her order by January thirteenth to ensure she receives them in May. Are you sure you don't want to drive back with me?"

"I'm sure. Madame would see my leaving as walking away or being weak. I *have* to stay and earn back my position."

"I guess I knew you'd decide to stay. I'd do the same in your position." Her mom stood and kissed Marta's cheek. "Take care of yourself, sweetie. I know you'll be fine. Call me Sundays, okay?"

Marta nodded and wiped away her tears. "Be careful. I'll miss you." She wheeled to the window and watched her mom's car disappear down the street. The tap, tap of the sleet broke the silence of the empty house.

Around noon, Lynne walked in covered in snowflakes. "Hey, thought you might like company. Hope you like peanut butter and banana sandwiches. That's all I have in my place until I get paid."

"Sounds perfect. Can you stay and help me exercise?"

"No problem. Classes don't resume until two."

They sat in the common room to eat and talk before they began the exercises. "Thanks for coming over and bringing lunch. Mom just left. It's so quiet here during the day."

"Bet it is. Nothing is quiet at the company. Madame's all twitchy about our next performance. With you out and Bartley a no-show, she's having a fit and daring everyone to complain about anything smaller than a serious illness. Jer sneezed, and she gave us a lecture on staying healthy. I'm so busy learning extra choreography that my head is spinning. She may call up two dancers from the local dance school to fill in as peasants."

"I'm sorry. She must know I didn't plan to get hurt. No wonder she hasn't contacted me."

"And on top of that there's the *Giselle* costumes. She says they need more repairs than the seamstresses have time to do."

"I could help. Once my hand is stronger, I can repair or replace embellishments."

Lynne helped Marta exercise her upper body with resistance pulls and pushes with her right arm. "I'll mention it to Rosemary. I'm surprised you didn't go home. I'd take you to my place if it would help."

Marta shook her head. "I'm fine here, except for needing to exercise twice a day. Now, tell me how the *Giselle* choreography is shaping up."

"It's okay. We've completed most of Act One, the peasant scene. Lots of *balancés* and partner dances. I even have the privilege of partnering with Marguerite."

"I remember that act as being lots of mime and village dances."

"It is. Not much to audition for unless you want to be noblewomen, but they don't dance. I'm auditioning for Myrtha, the Queen of the Wilis. She's one heartless ghost. That's right up my alley."

Marta smiled. "I always wanted to dance as a Wilis. Those white dresses and the spooky gravesite in the moonlight look magical."

Lynne massaged Marta's back and shoulders as they talked. "You should see Patrice. She's amazing as Giselle. She must have a hundred turns, yet she hardly breaks a sweat. It's exciting to watch her learn new choreography. She struggles as much as we do, but she's expected to learn things more rapidly than corps members. If we want to move up in the company, we'll need to work on our technique and stamina all summer."

"Are you signing up for any summer seminars?"

"A few. Marta, we could to apply together. Wouldn't that be a hoot?"

Marta shrugged. "I'd need Madame's or Damien's approval. It's too soon to know if they'd approve."

Lynne stood and carried their empty plates into the kitchen. "Is there anything else I can do for you?"

"Yes. Two things. Please bring down my ribbons box and...help me write an article about *Giselle*."

"A box I can do. No to the writing, Marta. I can't write."

"You don't have to. We just need to tell the story, put in the names of the principal dancers, then Steve or Susan will do the rest. Please?"

"I guess I could help you. Damien is letting us shadow the principals, so my days are longer than normal. I'll come over for dinner later this week and we can work on it. Just promise you won't volunteer me ever again."

Marta raised her right hand. "Promise. Now, can you get the box?"

After Lynne left, Marta wheeled to her room and closed the door. She pawed through her ribbon box and smiled. Her stash of diet pills remained tucked away under her *pointe* ribbons. She counted nine. Maybe a pill or two a day would help her eat less and boost her energy. That meant she'd need to call the drug store before this weekend and have them deliver several packs to replenish her supply.

On the last Sunday in January, the girls worked on ideas for the article. Lynne read it aloud to Marta.

> *Giselle is a romantic ballet about a young noble-*
> *man, Albrecht, who falls in love with Giselle, a village*

girl, the night before he's to marry Bathilde, a noble-man's daughter.

The ballet has two acts: one shows the peasants at harvest time, the other takes place in the graveyard where the ghostly Wilis (the spirits of young maidens) dance at night.

"Sounds good," Marta said. "Should we mention that Patrice Royal performs as Giselle?"

"Yep." Lynne wrote out the information. "And we must mention that Neil Barstow is in town to play Albrecht. Let's leave the composer information and other details for Steve. He needs to do some digging for his article."

"True. When he comes over, I can go over whatever he needs before he finalizes the story for Madame to read."

"I still think I'd rather go to the dentist than write." Lynne picked up her purse and danced to the front door. "I'm going home to clean up my mess, then sleep ten hours so I'm the brightest corps dancer in the company. Night, Marta."

෨

The next evening as Marta read their ideas to Steve, he chuckled. "You two saved me a bunch of work. I'll add details, then send it to Susan, who'll run it past Madame. Watch for it in the paper over the weekend."

෨

When the phone rang early Friday morning, Marta answered. It was Damien. He sounded tense. "It seems you and Lynne wrote an article about *Giselle,* is that right?"

"Not exactly. We gave the reporter the outline of the ballet."

"Madame will not allow it to be printed."

"Why?"

"Because you're not an active member of the company."

"But my name isn't on it."

"It is, Marta."

"Well, take my name off."

"It's too late. Madame put her foot down. Sorry."

As Marta hung up the phone, it rang again. It was Steve. "I just heard. I'm sorry, Marta. It's my fault. I put your names on so people would know that people who knew the ballet contributed to the article. Susan said she'd talk with Madame and try to salvage it."

Lynne stretched her arms and shoulders as Marta relayed the message about the article. "No wonder Madame looked at me like I had two heads. Let's just forget the whole thing and get back to your exercises. I need to get back for afternoon rehearsals. With the *Giselle* dress rehearsal in four days, I'm afraid she'll send out her bloodhounds looking for me. Did Bartley call or come over?"

"Nope. I'm afraid something terrible has happened to her. She's been gone almost a month."

While they worked, Marta distracted herself from her pain by asking Lynne about the company. "How's Jer doing?"

"He's the understudy for Hilarion, the game keeper. He's very strong. If he follows through this summer and accepts a regional invitation, his poor girlfriend won't see much of him, but he'll get solos next year."

The phone in the hall rang, and Lynne hurried to answer it. "Bartley! We were just talking about you. Where *have* you been? Oh. Uh-huh. Seven. I'll tell her."

Lynne shook her head. "Strange. Bartley said we're to get dressed up. She's taking us out to dinner at the Granary so she can explain everything."

"I can't go to dinner."

"Sure you can, Marta. I'll swing by at six and help you get gussied up. When we see her we can decide if we'll forgive her."

"But the wheelchair."

"So? I helped you get in here from the hospital. And with that ramp James and Shorty built, it won't be a problem. As long as you don't try to roll away and leave me behind."

The Granary hostess directed Lynne and Marta to the dining room, an upscale area with tablecloths and straight-backed chairs. Bartley stood and waved as they approached. The copper crepe organza sheath she wore made her look like a paper-thin goddess.

"Good grief," Lynne said. "You really meant it when you said get dressed up."

Bartley's new thinness startled Marta. How and why had she lost so much weight in such a short time? Marta took a deep breath and smiled to hide her concern and her wanting to crawl in a hole to hide her plain cotton shirtwaist dress.

Bartley leaned down to hug Marta. "Oh, Marta. Are you okay? Can I do anything for you?"

Marta smiled and straightened her back. "Just tell us what's going on and where you've been."

"I've been in San Francisco. I had an audition."

"Whoa. San Francisco?" Lynne said.

"I've quit the Intermountain Ballet Company," Bartley said.

"What!" both girls said together.

"When?" Lynne said.

"Why?" Marta asked.

"I had an audition the day after Christmas. That's why I left right after the last *Nutcracker* performance. I didn't want to tell you about it and then not get a position. I stayed on to visit relatives and begin dancing with the company. This was my first chance to come back to see you guys and Madame."

"What did she say?"

Bartley shook her head. "You don't want to know."

"That's amazing news." Marta struggled against the lump that settled in the pit of her stomach. Bartley had all the luck and good fortune. She'd be dancing solos before her own recovery was complete.

"I only flew in to get my belongings packed to be shipped. I fly back to San Francisco tomorrow. You two could tryout next year if you each grew three inches taller. Then you'd meet their height requirement."

"Fat chance of that," Lynne said. "Guess we're stuck here in cowboy land."

"Think of it this way. Now you have a place to stay in San Francisco, and I have one here as well, okay? Let's celebrate." Bartley signaled the waiter, who poured three glasses of sparkling cider. She lifted her glass. "To our friendship and the rest of our lives."

While the three ate shrimp cocktails, Bartley shared more information. She'd be living with her grandmother in San Francisco on Russian Hill. When they came for a visit, they'd go to Fisherman's Wharf, Coit Tower, and Chinatown.

Lynne hoisted her glass. "Happy Groundhog Day, everyone. Looks like it's going to be spring for Bartley and more winter for us. To Bartley Timmons, the next prima ballerina in California. You're an amazing dancer as well as a good friend, even if you are deserting us."

"Thanks, I guess. Please be happy for me."

"We're happy for you and a lot jealous," Lynne said. "You deserve this, but we'll miss you. Right, Marta?"

Marta nodded, swallowing down an explosion of tears with her sip of cider.

Later that evening, Marta sat alone in the common room, looking at the television but not seeing the program. Bartley's leaving shocked her, but what a great opportunity. She stared at her cast. Would she ever dance for a prestigious company? Heck, would she ever dance again?

The doorbell rang. Mrs. B. answered. "Hello! She's inside."

Expecting Steve, Marta startled when Bartley walked in.

"Hi, Marta. Mind if I join you?" She sat on the couch next to Marta's wheelchair. "You didn't eat much tonight. I hope you're not mad at me."

"No, not at all. That's amazing news. I'm just not very hungry these days. Your leaving surprises me. I had no idea you were unhappy here."

"I wasn't unhappy. When I heard about the vacancy, I wanted to audition. I...I'll miss you."

"I'll miss you too, but I'm proud of you. Wow. The San Francisco Ballet!"

"Exciting, huh? I wanted to be sure before I told anyone. My parents are still in Europe; they don't know what I've done."

"They'll be proud of you."

"Maybe. But they've never come to visit or see me dance."

They sat in silence holding hands until Bartley patted Marta's arm and stood. "I'd better get going. I need to finish packing. I'm sorry I wasn't here for you."

"Bartley, it's okay. I'll be fine."

"Promise? How about I come back next summer for a visit. We'll drive to San Francisco and spend a few days acting like tourists."

Marta looked down at her hands, then smiled. "Sounds perfect."

"Good. It's a date." Bartley scanned the common room and sighed. "You know, I envy you."

"Me? Why? You're going to dance with the San Francisco Ballet. I'd rather be you."

"You live in a cozy house, ride a bike to the company, and you're happy. I know you'll dance again." After she hugged Marta, she rushed out the door.

The phone jangled as Marta sat by the bay window watching Bartley drive away. She answered, "Belvern Boarding House, may I help you?"

"Yes, I want to talk to the prettiest girl in the house. Would that be you?"

"Hi, Steve." She felt a tingling of happiness at hearing his voice.

"I've got something to tell you. I'll be right over, okay?"

"Will it keep until tomorrow? I'm really tired. Come for dinner."

"O-kay. I guess it will keep. Can we go out on a date after dinner?"

"If you'll haul me around. Now, give me a hint about your news."

"Marta, Marta. Miss Impatient. I'll tell you tomorrow. Sweet dreams. Think of me. I'll be thinking of you."

*A*fter dinner the next evening, Steve and Marta drove to The Rims. The city lights sparkled like stars hovering near the ground. Headlights and tail lights moved like ants along the streets. Marta never tired of the view.

Steve angled his family's station wagon, allowing Marta the panoramic view from her backseat perch. He reached over the seat for her hand.

"Wish that cast fit in the front seat. I'd like it better with you sitting beside me."

"Me too," Marta said. "Thanks for bringing me here. Now what's your news?"

"I'll get to that. First, I want to remind you that you're extra special to me. I'd like to keep you to myself, as my girlfriend."

"I know, but I'm—"

"You're not ready. I know." He cleared his throat. "But I needed to bring it up. Things have changed. Dad set up an internship for me at the *San Francisco Chronicle*."

"What? You're leaving? When?"

"Soon. It's a great opportunity, but it means leaving Billings and you until the end of spring or longer and moving 1250 miles away."

"You checked that pretty close."

"Yeah, I did."

"You don't sound excited about it."

"I'm not. Well, I am excited, but I wanted to stay closer to home. My dad jumped in; didn't bother to consult with me. I'd started asking around on my own to newspapers in Montana and Wyoming. Now he's set this up, and I'm obliged to go."

"Isn't it a great opportunity? It's like my being asked to dance for the New York City Ballet."

Steve shrugged. "Interning at a large city paper will improve my chances for a better job after I graduate. I know he's right, but I wanted to find an internship myself. Plus, it moves my graduation back a semester unless I continue with my classes as a long distance student. I'll be working through the summer sessions instead of having time to be here with you."

Marta wasn't sure how she felt about that. She was happy for him. But he helped her escape from herself. If he left, she'd be more alone than ever. Why couldn't *something* in her life stay constant? "I know it changes your plans, but if it helps your career, that's good, isn't it?"

"It's better than good, but I won't know anyone."

"That's not true. Bartley joined the ballet company there."

"Really? When did that happen?"

"Just this week."

"That's interesting. Do you think she'd want to hang out? She *is* snobby, kinda icy, not friendly like you, but maybe her family has contacts. A newspaper man needs contacts."

"Steve! You certainly jumped on that information quickly. You didn't want to go and now you want to *use* her?"

"Her family's rich. She may know people who will get me in the door to some important interviews."

"That's just wrong, Steve. Sometimes you're a self-centered jerk."

"Ah, Marta." He kissed her fingers one by one. "How about thinking of me as a nice, sweet, adorable guy who'll really miss you?"

Marta pulled away. "Promise me you'll treat her like you treat me."

"You mean like a girlfriend? Ruffle her hair, hold her hand and..."

"No, Steve. You know what I mean. She's sensitive about her family being rich."

"Relax, Marta." Steve reached through the dusky night, took her hand, and massaged small circles on it. "I understand what you are saying. But I need you to let me finish." He turned on the wagon's interior light and fumbled around in the glove box. "Ah… found it," he said.

He lifted his hand like a magician about to share a trick. A small blue velvet bag with a satin tie dangled from his fingers. "My surprise will prove my intentions." He handed Marta the bag.

Her fingers trembled as she unknotted the satin strings and removed a tiny blue velvet box. When she opened the box, light ricocheted off a tennis bracelet of ruby-colored stones and oval diamonds. She gasped.

"It belonged to my grandmother, a fiftieth anniversary present from my grandfather. I want you to have it, as my promise that I'll return to be with you.

"A promise? She wasn't ready for a promise. "What if I'm no good as a girlfriend?"

"You're a great girlfriend. How can you say that?"

Tears raced down her face. She closed the box, shook her head, and handed it back to him. "I can't."

"Why not? I thought you cared for me and that we made a good team."

"I do. We do. But you hardly know me. Right now I need to focus on my recovery. I don't have the energy to think about all this."

"What does 'all this' mean, Marta?"

"You know."

"No, I don't know. I care about you so much, and now I'm leaving town for months."

"You want us to be a couple."

"So?"

"I'm not ready to be a couple. I've never dated anyone but you. Besides, I need to focus on myself, and you need to focus on your internship."

Steve took back the bracelet, placed it in the tiny box, and tossed it on the front passenger seat. "You confuse me. I thought you'd want a commitment from me."

"I care about you, but I don't need you to make a commitment."

"Fine." Steve sat in stony silence.

She leaned against the back of the seat and took a deep breath. "Steve? I'm sorry it's just--"

He raised his palm, stabbing the air. "Don't say anything. Please." He turned off the overhead light, started the car, and backed onto the road.

Marta felt his verbal slap; her refusal of the bracelet devastated him. Maybe she should have taken the bracelet and worked out her feelings over the time he was away. Why hadn't she seen something like this coming?

She kept silent but studied his tight jaw as they passed street lights. His death grip on the steering wheel and his silence continued on block after block through town. She had no idea how to start a conversation. She might as well have been riding with a stranger.

At the boarding house, Steve lifted her out, carried her inside, and left her sitting in her wheelchair in the front hall. When she reached out to touch his arm, he stepped away.

"Not now, Marta."

He stalked to the front door and slammed it closed behind him.

༄

Hours and days passed at a snail's pace. *Giselle* performances began. Lynne reported the ballet's success to a tight-jawed Marta. She worked on bodice repairs for the ballet company, all the while replaying her last minutes with Steve. She should have found words to explain herself, but how could she tell him when she couldn't understand her own reluctance? Now it was too late. An ache deep inside her body told her she missed him more than she had anticipated.

James and Shorty sensed a change in her mood. They carried the basement record player and records to her bedroom and installed it on a TV tray beside her bed.

"Is there music you'd like us to get for you?" James asked. "The record shop is on my way home. I can stop in tomorrow."

"No, these records are fine, thanks."

When they left, she placed the *Nutcracker* on the turntable. She watched the needle slip into the first groove. The open strains reminded her of the excitement of performing on stage in Billings just weeks earlier. With each new ring of music, she relived her various roles: Mother Ginger, the Waltz of the Flowers, background corps dancing, as well as the understudy roles she'd rehearsed with Lynne and Bartley.

At meals she picked at her food. Dinner conversations blurred. She looked up when she heard her name, answered, and went back to pushing the food around her plate. After helping with the dishes, she wheeled into her dreary downstairs room and watched the sky turn as black as her mood. The quiet permeated the walls, the furnishings, and the air in the room.

Lynne's calls and her attempts to entice Marta to "spill the beans" were ignored. During the day she sat in her wheelchair in the common room and stared at the phone, willing it to ring, willing it to be Steve.

Had he already left for San Francisco? She'd told him she couldn't focus on him *and* her recovery. Now she could focus on nothing else.

Over the next week, her costume repair tasks ended and she worked on intricate embellishments for costumes for April's *Serenade*. Luckily the stiffness in her left hand disappeared, because adding tiny beads on the bodice made her hands ache almost as much as her iron injections made her *derrière* ache.

Every two weeks, the nurse took blood from her arm. Then she stuck a large needle of an iron supplement in Marta's *derrière*, smiled, and said, "See you next time."

One evening Lynne stopped by for dinner and stayed for conversation. They sat alone in the common room. When the phone rang at a little after nine, Marta jolted and dropped her hand sewing. The caller wanted to speak with Shorty.

"Boy, are you jumpy!" Lynne said. "You miss Steve, don't you? Does he know?"

"I hope so."

When the hall phone rang again, she held her breath. Mrs. B. called out, "Marta?"

A nervous bubble zigzagged through her. "Coming." She wheeled herself to the hallway phone.

"That's my cue to exit stage left," Lynne said. "Might be Mr. Wonderful. Call me if you return to earth anytime soon."

"Hello?"

"Hi, Marta," Steve said.

The next afternoon, Lynne returned and dropped a large box on the floor beside Marta. "You didn't call. Was it Steve on the phone? If so, did it get steamy or what?"

"We got things straightened out."

"What things? Spill it, Marta. You've got a smile glued on your face."

"He apologized for going all crazy and not saying good bye. He's stressed about his dad making plans and not consulting him. When I turned down the bracelet, he said it broke his heart. I apologized and told him I missed him."

"And?"

"He'll call every evening. I don't know what I'll have to talk about, though."

"Marta, he just wants to hear your voice. You could probably read him the phone book and he'd be happy."

"I hate to admit it, but I miss him. He had a way of making me forget about myself. I could use that now with this cast." Marta fidgeted and brushed aside her straggly hair. She repositioned the sharp hairpins against her scalp.

"Told ya. 'Bout time you got off the dating fence. Now, back to the real world." Lynne opened the box, revealing a pile of white bodices. "Rose said to copy the design from the old bodice onto the new ones. She needs them in two weeks."

"No problem. Sewing keeps my mind from spinning empty circles."

"You're coming to see *Giselle* before we end, aren't you?"

"I don't know."

"You're coming. I'll save you two tickets so you can bring Mrs. B. or someone to help you maneuver through the theatre. You have to see me dance as a Wilis. I love being a ghostly spirit who haunts people and dances on graves."

Carol entered and sat on the couch directly across from Marta and Lynne. "Where's your boyfriend these days? Tired of you and your cooking, I imagine."

Marta bit her lip to keep from answering Carol, or better yet, ramming her with the wheelchair.

Lynne stood, grabbed her purse, and stopped almost on top of Carol's slippered feet. "See you Marta. Too bad about Steve getting an internship with a prestigious paper in San Francisco. Night, Carol. Too bad you're going to be an old maid. I'd love to haunt your..."

"Lynne!" Marta said. "Call me tomorrow."

As the front door closed, Carol squinted her eyes and looked Marta up and down. "I hear San Francisco girls are stylish."

Back in her room, Marta stared into her mirror. Carol might be right. Steve could meet a stylish California girl and become infatuated. Who'd stay serious about a teary-eyed girl with a limp? She wondered again if she'd been wrong to refuse the bracelet. He wanted to commit to her. Why couldn't she accept that and return his commitment?

She sat in front of the mirror that hung over her sink and stared at her hair. As she dragged a comb through it, she turned her head side to side. Yuck. Her hair hung in scrawny kinks. If she trimmed it, the natural curl would hide its thinness. It might also perk up her evening. She reached for the scissors.

*S*nip, snip, snip. Strands of hair dropped away, covering the bottom of her wastebasket. Marta doused her hair in the sink, then towel-dried it as ringlets curled around her face. Kinda short. Oh well, she had time to grow it out before Madame saw it in June.

A quick ruffle of her hair and a shake of her head and she'd be ready to go. If she looked perky, maybe she'd feel perky. No way could Lynne say she didn't take chances now.

When Lynne arrived for dinner the next night, she stared open-mouthed. "What did you do, back into a lawn mower?"

"I cut my hair."

"I can see that. But why super short? You're nearly bald."

"It's easier with my wheelchair and taking showers and all."

"Madame will kill you."

"No, by the time she sees me, it will grow out. Besides, no one notices me."

"Doubt that, Harpo." Lynne circled Marta. "Does your hair grow fast?"

"I don't know. If it doesn't, I'll buy a hairpiece."

"Like that will work. So, what's for dinner? I'm hungry as a bear."

"Tonight is chicken and dumplings with mixed vegetables, a salad, and a pudding cake."

Lynne yawned. "Just what I need; a hearty meal before I flop into bed."

After dinner, Lynne yammered on and on about rehearsals. Marta visualized each dance, wishing she could lift out of the wheelchair to perform a simple series of *balancés*. Embroidering costumes paid a few bills, but costumes were window dressing and had little to do with the art of dancing. Most dancers would wear black leotards and be content, as long as they could dance.

"News flash," Lynne said. "Madame's threatening to look for replacements before audition season begins. She's so steamed at you and Bartley that she paces and talks about loyalty and respect and people risking their careers. But you'll prove her wrong when you come back next season. I'm anxious to watch her eat her words. I'll bring the ketchup."

Bartley began calling Marta and Lynne Sunday afternoons at Marta's. The girls sat close, sharing one phone, comparing their weeks, and talking ballet.

"Is Madame still mad about me leaving?" Bartley said.

Lynne laughed. "Almost never comes up, just every day. Calls you a disloyal, ungrateful girl, but doesn't mention your name."

"Oh, guys, I'm sorry, but only because of you. I loved it here the minute I arrived. The ballet mistress is nothing like Madame. She treats us like Damien does, as human beings. I belong here; so do you."

"Don't worry. Marta and I are fine. Hey, do you really have room for us to come visit?"

Bartley laughed. "The entire company could move in and there'd still be empty space."

"Has Steve called you?" Marta said.

"He left a message with the butler, but I haven't seen him yet. I'm sure he's busy settling in. It will be nice to see a familiar face from Billings."

"Too bad you're not here, Bartley," Lynne said. "My aunt has a brainy idea. She wants us to give ballet lessons to the little girls in her church's after school club starting in March. Looks like Marta and I will have to do it without you."

"That sounds fun. But where will you meet?" Bartley asked.

"Wait. Lynne, when were you going to tell me?" Marta said.

"I just did," Lynne said. "Tomorrow, I'll ask Madame about using a small practice room. What could it hurt?"

The next evening Lynne paced Marta's bedroom as she relayed her encounter with Madame. "You'd think I'd asked her to pay us more money or make us prima ballerinas next week. I thought she'd have a heart attack. Her face got blotchy, and I thought the mole on her face might burst." Lynne crossed her arms and lifted her chin. "And, I quote... 'We can't let you in and out whenever you *feel* like dancing or giving lessons.' I couldn't think of anything more to say, so I backed out of her office."

"Ouch." Marta wheeled to the window in her bedroom and turned her chair to face Lynne. "I've got an idea. And Madame won't have anything to say about it."

Mrs. B. stood by the kitchen sink scraping carrots. Marta watched the easy way she kept the peeler moving down and around each carrot.

"Having a good day, Marta?"

"Kinda. I need to ask you something. If you say no I'll understand."

Mrs. B. stopped peeling and turned to face her.

"Is there any way Lynne and I could use my basement studio space to teach ballet lessons? Lynne's aunt supports the after school program at her church. She thought ballet lessons would interest some of the girls, but Madame said no to our using a rehearsal room."

"I bet she did." Mrs. B. wiped her hands on her apron. "So, what's your plan?"

"The church bus will bring the girls here twice a week at a quarter after four and pick them up at five-thirty. When Lynne has late rehearsals or performances, the lessons will be canceled."

Mrs. B. turned back to the sink. Marta watched her pick up another carrot and continue peeling.

"When would it start?"

"The first part of March. The girls would be supervised at all times, even going to the bathroom."

Mrs. B. turned to Marta with a grin. "Sounds good to me. The girls may use my private bathroom. But I have two questions: will they need a snack, and do you and Lynne get paid?"

"The girls will have a snack before they arrive, and Mrs. Meadows said we'd get a small stipend. We could share it with you."

"No, no, dear. I wanted to be certain you two women were paid for your time and your skills. And seeing a happy face on you will be wonderful."

"It will be fun. Thanks, Mrs. B."

Marta wheeled plates and silverware to the dining area. Carol sat by the bay window with a book in her lap. Seeing her brought up one last question. On her return to the kitchen, Marta approached Mrs. B. "What about the boarders?"

Mrs. B. smiled. "I'll handle Carol."

Marta called Lynne from the downstairs phone as soon as Carol headed up the stairs. "Mrs. B. sounds as excited as we are."

"Good," Lynne said. "Let's plan it out tomorrow."

The following evening, Lynne joined the boarders for dinner. Marta caught Carol eyeing Lynne at regular intervals. It didn't appear that Carol knew about the arrangement yet.

After dinner, Lynne and Marta disappeared into Marta's room and closed the door. Lynne lounged on the bed while Marta sat in the wheelchair with a tablet on her lap. "How shall we start?"

"Like we do, with *barre* exercises," Lynne said. "They'll need to wear shorts and undershirts so we can see their bodies until they get leotards. I'd hate for them to start bad habits. My aunt will buy what we need. I'll have her pick up rug samples for them to sit on, plus scarves and beach balls for movement activities."

"I'll make totes," Marta said. "We can ask the church auxiliary to purchase ballet slippers once we know if the girls are interested."

While Lynne continued to throw out ideas, Marta absentmindedly opened a box beside her nightstand and took out a pair of scissors and four old *pointe* shoes. She cut off the ribbons and rolled them up.

"More ribbons?"

"I just found these in a bag in my closet. They may be the last ribbons I'll ever have."

"Come on, Marta. Don't talk like that. If you don't believe you'll recover, who will?"

Lynne had a good point. She needed to stay positive. She closed the box and shoved it under the bed.

At nine-thirty Lynne stretched and grabbed her coat. "We have enough to get started. Let's decide records later. I doubt the girls will appreciate Shorty's *Overture of 1812*. This may be the kick in the *derrière* you need. I'm tired of coming over to find you all gloomy about dancing and Steve and Bartley and getting fat."

"By then I'll be out of this cast, so getting to the basement will be easier."

Lynne put her hand on the doorknob. "If it weren't for you and Mrs. B., we couldn't do this." Lynne bowed. "Thank you, Miss Selbryth."

As Lynne turned the knob, footsteps scuttled away. She closed the door and stepped close to Marta. "We have a spy in the hall. Let's make up an outlandish idea to entertain snoopy Miss Carol."

"Naw. She's not worth the time and energy."

Excitement over working with the girls raced through Marta. The next morning, after Friday's breakfast dishes were done, Marta placed an early call to Bartley, trying to catch her before she left for practice. The phone rang and rang.

"Hello?" A man answered.

Marta didn't speak.

"Hello?"

She set the phone back in its cradle. Her spirit sank into the floor. Steve answered the phone. He must have been there all night.

Her hands were shaking as she wheeled to her room. He'd played with her emotions, and she'd almost fallen for it. How could he? She decided to bake bread to fill her mind and her hands with activity.

Minutes later she banged bread dough against the kitchen worktable. Thunk. Steve stayed at Bartley's all night? Thunk. What had she been, a naive girl to laugh about? Thunk. Her heartache promised to linger.

The dough looked overworked. She stopped, wiped her hands and wheeled to the back porch. The unseasonably cool morning soothed her overheated face.

The phone rang. She ignored it.

"Marta? Phone call."

Mrs. B.'s voice jangled in her ears. She turned back inside and took the call.

"Hey, Marta," Lynne said." No practice today. The Valentine Festival starts today in Livingston. We're going. I'll be there by half past ten. We need a change of scenery."

Marta focused on the countryside west of Billings, too embarrassed to tell Lynne about hearing Steve's voice on Bartley's phone. Lynne would tell her to stop leaping to conclusions. Right now, she wanted to forget most everything and everyone.

"You're quiet today, Marta. Got a lot on your mind?"

"No. There's nothing I want to say right now."

"Right."

"I can't talk about it, okay?"

"Okay." Lynne pulled into the play field parking lot. "Now, Miss Selbryth, we are going to wander around. So hang on to your wheelchair handles and expect a few bumps. We're going to have a good time, even if it kills us."

The trip proved to be exactly what Marta needed to keep her mind busy. The community center had rows of tables displaying a sea of handmade afghans, quilts, preserves, and crafts. Lynne wheeled Marta past every exhibit. They shared chili with corn bread and sat people-watching.

Marta loved the way people acted happy, gave each other flowers, and sent out cards declaring their love. One elderly couple worked together in a woodcraft booth. Marta couldn't keep her eyes off the way they touched hands and shared private smiles. Her mom didn't have the chance to grow old with her dad. Maybe Robert would be there for her. She wondered what it would be like to share her life with someone, especially Steve. Too late for that. He'd moved on to share his life with someone more sophisticated.

Returning to the boarding house, she ate her traditional Saturday dinner a day early: a spoonful of peanut butter, but she skipped the bread and jam. She moved to the common room to finish the costume embroidery.

Every stitch became a stab. While she sat sewing, Steve was no doubt entertaining Bartley in a posh club, laughing all huddled together, then dancing cheek to cheek. She and Steve had never danced.

When she looked at her embroidery, the tight, angry stitches puckered the material. Now she'd need to redo everything.

The phone rang. Marta answered, "Belvern Boarding House."

"Marta? Hi, it's Steve."

"Who?"

"Very funny. Happy Valentine's Day. I miss you so much. I'm sorry I didn't call earlier."

"That's okay. Lynne and I were out most of the afternoon."

"I've been on assignment. I hardly remember my own name. Got back late Thursday, then Bartley asked me to drive her to the airport early this morning. It's been hectic."

"You drove Bartley to the airport? Why?"

"She had a family emergency. Flew home for a few days. She asked me to tell you."

Marta felt the pressure in her chest float away. So that was what had happened. "Did she give you any reason at all?"

"No. She'll probably fill in the details once she's back. It must be serious. She looked tired and even thinner than I remember. She worries about things even more than you do."

Marta couldn't think of what to say next, so she sat waiting for Steve to pick up the conversation. The phone line hummed with silence.

"Marta, are you okay?"

"I'm fine. Tell me about your week."

Steve rattled on and on about security and inspections for his trip onto a military base. "You'd have thought we were trying to carry *in* weapons the way they checked us. I wish you could have seen me. I feared they'd kick us out, so I didn't crack a single joke."

"Good thinking."

"How did your week go, Marta?"

"Nothing new."

More silence hummed on the phone. Steve tapped his mouth piece. "Marta? Are you sure you're okay?"

"I'm fine. But, Steve, I've got to go."

"OK. I'll call you tomorrow night. Sweet dreams. Think of me."

"Sure. Night." After hanging up, she placed a collect call home to surprise her mom.

"Will you accept collect charges from Marta?" the operator asked.

"Yes. Hello?" answered a baritone voice.

Hearing a man's voice surprised Marta. "Is my mom there?"

"She's got the flu and she's sleeping right now. I'm Robert Marsden, Elle's friend. May I take a message?"

"Yes, thanks. Wish her happy Valentine's Day."

"I will. I'll tell her you called. She'll call you when she's feeling better."

Marta's loneliness turned to sadness, then concern. Maybe she should have gone home to keep her mom company. No, Robert took over *that* job. What help could she be from a wheelchair anyway?

As she moved to her bedroom window, tiny snowflakes drifted down. In minutes a wind whipped up, changing them to a wild blur. Another storm passing through. That would keep Lynne holed up; she hated to drive in snow.

Marta imagined the icy flakes glancing off her cheeks and dropping onto her out-stretched tongue. In reality she was stuck inside with no hope of escape.

The front doorbell rang. Marta heard quiet laughter, then footsteps in the hall and a knock on her door.

"Come in," she said as she ran her hands through her hair.

Steve walked in.

Marta gasped. "I thought you were out of town."

"I was, but I wanted to be with you for Valentine's Day." Steve closed her door with a quiet click.

"But you called me."

"From the Billings airport. We landed before the storm blew up. Did I surprise you?"

Marta saw Steve's smile change to a quizzical look as she started to cry.

"Hey, don't cry." He tossed his overcoat on her bed and knelt beside her wheelchair.

She wiped her eyes and stared at his face. "I've missed you so much."

He touched her hair, moving it away from her face and kissed her forehead. "Good! That's the welcome I'd hoped for."

"I...I'm glad you're here. I've been... Did I say hi?"

Steve laughed. "In your own way." He stood, put on his coat, and pulled hers from her closet. "Let's head out and watch the snow."

"But it's becoming a storm."

"I love to drive in snow."

He helped her into her winter coat and carried her to his family's station wagon. After he settled her into the back seat, he surrounded her with blankets, then slid into the driver's seat. "We're off."

"I hope you mean to The Rims."

Steve laughed. "Even after the bracelet fiasco? I'm pleasantly surprised. I was afraid you'd not want to return there."

"I love The Rims almost as much as walking to the bay back home."

They sat on the side road of The Rims where the snow created a fast-moving screen, isolating them from the town below. It was like being inside a snow globe. The flakes reminded Marta of the ending of Swan Lake when paper snow fluttered onto the stage. She leaned her face against the cold window glass and closed her eyes.

"Warm enough?" Steve asked as he stretched his legs around the gearshift in the front seat and reached for her hand. "God, I've missed you."

"I've missed you too."

"This reminds me of being snowed in at my parents' cabin. We should go up there since you didn't get to stay over New Year's. Let's go now. I've got time before I need to fly back."

"Won't the roads be icy?"

"We have chains. Let's do it. Okay?"

"Now?"

He backed away from the ledge and drove onto the main road.

A twinge of uncertainty climbed through her body. "I don't have clothes or anything."

"It's just one night. You're fine."

"What about food?"

"I've had lots of practice cooking meals from canned food lately."

"What about my wheelchair? Steve, I—"

"We'll manage without it. It'll be an adventure."

Marta swallowed down her uneasiness. He'd come all this way to see her. Now he wanted to go to the cabin. In a snow storm. How could she say no? She'd wanted an adventure; now she'd get one.

They stopped in Laurel, and Steve phoned Mrs. B. She promised to let Marta's mom know where she'd gone, if she called.

Few cars ventured out along the main highway, fewer still once they turned onto the mountain road to the cabin. Marta relaxed, enjoying her escape from the boarding house, certain Steve could handle the icy roads. But how would it feel going back to the cabin so soon after her fall?

As Steve carried her up the steps, she looked around for any sign of the broken porch railing and the chaos of the woodpile that had buried her.

"You cleaned up everything."

"All back to normal. Good as new."

When they entered the cabin, their warm breath hung in puffs whenever they spoke. It felt colder than when she and Lynne had come up.

Steve settled Marta onto the sofa by the fireplace and covered her with quilts. "I'll get wood to start a fire."

"Be careful!"

"Relax, Marta. I'll be fine."

As they waited for the fire to take the chill off the room, Steve pulled up a chair and sat holding her hand. "How's this?"

"It's wonderful! Thank you for bringing me. I've been lonely."

"I could tell. I'm sorry your mom is sick and that I've been away so much. You need to think happy thoughts."

"Like what? Sewing beads on costumes until my hands cramp? Or not being able to go anywhere unless people haul me and my wheelchair around?" She recognized the anger in her voice, wishing too late she could take back her words.

"How 'bout me? Doesn't thinking about me make you happy?"

"Yes, but you're busy or gone."

"Ouch, you're mean today. Does Marta Selbryth need a kick in her back side?"

"Maybe. I'm so tired of sitting. It's ten days before I get this cast off."

"And each day you're closer to walking and dancing. Focus on that." Steve stood, kissed her cheek, and headed for the kitchen area. "Ready for a cup of hot tea?"

"That depends on whether you'll carry me into the bathroom later on."

"No fear, fair maiden. We can handle any situation." Steve settled the tea kettle on the stove, then filled a small coffee pot with water and scoops of coffee for himself.

The bathroom experience didn't embarrass Marta like she thought it might. Steve carried her inside, set her on the edge of the bathtub, and got a stepstool to elevate her leg. When he returned, he moved her to the couch and set her down with a grin. "You are light as a feather. Let me find some food to fatten you up. That cast must take lots of energy to haul around."

Steve whistled as he rummaged through the kitchen cabinets. His off-key tune made her smile. She'd missed his being around. His presence pushed away her sadness. Could this be how love felt?

His foraging produced chicken noodle soup, Cheese Whiz, a carton of sugar wafers, and a jar of Planter's peanuts. After he started heating the soup, he set the coffee table in front of Marta. "So, now what, Miss Fluff? Hungry? Tired? Want to play cards?"

"I'm fine sitting here watching you work. Are you sure we should stay overnight? Maybe a few hours is enough."

"It's beautiful when we get snowed in. It's quiet and we're all alone—"

"Wait. Where will I sleep?"

"Relax, Miss Worry Wart. You can sleep on the couch, and I'll sleep in the loft. Come on, Marta. It'll be fun."

"I, ah...okay."

Steve grinned and rubbed his hands together. He took down a game box and handed it to her. "Okay, I challenge you to Monopoly. The winner decides how long we'll stay. Sort out that mess of play money while you still have a reason to smile."

Marta toyed with the bowl of soup. She turned down Steve's offerings and his extra "treasury of foods": pimento cheese and canned deviled ham.

"Aren't you hungry? It's been hours since you ate."

"No. I'm fine. But is there something to drink?" Marta reached for her diet pills. Her pockets were empty. She'd be without pills until she got back to Billings. Drat.

Steve found an Orange Crush, two Pepsi-Colas, and a bottle of Squirt. He lined them up on the table next to the bottle opener. "There, just in case we get into the game. I don't want to turn my back on you in case you decide to cheat."

Marta threw a pillow at him. He caught it and grinned.

They played for hours, taking turns buying property and spending time in jail. When she surrendered her last property, he raised his bottle of soda, toasting it against hers, tipping her remaining soda into her lap.

"Hey! Take it easy!"

He stopped laughing and grabbed a towel. "Sorry."

"I'm sticky and you want me to forgive you? Maybe if we have a Monopoly rematch tomorrow morning..."

Steve wiped off the blankets and smiled. "You'd like that wouldn't you? For now let me get my mother's robe."

"You do realize I have soda in my hair, don't you?"

"I'll help you wash it out. Can't have you be a sticky loser, can we?"

In the next five minutes, he'd carried her to the bathroom, she changed into his mother's robe, and he'd carried her to a chair by the kitchen sink.

Steve gathered shampoo and towels. "Lean back and leave everything to me."

She closed her eyes, feeling his hands and the warm water circling through her hair. "This feels wonderful. I'm floating on a cloud."

"Who cut your hair so short?"

Marta laughed. "I did it one night. It's a long, boring story."

"Well, I like it. And, I doubt anything about you is boring." Steve's hands stopped moving.

Marta opened her eyes. With his hands tangled in her curls, she couldn't turn away.

He leaned down and kissed her wet face and her lips. "Okay, Miss Fluff. Now I've got you where I want you."

He kissed her lips again. Her usual panic didn't arise. A mellow glow roamed her body. Were Steve's kisses or not taking the pills the reason she felt so good?

Steve stared down at her. "Ready for more?"

"Keep doing your job, Mr. Sticky, if you want to be forgiven." Marta closed her eyes and let the sensation of laying in the ocean surf on a hot summer day wash away her sadness.

Steve's hands stopped again.

She opened her eyes.

"You're beautiful. I want to keep doing this. That way I can watch you," he said as he brushed wet curls off her face.

"I'm not beautiful."

"Sh-h. You're beautiful and I love you. Being away from you is torture. Spend the night with me."

Marta bolted upright. "I—" Her heart pounded faster than a jack hammer.

"I'll keep you warm."

Marta grabbed a towel. "My hair is probably clean now."

"Hey, relax. Let me rinse out the shampoo."

Steve tucked the top quilt around Marta's neck. "Think you'll be warm enough? I can round up more covers."

"If you put on any more covers, I'll smother."

"Okay then." He kissed her cheek and slid around to kiss her lips. "Sleep well. Thanks for coming with me. Holler if you need anything."

She watched him start up the ladder. "Steve? Thanks. I know I've been hard to be around."

"Don't worry, Marta. This cast business ends soon. Night."

She lay awake, watching the fire until it became a pile of embers. Once she fell asleep, she became the firebird. As she danced the dramatic ballet, ugly birds flocked onto the stage plucking her feathers. The more she pushed them away, the angrier they became, biting and scratching her arms and legs until they drew blood. She cried out, "No! Stop! Stop!"

One bird grabbed her shoulder. She struck out with her hands.

"Marta! Marta!"

She opened her eyes. Steve knelt beside her, ducking her frenzied arms.

"What? Oh."

"Are you okay?"

Marta shuddered. "I had the worst nightmare."

"You're safe. We can talk about it in the morning. Go back to sleep."

Marta shook her head, trying to push the vivid scene away. "Stay down here with me? Please? I don't want to be alone."

He pulled one of the oversized chairs close to the couch. "I'll stay right here. All night."

When Marta awoke in the morning, Steve's head leaned awkwardly to the right. A small rhythmic snore escaped his lips. She watched him, thinking about how he'd flown home just to see her. Such a sweet thing to do. That's what made him so lovable.

Marta turned down Steve's offer of Sugar Pop cereal and powdered milk for breakfast. She closed her eyes when he started eating.

"Yum. Marta, you don't know what you're missing. M-m-m."

"Yes I do. That's disgusting. Turn around, I don't want to see those balls of sugar on your spoon. How can you drink powdered milk?"

He didn't answer. He just grinned and kept eating.

Steve moved to sit beside Marta by the fire and took her hands in his. He nudged her shoulder. "Hey Marta, remember our articles for the paper?"

"Oh my gosh. I completely forgot about them. We could write about their next ballet, *Serenade*."

"Great. But first, tell me about that dream that frightened you last night."

"It was from a ballet. It's not a scary story. It's a love story about a man who enters a magical kingdom and captures a firebird. She helps him win over the princess he loves."

Steve held Marta's hand and smiled. "Do I need a firebird to win you over?"

"No. You've done that on your own."

They drove back to Billings that afternoon. Untracked snow glittered like rhinestone dust across the open fields. Next time they'd plan to walk in the drifts and make fresh footprints and snow angels.

At the boarding house as they sat in the warm car, Marta leaned forward to touch Steve's sleeve. "I loved our trip."

"And, see, I remained a gentleman, right?" He kissed her fingers.

"Wish I could stay longer in Billings. But it's time for me to catch my flight."

Back in her room, Steve tucked her in, then hugged and kissed her before he backed out the door. "Bye, Miss Fluff. Think about me."

"I will. I'll miss you."

23

*T*he days dragged along. February 28, cast removal day, arrived with no new snow, making it easier to maneuver into the doctor's office. Marta fidgeted as she sat in the crowded waiting room surrounded by sniffling, sneezing, and restless patients. She thumbed through the dog-eared *Modern Screen* where Doris Day smiled from the cover. In a few minutes when they removed her cast, she'd be smiling too. She thought about how she'd start her recovery with *pliés* and stretches.

"Marta Selbryth?" called the nurse.

She wheeled down the hall beside the nurse. "After you're weighed, we'll do a blood test, then see about that cast."

Marta balanced on one foot, watching the nurse adjust the weight bar. Had she been careful enough? Her clothes fit the same.

The nurse made a notation on her chart. "Good. You've gained since your last visit. Anxious to get that cast off?"

Marta nodded with a stage smile. She'd gained weight? How could that be? She watched what she ate. She'd need to increase her regimen of diet pills and her daily exercise routine and decrease meal sizes if she wanted to return to the company. All the sitting around didn't help either.

In the exam room after the blood draw, Marta sat with a thermometer in her mouth. The room gave off a ghostly glare: white walls, white linoleum, white nurse's uniform with white shoes, white cast. In a short while she'd be walking and laughing at how she'd moaned over her "plaster stocking," as Shorty called it.

By upping her twice daily exercising to three times a day, getting her muscles toned and her energy back should be easy. Everyone would marvel at her rapid recovery—even Madame Cosper.

Dr. Wycoff entered the exam room scanning her chart. "Today's the day? Excited?"

"Yes, I am."

"Good. Let's get this cast off." He used a noisy saw and set the cast remnants aside. Next he cradled her calf and shifted her ankle from side to side. Marta grimaced and looked at the wall behind his shoulder. He pressed her toes forward.

"Ah!" She jerked back as an electric charge shot through her leg.

"Hm-m. Let's get an x-ray and see what's going on in there." He made notes on the chart and left the room.

Long minutes later, after her stint on the cold x-ray table, Dr. Wycoff returned and placed the x-ray film on the light box on the wall. "See that space on the top of your foot? The scaphoid hasn't healed the way it should. We'll need to recast."

"But you said seven weeks would be enough."

"Usually it would. But you're not healing properly. We'll recast and check again in four weeks. The good news is you may switch to crutches. In a couple of weeks you may add weight to your foot."

Before she had time to react, he tapped her chart, then looked up. "Your anemia concerns me. I thought you stopped dieting."

"I've never dieted."

"Hm-m." Dr. Wycoff kept writing. "We'll continue iron injections until I see improvement. Any questions?"

"Can't I begin exercising sooner? My position with the dance company is coming up for review."

Doctor Wycoff looked from her leg to her face. "If you add pressure too soon, you'll prolong your recovery or cause permanent damage."

Marta sucked in her bottom lip and bit down to keep from crying. Four extra weeks; might as well be four years. She needed as much time as possible to prepare for a June audition.

"The nurse will apply a walking cast to support your foot and ankle. It will let you maneuver more easily."

She nodded. Her earlier excitement washed away like water sliding down the drain. She half-expected to see a puddle on the floor.

The new cast left her toes exposed. When she stood, the knob below her foot forced her to lean to her right. The nurse steadied her and brought in crutches. "Follow the doctor's orders. Exercise your healthy leg, and only your healthy leg, understood?"

Marta nodded, then hobbled to the waiting room. She thumbed through the dog-eared magazines and watched the clock: noon, 12:15, 12:30. The reception room emptied.

Lynne bounded into the waiting room, nearly crashing into Marta's crutches that stretched out beside her chair. "Hey! I thought you'd get your cast off."

"So did I." Marta swallowed and looked around. "Let's get out of here."

As they drove through town, Marta asked, "Can we stop at Olson Drugs? I need a bunch of personal things."

"Want me to get them so you don't have to get out?"

"No. But, if I'm too slow, come get me. I don't want Madame on your back because I made you late."

Marta made her way around with a tote collecting a *Seventeen* magazine, two packs of Chiclets, diet pills, and laxatives. As she stood at the
counter paying, Lynne walked up behind her. Marta closed the paper
bag to hide her contraband.

"Ready?" Lynne said, checking her watch and taking the bag from
Marta's hand. "You worry about walking, I'll carry your bag."

Marta twisted to free the knots in her back and shoulders before heading to the front of the store. The thumping sound her crutches made on
the wooden floor sounded like Madame's cane. She shuddered.

On the drive to the boarding house, Lynne flipped through radio sta-
tions, stopping at Buddy Holly and the Crickets singing "That'll Be The
Day." Marta closed her eyes. When would it be her day?

"Want to go for a drive later?" Lynne said. "Maybe a movie? I need
a break from dating, Madame, and everything else. You should see the
mess I've made in my apartment."

"No, not today," Marta said. "I'm exhausted and maybe a little grumpy
about this new cast. I'll call you."

Marta entered the boarding house and sat slumped on the hall bench.
Her arms ached from maneuvering the crutches. She looked up the flight
of stairs. Today didn't appear to be the day to return to her room. Maybe
tomorrow or the next day she'd have the strength. She made her way to
the downstairs room and flopped across the bed.

Her shorter cast exposed pale skin. It reminded her of the bleached
driftwood near Kalaloch: dead and useless. In her head she felt a scream
building. If she could let it out, she'd feel better. No, she needed to handle it, not let frustration overpower reason. She settled for beating her
fists into her pile of pillows.

The following Monday, Marta sat in the common room. She picked
up today's newspaper dated March 3. Postage would soon increase to

four cents for a letter. The latest on the British expedition crossing Antarctica announced they were approaching the South Pole. The grocery store ad said bread had risen to nineteen cents a loaf, and oranges were five pounds for forty-nine cents. Food costs increased each month. When would it stop?

With her sewing projects ending, she needed to look for other income.

She turned to the newspaper's classifieds and circled half a dozen help wanted ads. Over the next hour she called the grain company office, one movie theater, the library, a physician's office, the Montana Inn, and an alterations shop.

Two had job openings: the Montana Inn needed a night clerk Monday and Tuesday from eight to eight. The Grand Theater wanted a ticket seller all day Sunday, plus evenings Thursday through Saturday. Both had no problem with her being on crutches. And, if she'd figured correctly, she'd earn more than dancer's wages.

When Lynne dropped over two nights later, Marta showed her the schedule she'd drawn up.

"Good grief! You're working long hours. How can you add this much and still sew? And what about the girls we're supposed to teach?"

"Sewing's ending. The new jobs will pay my rent so I don't dip into my mom's savings. If we delay the dance lessons a couple of weeks, I'll be able to manage the steps to the basement."

"You didn't mention Steve. Is he back? Can he drive you around to all your jobs?"

"No. He's still interning. I've arranged with Mrs. B.'s nephew to drive me. He needs pocket money. Once I get rid of this cast, I'll quit working."

"Until you do, I'll never see you. What about Steve?"

"He'll be too busy to notice me."

"There's no way he'll not notice you, Marta." Lynne pulled out her lipstick and refreshed her makeup.

Marta watched Lynne stretch her lips taut, draw an outline, and fill-in with hot pink. After she smudged her lips together, she smiled and turned. "You're trading shifts and coming to watch me be amazing in *Serenade*, aren't you?"

"I doubt it. No one wants the night shift. That's how I got it. I'm sorry, Lynne."

"It's okay." Lynne stashed her makeup and zipped her purse closed. "You've gotta work. I get it."

"We'll see each other when we work on the *Serenade* article. Madame gave the okay as long as my name isn't on it. I need your help explaining the choreography."

Lynne shook her head. "You're on your own. I'm not getting in trouble with Madame over a newspaper article. I'm hoping to be selected to perform one of the small group dances in *Serenade*." She headed for the door and turned back. "Take care of yourself. Call me, okay?"

Marta nodded as Lynne slipped out the door. The quiet deafened her.

Marta began her exercises with leg lifts while seated in a straight-backed chair. Her right leg felt weightless compared to hoisting the cast on her left. Next, she used the chair arms and pushed her body up, then slowly lowered herself back into the chair. Sweat covered her face long before she stopped to rest.

Last month she'd increased her arm raises from lifting soup cans to large cans of chicken and dumplings. Each time she curved her arms over her head, she gritted her teeth. Her arms quivered, but the line of her *port de bras* improved. Tomorrow she'd use her new strength to move upstairs to her bright space, the rocking chair, and the quiet.

After dinner that next evening, the men in the boarding house helped carry her belongings. Marta stood beside her upstairs bed and looked around. With everything tucked away, the space felt homey, inviting her to sit and rock. Her room, so far from the furnace, held an icy edge, so she grabbed a sweater, wrapped her plaid scarf around her neck, and covered her legs with Gran's quilt. Thank goodness the braided rug tempered the icy floor beneath her cast.

She woke with a start, not realizing where she sat. Once she got her bearings, she moved to the window and trailed her fingers over the frosty bursts of ice that crossed the cold glass. Below, the walkway lay buried between two rows of white-capped bushes. Cars followed snow trails, their headlights glowing like cat eyes. The snow that she loved back in December had returned to box her in during March.

At least she'd get outside for a few minutes when she traveled to and from her new jobs.

The receptionist job at the inn turned out to be simple: sit, sign in guests, pass out keys, answer the phone, and smile until ten p.m. Then lock the front and back doors and sit in the office awaiting emergencies. At five a.m. she unlocked the doors, began wake-up calls, answered incoming calls, and accepted payment from outgoing guests. Eight a.m., her end of shift, refused to be rushed.

At the Grand Theater she worked in the ticket booth from four thirty until closing at nine. She sat in the glass enclosure on the sidewalk under the marquee, trading half dollars for tickets. Time passed slowly except for Friday and Saturday evenings and the kids' matinees on Saturday; both attracted large crowds.

Sleeping strange hours and not knowing the day of the week frustrated her. She upped her diet pill regimen to boost her energy and found meals no longer interested her. Free time she filled with exercising, baking for the boarding house, or napping.

Sunday matinee hours dragged. Marta yawned and stretched her back. A tap, tap, tap on the glass startled her.

Lynne smiled and moved around to the front of the booth. "You remind me of Sleeping Beauty, awakening in her glass box. How does it feel in there?"

"It's eerie. I'm alone, but I'm on the sidewalk in view of everyone that passes. People stop and look over the coming feature posters but don't look my way unless they buy tickets."

"Need your Prince Charming to come and give you a kiss?"

"He's not my prince anything, Lynne. He's in San Francisco for another two weeks."

"Too bad. And now you'll miss Bartley's Sunday call, if she calls. She's probably too busy going out with a rich guy and eating caviar to remember us."

Before Marta answered, a large group approached the ticket window. Lynne waved and walked toward the Granary. After dispensing tickets, Marta sat alone, staring at the massive, four-sided face of the jeweler's clock across the street. It stood atop a column on the edge of the sidewalk, silently ticking away the seconds. Did it always move so slowly?

The following night, Marta sprawled on her bed with a pocket size calorie counter book she'd picked up at the drug store. She thought she'd kept to less than eight hundred calories a day, but at her latest weigh–in she'd gained two pounds.

Page by page she located everything she'd eaten this past day.

Breakfast: oatmeal with fruit and milk—260 calories

Lunch: fruit cocktail and 7Up—160 calories, peanut butter and jelly sandwich—220 calories

Dinner: beef, string beans, a dinner roll—500 calories

That totaled 1140 calories in one day, and her stomach still growled.

Marta sent the book flying across the room. Whap! It hit the closet door and fell to the floor. She glared at it, willing her calorie intake to shrink, knowing it didn't change by wishful thinking.

She retrieved the book and scoured its pages to locate low calorie foods: green beans, club soda, canned mandarin oranges, and not much else. How depressing. When hunger gnawed at her, she could chew a yucky Feen-a-mint laxative. Whoever thought it tasted like chocolate must not have taste buds!

Marta stepped on the bathroom scales and gasped. She'd gained ten pounds. Even counting the weight of the cast, if she didn't slim down she'd never be accepted by Madame. Not if she weighed 110 pounds.

What more could she do? Give up eating altogether? She exercised as much as she could. Obviously the diet pills weren't helping. Maybe a shower would inspire something she could do.

Just then, the phone rang. Marta answered upstairs. It was Steve.

"Hello, Marta," Steve said. "How's the leg?"

"Don't ask. He gave me another cast."

"No. Oh, Marta. What happened?"

"It's taking longer to heal than expected. But I don't want to talk about it."

The phone line was quiet for some time. "Okay. But Marta, what happened?"

"Don't you get it? I do not want to discuss my leg." Marta squeezed her eyes closed and waited. The phone line buzz stretched on.

"Maybe I should call back later. Marta?"

She swiveled her neck and exhaled. "No. I'm sorry, Steve. I'm disappointed, that's all. Let's talk about your week."

"Um-m, I'm busy doing research for my mentor. Not nearly as exciting as working on my project or out doing interviews, but it's part of the job. I bummed around my neighborhood, then called Bartley. She's still gone."

"We haven't heard much from her either." Marta twisted the phone cord around her finger while she searched for something to say. "Are you still coming home in two weeks?"

"I'm not sure. I need to finish my research on the issues for agriculture workers and other projects before I'm done here."

Marta sat, waiting for him to continue.

"Say you miss me as much as I miss you, Miss Fluff."

"I do. It's too quiet with you gone. Lynne nearly backed out of helping me write out ideas for the *Serenade* article. I coaxed her into helping me, but promise me our names will not be anywhere on it."

"I promise. Read your ideas to me. I'll edit and send it on to Susan."

Marta hobbled to retrieve her tote and the pages she'd written. Dumb cast. Why were things always somewhere else when she needed them? She used her time away from the phone to calm the tension building up in her chest. Why was she taking out her frustration on Steve? He called to talk to her because he cared about her. She shook her head, took a deep breath, and read what they'd written.

> Serenade is a ballet with a musical story instead of being based on a well known fairy tale or folk tale. It is named for the music written by Tchaikovsky: Serenade in C major for String Orchestra. It's a series of dances that explore moods. Patrice Royal is the company's principal dancer. She performs with soloists and corps members to interpret the music. The ballet runs April 3 through 20.

Steve remained silent for several moments. "Okay. I got it."

Marta inhaled, then sank down in her chair. "Is there anything else you need?"

"It would be nice if you were happy to talk with me."

Marta pulled in her lips to hold back her words.

"Marta? Are you there? I miss you."

"I know."

"I'll be back soon. Maybe I can distract you from your cast. How's that?"

"Good. But I need to go. I'll talk to you soon." She hung up the phone, gathered up her tote and crutches, and returned to her room, feeling the weight of their conversation twisting in her heart.

Hour to hour. Day to day. Marta's energy lagged. She staggered from one job to the next. When the low calorie green beans and mandarin oranges didn't give her enough energy to walk, let alone work, she increased her doses of diet pills and went back to eating peanut butter sandwiches.

As she left the hotel Wednesday morning, she began her free day. She leaned against the entry wall of the hotel waiting for Mrs. B.'s cousin to drive her home, anticipating a long nap.

In the late afternoon, she got up to work on dinner for the boarding house. Every step around the kitchen was a chore. She craved sleep even after her five hour nap.

Dinner conversation tonight only required head shakes. She pushed food around, ate small bites, and stifled several yawns. After clearing away the dinner dishes, Mrs. B. set a cake before James. "Tonight we have a celebration. James got a promotion to project manager."

James smiled. "Thank you. I even get an extra week's vacation starting this fall. Might go to Alaska, find out what's so special they're making it a state."

Everyone clapped as Mrs. B. cut the cake and passed out slices. "And soon we'll have more to celebrate when Marta gets that cast off for good."

Marta put on a performance smile as she accepted a paper-thin slice of cake. "Not long now."

Dish after dish she washed, rinsed, and set to dry. Her kitchen partner, Mrs. B., had left earlier for a guild meeting. The kitchen felt too quiet. After draining the sink, Marta retreated upstairs to repeat her evening ritual: exercising, rocking, thinking about everything and nothing, then trying to fall asleep. Why did sleep refuse to come when she dragged herself around exhausted all day long?

Each morning as she shut off her alarm, she struggled to remember the day of the week. Monday? Saturday? Did it matter? Today was Sunday, March 16. She crossed out the date. Her cast came off next week. Then she'd begin putting full weight on her leg.

Hobble, step, hobble, step. The smell of bacon and eggs assaulted her on the stairway. Another round seated amid disgusting, fattening food. Then more sitting, followed by still more. Her backside would soon be as wide as Steve's car. Not a pleasant image.

That evening Marta paced her room as best she could with crutches. Movement helped her sift through her tangled thoughts. The new cast created a definite setback. Could she prepare for returning to the dance company alone? No, she needed help exercising. Lynne was busy, Bartley was gone. So who could help her? Carol? No, that would never work. Maybe Lynne would make time.

She checked the clock. Only ten minutes had passed since she'd returned to her room from dinner. Time and remembering moved like a cup of molasses stirred into cookie dough. She knew she'd forgotten something; what was it?

A knock on the door startled her. "Who's there?"

"Mrs. B."

That's what she'd forgotten—the bread she'd promised to prepare. Marta inched the door open. "I know I forgot to start the bread." She opened the door with her crutch to step into the hall, but Mrs. B.'s hand on her arm stopped her.

"Wait, Marta. We need to talk."

Marta backed up and sank onto her bed as Mrs. B. stepped inside. Marta knew what she saw: rumpled clothes, tossed magazines, and litter. Too late to do anything about it now.

"I'm concerned about you, dear."

Marta picked at a knot on her quilt. "Did I forget something else?"

"No, dear. Forget about jobs for a minute," Mrs. B. said. "I'm concerned about what's going on inside you. You work all hours, skip meals, and disappear into your room."

"I have a lot to do and—"

Mrs. B. placed her hand on Marta's shoulder. "Stop, Marta. Listen to yourself. I told your mother—"

Marta's head whipped up. "You called my mom? Why?"

"Because we all care about you. Seven months ago, a delightful young woman moved into my boarding house. She danced, baked for us, laughed at Shorty's jokes, and spent time with her friends. I know this injury has been hard, but I think there's more going on than a broken foot."

Marta squeezed her eyes shut as tears trickled down her face. "Please, leave me alone. I don't want to talk about this."

"You need to talk with someone, sort through all that's happening in your life."

"It's not that easy. You don't know anything about this." Marta looked down at her leg. "This new cast is a huge set back. I can do so few exercises. I'm out of shape and getting fat. There's no guarantee I'll get my position back."

Mrs. B. took Marta's hands in hers. "You are anything but fat, dear. We can all see that you're not taking care of yourself. All the jobs you've taken on are too much."

"I need to pay my bills. I can't let my mom do it all." Marta shook her head. "I can't talk to anyone. I don't want them to know how I've failed at everything."

Mrs. B. sighed. She took a small card from her pocket and looked at it before handing it over to Marta. "This is someone who helped me after my husband died."

Marta stared at the card. "A psychiatrist?"

Paddy Eger

"She is a good listener, Marta. She helped me see myself and my loss in a very different way. I'm not sure I would have made it without her."

"I haven't lost anyone since my dad died," Marta said. "That was a long time ago."

"Visit with her once, then decide for yourself." Mrs. B. turned to go but stopped short of the door. "I think maybe you have lost someone recently. The one person you need to take care of and protect. Yourself."

The office building sat one block off Twenty-seventh, the main street of downtown Billings, not far from the dance company building. Marta climbed the slick granite steps cautiously, stopping to rest and adjust her crutches on each landing. The office she wanted was left off the stairway on the third floor.

The block letters on the opaque window read, *Marjorie Wilson, Counselor—Welcome.* Marta entered and took a seat. At first glance the room reminded her of a small version of the clinic waiting room where she saw Dr. Wycoff: chairs against one wall, a table with magazines, and art prints on the wall. But a closer look proved that observation totally wrong. This room held only three chairs. The table with magazines also held a bouquet of fresh flowers. The brush strokes on the art work indicated the painting was an original. The biggest difference: she sat alone.

Jitters and tightness cycled through her body like stage fright. She should have skipped the diet pills this morning. The quiet of the waiting room didn't help.

At precisely eleven, the inner door opened and a tall, gray-haired woman wearing a rose-colored blouse and a floral skirt walked out. She smiled. "Miss Selbryth? I'm Marjorie Wilson. Please come in."

As Marta entered the room, Miss Wilson gestured toward two blue club chairs and seated herself in the one closest to the desk. Marta sat down, laid her crutches on the floor, and folded her hands in her lap. She scanned the room: two more chairs, two windows, and two bookshelves. A high-backed black leather chair was tucked in behind a polished wooden desk; a mug of pens lay beside a closed black leather binder. What did this woman write in that binder? Probably everyone's deep dark secrets. Marta didn't plan on sharing any.

Silence hung like a velvet stage curtain.

"It's a pleasure to meet you," Miss Wilson said. "Let's get acquainted, shall we? I'm a native of Montana and have worked with people over the last twenty years. I live along the Yellowstone, where I like to fish. I'm an avid reader, I love to cook, and I enjoy the arts. Now, tell me about yourself."

Marta pressed her lips closed. Why did everyone want to talk? If people left her alone she'd be fine. She had fulfilled her promise by coming. Now she'd try to out wait this stranger.

"Miss Selbryth?"

A breeze entered through the open window. Trucks rumbled down the street. A horn sounded. A cart rattled along the sidewalk. Inside, quietness blanketed the room. Marta bit her cheek and kept her face down to keep from answering.

The room remained silent. Marta sneaked a look at Miss Wilson's shoes. The muted purple velvet high heels surprised Marta; Miss Wilson kept up with the latest trends.

Marta looked up to find Miss Wilson's green eyes locked on her. Now she knew a bird's panic when it flew in through an open window and couldn't find an exit. "I'm a dancer with the Intermountain Ballet Company. Well, I was."

"I love the ballet. This season's Nutcracker had great energy. What dances did you perform?"

"I did all the corps dances and Mother Ginger."

Miss Wilson smiled. "I loved Mother Ginger. You must be a patient young woman to handle those children popping in and out of your skirt and all while wearing stilts."

Marta shrugged. "It was a challenge."

"What challenge brings you here today?"

"A promise I made to someone."

"You must trust that person," Miss Wilson said.

Marta nodded.

"Does any of your reason for being here come from your injury?"

"Yes. When I fell off a porch and broke my ankle, my whole life changed." Saying the words triggered an ache so deep she thought she'd crack open.

"How is your recovery progressing? I notice that you use crutches. I broke my foot once. Crutches can be frustrating, can't they?"

The dam burst. Marta's body jarred through each sob.

Miss Wilson handed her a box of tissues and sat without speaking.

The aching subsided. Marta closed her eyes, then opened them and looked at Miss Wilson. "I don't know what to do anymore."

"Let's back up. Tell me about your typical day."

"Mostly I work a handful of part time jobs."

"How does that work with a cast?"

Marta looked down at her hands. "It's hard to be independent when you can't walk or get around by yourself."

"What do you miss about not being able to dance?"

"I miss my friends, learning new choreography, and being able to move freely. Dancing is all I've ever wanted to do."

Over the next minutes they talked about her early years of dancing and her coming to Billings. The longer she spoke, the more her heartache lightened. "All this sitting drives me crazy. Some days I'm so frustrated I want to scream."

"Describe how your anger feels."

Marta shrugged and scanned the room as if the answer might be encased in the walls or bookshelves or window shades. It wasn't.

"Where does your anger gather in your body?"

"Mostly in my stomach. It feels like a balloon is inflating and pushing up through my lungs and my heart. Other times my whole body aches like a giant cramp is squeezing and twisting inside me. I feel jittery and impatient. I can't catch my breath."

"Have you told your doctor?"

"No." She thought about Dr. Wycoff. If she told him, he'd start asking questions she didn't want to answer.

"You should. Maybe it's your medications."

"I don't take anything."

"Do you drink coffee? That makes many people jittery."

"No coffee." Marta leaned forward and reached for her crutches. "Are we done?"

"That's your decision."

Marta sat back and wiped her palms on her skirt. She needed to talk, but did she trust this stranger with a leather binder on her desk? How much could she share and still be in control of herself? She swallowed and looked around the room. A small sign behind Miss Wilson's desk caught her attention. It read: *Self-discovery leads to recovery*. Marta decided to stay.

Over the rest of the hour she spoke of events in her life she'd tried to bury: her dad's death, her mom's struggle to provide for them, her failed auditions early on, and her frustration over her injury. Miss Wilson asked a few questions; mostly she sat and listened.

Suddenly, the hour she'd dreaded came to an end. She'd talked all that time and didn't once feel embarrassed for telling a stranger her story.

"Would you like to return another time, Marta?"

"Yes. Do I need to take pills or anything?"

Miss Wilson tipped her head. "Do you think you need pills?"

"No. I just thought...no, I don't need pills."

"I don't prescribe medications this early in getting to know my clients."

Marta nodded. "I'm sorry I acted so sour when I arrived."

"That doesn't matter. How do you feel now?"

"Like I can breathe."

As Marta waited for her ride, a peacefulness settled down inside her. Talking to Miss Wilson cleared her view. Women walked along the sidewalk with jumpy young children who pulled away to study shop windows or hop over cracks in the sidewalk. Trucks idled with open tailgates delivering goods to shop keepers. She'd been so wrapped up with herself she'd stopped noticing the world around her. Maybe she'd also ignored her friends. How did she get so out of sorts and not notice?

Over the next couple of weeks, Marta returned to talk with Miss Wilson twice each week. Each time she left the office, her calmness lasted longer than the previous visit. Mrs. B. had been right; she'd needed to speak with someone.

After her latest visit with Miss Wilson, Marta finished the dinner dishes and moved to the back porch bench. She set the crutches aside, leaned back, and scanned the sky. The cold night air made her shiver, yet it refreshed her.

Familiar constellations glimmered in the inky darkness: Orion, the Big Dipper, Casseopia. Did Steve look up and see the stars and think of her? What about Bartley? Where was she?

Marta caught herself. Miss Wilson suggested she focus on herself and what she'd teach the little girls when she met with them tomorrow. They'd be fun to work with, but she'd need diet pills to keep up her energy. Could she ride a bike to the drug store with her cast? Doubtful. Time to request another delivery.

Marta returned to the basement practice room to do a final check. She'd cleaned, installed hooks for the little girls, and hung the totes she'd made for them. When she returned upstairs to her room, she stopped near Carol's door, where she saw light escaping around the edges. Must be hard reading and writing for hours every night, she thought. No wonder Carol continued to be such a grouch.

Carol's door opened. Marta stepped back, nearly falling over her left crutch.

"What do you want?" Carol asked.

"Want?"

"Yes, why are you standing in front of my door?"

Marta shrugged. "I'm not."

"Yes, you are." Carol stretched tall and crossed her arms as she looked down on Marta. "Stay away from my door. I don't appreciate spies."

"You don't? Really? Then why do I hear you scuttling away from my bedroom door and from the basement door all the time?"

"How dare you accuse me of spying! I have every right to be in the hall and in the basement. Even though you think you're Mrs. B.'s favorite, that doesn't mean you're special. I've seen the drug store deliveries you receive when you think no one is watching."

"What?"

"I know you're taking something you don't want anyone to know about. And I could have told you about Miss Wilson…"

The hair on Marta's arms bristled. "What did you say?"

"Ah, nothing," Carol stammered. Her face reddened. "Just keep away from my door." Wham. She slammed the door.

Marta's shock took her breath away. Carol spied on her and listened to the private conversations she'd had with Mrs. B.? Who had she told: the boarders, her college friends, who? And what did she know about the drugstore deliveries?

At breakfast the following morning, Marta surveyed the other boarders. Shorty and James savored their morning coffee and conversation. Carol ate with her head down. All the while, Mrs. B. kept a watchful eye on everyone and everything. It appeared that nothing had changed.

Marta relaxed as she dragged her spoon through her half-filled bowl of cereal. She made a mental list for the drug store: diet pills, chewable laxatives, tooth powder, deodorant, cotton balls, and two packs of bobby pins. Lynne predicted correctly; she'd cut her hair way too short. She'd need handfuls of pins to practice fastening on the hairpiece she'd picked up from Dolly's Hair Emporium last week. It would never do to have a mound of netted hair fly across the room during her audition. June was creeping closer; only a little more than two months left to prepare.

As she dried the last of the dishes, she thought about Miss Wilson. Focusing on what she could control took more energy than she'd expected. Working with the little girls promised to her keep her mind off the mountain of things she couldn't control.

Four o'clock. Marta sat in the basement studio. When the girls arrived, Lynne escorted them downstairs. Marta listened to their chattering as they clomped down the stairs. The basement door opened. The girls stopped talking as they entered. The group stood so close together it would have been impossible to slide a piece of paper between them. Lynne's aunt stood behind them, placing her hands on the shoulders of two girls. "Hello, Marta. These young ladies are excited to learn to dance. I told them you're both ballet dancers."

A tiny black-haired girl looked up. "Are you really dancers?"

Marta smiled. "Yes, we are. We want to teach you to dance. Will that be fun?"

"Yes, but, you have a cast. How can you dance?" another girl asked.

"I can't until my ankle heals," Marta said.

The black haired girl spoke again. "My mother said I couldn't dance on my tippy toes."

"You don't need to dance on tippy toes to have fun," Lynne said. "What's your name?"

"I'm Carmen. I'm seven."

Marta felt a chuckle rise in her throat. "Well, Carmen, and the rest of you lovely young ladies, let's get started." Marta pointed to the hooks she'd installed. "I've made each of you dance bags to store your dance clothes and carry them back and forth to our lessons. Carmen, Lucy, Tracy, and Brenda, check to see that I spelled your names correctly."

The huddle broke apart as each girl found her bag.

"How did you know our names?" Carmen asked.

"I told her," Mrs. Meadows said. "Now take off your coats, your shoes, any extra clothes, and put them in your dance bags."

The girls did as directed. The room remained breathlessly quiet.

Marta turned on the record player and sat back down on the chair. "When you are ready, sit on a rug square."

When the girls were seated, Lynne sat on the floor with them. "Let's find out about each other. I'll start. My name is Lynne. I love to dance. I have lots of brothers. I like to meet new people. Carmen, you're next."

Carmen wiggled around and smiled. Her short curly hair made her round face angelic. "I'm Carmen. I have two sisters who like to tease me. I like to swing."

"So do Lynne and I," Marta said.

The next girl looked down at her knees, letting her long straight hair cover much of her face. "I'm Lucy. I like to help my mother when she's too sick to cook alone."

"I like to cook," Marta said. "Maybe some day we'll cook together."

Lucy looked up and smiled, then tucked her face down toward her knees once again.

"Who's next?" Lynne asked.

The smallest of the four rocked back and forth on the rug square. "I'm Tracy. I like to read. I live next door to Brenda."

"So what do you girls play together?" Lynne said.

Brenda shrugged. "Mostly we do ballerina paper dolls and play dress-up."

"And we pretend dance," Tracy said.

"You all do so many interesting things. Now you will learn to dance together," Marta said. "Let's get started."

Lynne led them with simple stretches. Next, they practiced walking like dancers, putting their toes down first and lifting their arms like flower petals in the wind. When Lynne pulled out scarves, the girls danced and twirled, waving the scarves until they were called back to their rug squares.

"Next time," Lynne said, "we'll begin real ballet exercises at the *barre*."

That evening Lynne called Marta. "You'll never guess what happened. The girls chattered all the way back. They showed the rest of the kids what we did, and they're all excited about coming back. Looks like we have our first students."

Each class the little girls started with stretches at the *barre*. After floor exercises, they tried simple leaps and ballet steps. Their happy voices and quirky movements energized Marta, reminding her of her own early dance years. She forgot about her cast and set to work making costumes for the girls to wear when they danced for their families in June. Tomorrow, Tuesday, April first, her cast would be removed. Hopefully there'd be no fool's trick waiting for her at the doctor's office.

After the dreaded weigh-in, a blood draw, and an iron shot, Dr. Wycoff removed the cast. While the nurse washed her leg and applied lotion, Marta stared at the ghost white skin of her shriveled leg. She held her breath to stifle her disappointment at its condition.

Dr. Wycoff twisted and flexed her ankle. Marta winced, but experienced no sharp pain. He massaged her calf muscle and her ankle. "Do this daily to stimulate and loosen the muscles before you exercise." She nodded, wishing she could leap up and dance all the way home.

"Use the crutches for support this week. I know your leg looks bad, but with a few weeks of therapy you'll be fine."

"Therapy?"

"Yes. I suggest physical therapy twice a week for three to four weeks. The nurse will give you a list of names. Make a follow-up appointment with me if you experience any problems."

"Okay." Marta spoke to doctor's back as he disappeared out the exam room door.

She wiggled her toes: a little pain and a stiffness she'd never before experienced. She lifted her leg; it felt weightless without the cast. Her muscles trembled. When she tried to rotate her ankle, she found she had no flexibility. The nurse returned, handed her a therapy list and crutches, then walked her to the waiting area.

On the ride home she thought about her pile of still-unpaid hospital bills. Where would money for therapy come from? She knew her own body; after all, she'd spent ten years doing warm-ups and stretches two or more days every week. Therapy cost too much right now. She'd exercise by herself.

Marta stood in the front hall leaning on the crutches. Sixteen steps up to her room; sixteen steps back down. Maybe she should have stayed downstairs longer, but she'd missed her room. Besides, using the stairs provided exercise. She'd follow Dr. Wycoff's orders and take it slow for a few days, but then she'd practice every waking minute she wasn't working.

∿

Thursday. Two days since her cast came off. It was time. She smiled as she made giant flowers around today's date on her calendar. A thrill sizzled through her as she put on her ballet clothes for the first time since the Christmas break. She turned side to side and looked over her shoulder. Saggy and flabby described her backside. Exercise should help reverse the damage.

When she reached the basement studio, she smiled and inhaled, feeling her lungs expand, welcoming her back. Now the real work began.

Marta knew her feet had swollen. Her ballet shoes felt extra snug, more like *pointe* shoes. Maybe she'd start barefoot and work back into her soft shoes after a few days.

She swiveled her neck to loosen her muscles, then stood in first position at her makeshift bar and took a cleansing breath. As the adagio recording began, she performed a *demi-plié,* then rose. Her body remembered even though her legs jittered. She sank into another and another. Her left ankle refused to flex to its full extent, but she pushed herself, ignoring the pain.

Sweat gather under her arms; they ached from holding their positions. She'd exercised every day these past two months, why did she feel so weak? *Demi plié*, point to second, and repeat.

Fourth position, fifth position, both sides. Her muscles vibrated as she added *ports de bras*, reaching forward and back, lengthening her torso further and further the longer she worked.

Battements tendus next. Her right side looked strong and normal as she stretched her foot out to a point and brought it back to first position. Standing on her left leg caused so much pain she rested before continuing on the other side. At least her injured leg was off the floor now, doing the beats. The bad part: her foot cramped with every attempt she made to point her toes.

She inhaled, straightened, and pushed through her discomfort. Her foot cramped, locking her toes in a gnarled position. She reached for the nearby chair to sit and rub out the knot. I can do this, she thought, as the cramp continued to send a burning sensation up her leg.

On and on she worked: *grands battements*, beating the air with swift leg extensions, *ronds de jambes* creating imaginary circles on the floor. After dozens of *relevés,* unending lifts ending with *demi-pliés*, she stopped, grabbing the *barre* to keep from fainting or falling on the floor.

Twenty minutes later, she began again. Hours later she returned to her room and collapsed without taking a shower or removing her soaked dance clothes.

When she woke, her body shivered. It was dark outside. Her clock said eleven. She sat up, trying to orient herself. She gasped. She'd slept through dinner and her job at the theater.

When she turned on her bedside lamp, she saw a message lay under her door. It read,

You missed your shift at the theater. Your unpaid wages will be mailed to you. Don't bother to return.

$\mathscr{M}$arta and Lynne taught the little girls *pliés* with the matching *ports de bras* so their body and arm movement positions aligned. They taught curtsies, flowing hands, jumps, and standing with straight backs. They taught them *glissades* and *balancés*. Whatever they taught, every lesson ended with the girls encircling Marta and Lynne with hugs before they hurried onto the waiting bus.

One evening after dinner dishes, Marta and Lynne sat in the dusky light of the common room talking. Marta massaged her leg and ankle, now an every day routine.

"How much longer do you plan to continue working at the hotel?" Lynne asked. "You look so tired you make me want to take a nap."

"I need money, so I'll stay on a while longer."

"Have you contacted Damien yet? Checked on the audition date?"

Marta shook her head. "I want to be able to walk in without limping. He'll not let me audition if I can't walk."

"Call him, Marta"

"I will. After I lose five pounds, I—"

"Forget the pounds. You're making excuses. Call him tomorrow. Promise."

Though Marta knew she should call, how could she when those extra pounds hung on her like dead weights? She'd call soon; just not tomorrow. Maybe by the end of next week.

Between working at the hotel, instructing the little girls, and baking for the boarding house, Marta anticipated she'd drop her excess five pounds like water off a raincoat. It hadn't happened. Her energy remained the only thing that dropped.

Tomorrow Steve returned. He'd stayed on in San Francisco to finish his project. Their nightly phone calls became once or twice a week because of his work, giving her more time to worry about everything. Miss Wilson would not be pleased.

What should she say when he arrived? She hadn't seen him since Valentine's weekend. Phone calls weren't the same as sitting next to him, watching his face, listening to his voice, or feeling his lips brush hers. What should she wear? When would he arrive?

Marta yawned as she set the breakfast table. She'd grabbed her clothes from yesterday, planning to shower once the boarders left. Mrs. B. finished scrambling eggs and frying the bacon. The front door opened and closed. Footsteps approached the dining room.

"Morning, Marta."

She froze with the breakfast napkins clutched in her hands. "Hi." Steve stood inches from her. He'd come back. She laid down the napkins, brushed back her hair, and stared at his face. "Wow. You're really here. I didn't expect to see you—and so early."

"Surprise. I wanted to see you as soon as possible, so I drove through."

Marta studied him. He looked tired, rumpled, and yet more handsome than she remembered.

Mrs. B. walked in with a bowl of fruit. "Steve! Welcome back. Ready for breakfast?"

"That would be wonderful."

Marta stood frozen in place. "Yes, welcome back." She reached out and took his hand, feeling its familiar warmth spread contentment through her. He'd come back to her.

When Mrs. B. returned to the kitchen, they shared kisses and hugs. Lips touching lips. Arms around arms. Heartbeat against heartbeat. The ache of his being away became the ache of longing to stand entwined. Only the arrival of the boarders broke their attention on each other.

Steve sat beside Marta and answered questions from the boarders: Did he like San Francisco? What projects did he work on? Would he want to go back? He answered each one but kept his eyes focused on Marta.

She didn't eat a bite, afraid her hands would shake and give away her excitement. This time she knew it wasn't diet pills; she'd yet to take any today.

After breakfast Steve helped her clear the table and finish the dishes. Then she banished him to the common room while she put dishes and breakfast condiments away.

When she looked in on him, he'd fallen asleep. She watched his steady breathing, the way his head lay to one side, and heard a faint snore flutter from his lips. Poor guy. He must be exhausted from the long drive. She touched his hair and brushed it off his forehead; she'd let him sleep while she rushed upstairs and took a quick shower.

Marta's hands shook as she showered. It was like stage fright; or was it excitement at seeing him here in the boarding house? She dressed quickly, grabbing whatever looked clean and reasonably wrinkle-free. As she returned downstairs, she heard his laughter. He was on the phone. "I'll be home in a little while. Just wanted you to know I'm with Marta."

Ease spread through her. She relaxed, knowing he'd returned and chosen to see her before heading home. She smiled as she turned the corner and saw him smiling back at her.

"All set? I must say you look great, Marta. Prettier than I remember."

She felt heat rise through her body. "So do you, I mean, you look good too."

He grabbed her hand. "Do you have time for a drive? I'd like to have you to myself for a little while. Dad said I should get to the paper by noon."

They drove east along the Yellowstone and crossed the river. Steve held her hand as he drove. Soon they pulled into a ranch that sat back from the main road. "Since you like tossing rocks and you keep a bag of polished rocks in your room, I wanted to bring you out here to see an interesting rock called Pompey's Pillar."

"Who's Pompey?"

"Sacagawea's son. Clark called him Pom and named the rock for him." Steve circled the car, opened Marta's door, and pulled her to her feet. "Now that you can walk, I want to show you the view."

"But isn't this private property?"

"Yes, but my dad knows the owners. It's okay that we're here."

They climbed around the edges of the pillar, finding foot and hand holds in the sandstone butte. Steve pulled Marta up the last few feet. At the top she made a slow turn, looking from the Yellowstone to the surrounding grasslands. "This is amazing. How do you know Clark came here?"

"He signed the rock. We'll see it on the way back down. It's a great place isn't it?"

They stood holding hands, listening to the wind rustle the grasses. The sound reminded her of hands rubbing together, creating small moments of heat on a chilly day.

"The owners, the Foote's are letting the paper do a story about the pillar. They're considering letting tourists visit the site. I'm putting my bid in to write the article."

Marta hugged Steve. "It's good to have you back. I missed you."

Steve smiled and brushed his hand against her cheek. "I missed you too." He kissed her forehead and stepped back. He scanned her from head to toe, held one hand, and twirled her around to look at her. "Let's go where we can talk away from this wind; maybe share a few more kisses."

They drove across the river and along a windy road heading west back toward Billings. At the end of the gravel road they parked and walked toward a wall of rock. This early in the morning they had the area to themselves.

"I wanted to bring you here this morning so you could see the prehistoric carvings in these three caves. On the drive home I realized we've never come here. The effect of the early morning light is worth the trip."

They followed a narrow gravel trail under the overhang and stopped at the first cave. Marta looked up. High inside the shallow cave the morning sunlight cast spotlights, highlighting the stick figures and animal petroglyphs.

"This is amazing," Marta said. "The air feels cool even though the trail up here has heated up. Must have been a great place to cool down on a hot day."

"Archaeologists think the local Indians used these caves as shelter. Come on. I want to show you my favorite—the ghost cave. Wait until you see the rock formations."

The ghost cave did not disappoint. Its large boulders looked to be cemented into the wall of the cave, as if they had rolled down the wall and gotten stuck.

"What do you think, Marta?"

"It's interesting, but why did you want us to come here this first morning you're back? Are you thinking of doing an article?"

"Yes, I'm hoping to, but I wanted you to see it when the light makes it magical. It's only this time of year that it's special. I might be gone this time next year."

They sat under a box elder tree and held hands while they shared a dozen kisses. Steve leaned back and looked at Marta. "Thanks for driving out with me. I know we both love the lake and The Rims, but I also like the snugness out here, being boxed in this hollow, away from the river and the big view. Probably not a great story."

"It's a great idea for a story. I doubt many people think of coming here, especially so early. They will after you write the story. Then we'll need to find a new place to be alone."

Steve laughed. "I have lots of cozy places left for us to explore, but I think I'll keep a few just for us."

"I'd like that." Marta kissed Steve's cheek and closed her eyes, enjoying the quiet.

"So, Miss Fluff, how's your leg?"

"Better. I'm back to exercising. My limp is less noticeable, isn't it?"

"You walk like a dancer." Steve held both of Marta's hands and stared at her face. "I've missed you so much." He kissed her fingers. "You look thinner. Have you lost weight?"

Marta pulled her hands free. "No. Let's not talk about me. Tell me what your plans are now that you are back."

"Back to school and back to the paper. Then start looking for a job by Christmas. I don't know if the paper in San Francisco will consider me for a job."

"Would you want to go back?"

"In a heartbeat. Starting my career at a large newspaper is the chance of a lifetime. It could shave years off my getting a byline. If they offered me a job, would you move there to dance and be near me?"

"Maybe. It's not that easy to get a position in a dance company. I'm like you, focused on my future. My audition to rejoin the company here is coming up."

"At least you didn't say no." He stood, pulled her to her feet, and bowed. "I am getting smarter. I'm not planning on handing you any small boxes; at least not right now. Come on. Let's get you back. I need to head home, shower, and get to the paper."

Marta watched Steve's car disappear around the corner. She sat on the porch swing, thinking about his plans. If she regained her position here, would she give it up and move to San Francisco to be near him? One of Miss Wilson's "out of my control" questions. It was something she couldn't control, but there didn't appear to be a way to erase it from her mind.

That afternoon the basement pulsed with excitement when the four young dancers learned they'd have a June recital for their families and friends, complete with costumes. Questions flew about jumps, solos, swooshing scarves, and twirling dances.

Lynne held up her hand. "Slow down, ladies. There's lots of time. We'll create a solo for each of you to do in addition to the group dance. Now, head for the *barre* to warm up."

Marta felt a tug on her leotards. Lucy stood close and signaled Marta to bend down. "Can I do a dance with a fairy wand? My mother gave me one for Christmas."

"Of course you can. Bring it to class. We'll figure out how to include it in your solo."

Lucy skipped to the *barre* and smiled as she began her first *port de bras*.

Marta marveled at the way the girls absorbed every new part of their routine. At seven and eight, they demonstrated amazing focus at the *barre* and during center work. Their eyes shimmered as they danced around the small basement space. Maybe one day some of them would dance on a real stage. She had, and the thrill of the first time in front of the lights lasted as a treasured memory.

Marta's weekly visits with Miss Wilson continued to be a highlight in her life; almost as important as seeing Steve. She realized she spent more time with Miss Wilson than Steve. Since his return, his free time shrank from hours to minutes and from every day to once or twice a week. Phone calls replaced face-to-face time. Marta longed for their walks and talks but settled for brief updates.

Now, as Marta sat in the blue chair, she relaxed and ignored the leather notebook on Miss Wilson's desk. Quite a change from her first visit.

"We have a few minutes left today. What else do you want to talk about, Marta?"

"My mom. Her life's changing now that she has a boyfriend. It sounds strange to call a forty-year-old man a boyfriend, but that's what he is."

"Does that bother you?"

Marta thought for a long minute before answering. "Some. But I want her to be happy. She's been alone for several years, working and taking care of me. She deserves someone who cares about her. But Robert will never take my dad's place."

"He may provide an important change for your mother."

As she walked the four blocks to the ballet company, she thought back on what Miss Wilson said. Her mom might be ready to move ahead with her life. Was she also ready to move ahead? Steve had stepped back into her life, although not with the frequency she'd hoped. Their relationship had changed since they met. Was that a good change or just the next step? Both their careers remained unsettled. Perhaps that was the change to deal with first.

Marta approached the dance company building and flashed back to her first day waiting on these steps. She revisited the anxiety of that day as she opened the heavy double doors.

Karl sat in his little room, reading a newspaper. "Can I help you... Marta? How's the leg?" His eyes drifted to her foot.

"Better. Are Damien and Madame in?"

"They are. Go on up. You know the way."

Marta inhaled the familiar smell of rosin and sweat as she climbed the stairs. Her heart raced like the first day. Maybe she should have prepared what she wanted to say. Maybe if she waited a few more days she'd feel more confident. At the office door she paused, took a deep breath, then knocked.

"Come in," Damien's voice called out.

Good, she thought; he's alone. Marta elongated her spine and plastered on a stage smile as she walked in. She stood behind a straight-backed chair that faced his desk, hoping the throbbing of her heart didn't drown out her voice.

Damien smiled. "Marta! Welcome!" He set aside his paperwork and indicated she should sit. "How's the leg?"

"Better."

"Feeling strong enough to start dancing?"

"Yes. I exercise several hours every day. I came by to find out if you'd set the date for my audition."

"Yes. I'd planned to contact you this week. Let's see." Damien flipped through his calendar. "It's May twentieth after rehearsals. We'll use the first section of the ballet I've choreographed to Gershwin's *Rhapsody*

in Blue. It's part of our musical tribute to America. The corps begins rehearsals next Monday. I'll call you with specific times."

Marta nodded. A shock wave traveled through her. One week? Only
one week to become ready to rejoin the other dancers. "Thanks. It will
be good to get back." She turned to leave.

"Wait," Damien said. "Do you want coaching or extra rehearsal time
to help you prepare?"

"That would be wonderful, but I don't have money for lessons."

"How about a trade? I hear you are a great cook. Our family life is
hectic. My wife runs a gallery, and by the time she gets home it's catch-
as-catch-can dinners. Our kids would love a few kid-friendly meals.
Want to trade cooking for coaching?"

"Sure. I love to cook and bake."

"Great." He scribbled a short note and handed it to Marta. "Here's my
wife's phone number at the gallery. Call her to set up a schedule. She'll
be overjoyed."

As Marta reached the bottom of the stairs, Lynne appeared. "Hey!
What's going on?"

Marta explained and started out the door.

"Wait. We're done for the day. Want a ride home?"

"That would be great."

"Let's stop at the burger shop out on Russell. Haven't had my fatty
food fix this week."

Marta ate a small salad and sipped iced tea. Lynne worked on a double cheeseburger and a shake. "I'm starving today. I could never get by
on your skinny salad. How are you feeling?"

"Good. I hope I'll feel ready to dance with the corps by Monday."

"I'll come over and help you get ready. It will be fun to see you every
day."

დ

Marta's ankle ached as she straightened the paperwork in the hotel office before her shift ended. This last overnight had been crazy. A convention of farm equipment companies stayed in the meeting room long after twelve. Then she'd stored the tables and chairs and swept. Stale beer and sticky splotches covered the floor. She'd mopped the entire floor twice. Quite a way to end a job.

Now she sat in the boarding house common room waiting for Lynne to arrive for their afternoon with the little girls. Having the consistent time with her and the girls gave Marta focus. What would she do without Lynne's craziness?

The front door opened, followed by Lynne's usual jump directly into a conversation. "I tried calling with your rehearsal schedule; no one answered."

"I must have slept through it."

Lynne handed Marta the schedule. "Not many days for you to pick up the choreography, but you'll get it, and I'll come over and help you."

Marta shrugged. "At least we can continue with the little girls. Their solos are coming along. Lucy is so excited to show her mother what she's learned. She's got a natural grace when she moves. Reminds me of Bartley."

"I see a lot of you in her as well," Lynne said.

The bus arrived before Marta answered. Soon the basement filled with laughter and music, creating a great way to end any day.

28

$\mathcal{M}$arta listened as the phone rang several times. She nearly hung up, but then a man answered. "Russell-Smyth residence."

"May I speak with Bartley Timmons please?"

"Miss Timmons is not here. May I take a message?"

The business-like voice surprised Marta. "Are you Bartley's grandfather?"

The man on the phone cleared his throat. "I'm the Russell-Smyth butler."

"Oh," Marta said. "When do you expect Bartley?"

"Miss Timmons has gone home for an extended period of time. Is there a message you'd like me to relay?"

"Home? Isn't she dancing? I thought she'd be back by now."

"Your message, Miss?"

"Please tell her Marta called. Or, could you give me her home phone number? I'll call her myself."

"I'll deliver your message."

Click. The phone line went dead.

Marta looked at the phone as if the ear piece might divulge information. Then she hung up. Maybe Lynne knew something. This was getting too strange, even for Bartley.

$\mathcal{T}$he basement felt stuffy. Marta opened the window and continued to exercise. After two hours of movement, her left ankle ached and her calf muscle tightened. She needed a break; maybe a small lunch. She walked through the quiet of the boarding house, feeling its emptiness.

The month of April dragged more than she did; each day blurred into the next. Lynne remained busy with the final performances of *Serenade*. Steve's schedule limited their time together as well. The latest news from Bartley dried up. Then the phone rang.

Marta answered, "Belvern Boarding House, this is Marta."

"This is Alexandra Belfor-Timmons III, Bartley's mother. Are you the Marta who broke her foot?"

"Yes, I am" What a strange question. Mrs. Timmons' voice sounded so formal; more like a receptionist than a mother.

"Bartley asked me to call. She's wondering if you'd come for a visit."

"I'd love to see her. Is she back in San Francisco? I could take a bus..."

"No, dear, she's not in San Francisco. A bus trip to Philadelphia would take too long. I'll arrange a plane ticket."

"A plane ticket?" A small warning tightened in Marta's throat. "Is Bartley okay?"

"She'll be fine. She asked to see you. She needs you."

Marta felt faint. *Needed* her? She held the phone with both hands to keep from dropping it. "I can come the end of the week. Is that soon enough? I need to be back by Sunday night."

"Thank you, Marta. I..., please keep this trip and this call between us."

"Okay. Give Bartley my love."

Marta stood by the phone in a daze. How could she not tell anyone? How could she not tell Lynne?

ৼ

Saturday morning long before dawn, Marta dressed in her best outfit: a blue wool sheath with a lace-edged Peter Pan collar, her gray winter coat, and her plaid scarf. She tried on her two pairs of pumps, but her feet were swollen, so she wore black flats. No sense in creating deliberate pain.

A cab left her outside the airport. Her stomach had been dancing flip flops ever since Mrs. Timmons called. She'd covered her bases by making excuses to Mrs. B. about going out of town and by avoiding Lynne's calls. She'd called her mom early since she'd return too late to place her traditional Sunday call home.

Once she entered the tiny airport, she moved to wherever people told her to move, handed over her suitcase, and took her ticket. She followed the line of passengers crossing the tarmac to the plane. A perky stewardess greeted her at the top of the stairs and showed her to her seat.

Marta sat by the window with an empty seat beside her. She kept her coat on but removed her scarf, hat, and gloves, gripping them like a lifeline as the plane vibrated down the taxiway.

Once the plane lifted into the sky, a cottony cushion of clouds covered the land below, blocking her view. For years she'd dreamed of flying but knew she'd not be able to afford it for some time. Now as she sat looking out the window, the joy she anticipated never materialized. All she could think about was why Bartley "needed" her.

When the flight attendant touched her arm offering her a soft drink and breakfast, Marta nearly upset the tray. The food smelled horrid, like cooked breakfast at the boarding house. She smiled and refused the tray even though she hadn't eaten since last night.

Her body trembled. She decided the jitters came from nervousness about flying and wondering about Bartley. Surely it wasn't the diet pill she'd taken.

When Marta exited the plane, she watched for a sign with her name on it. A portly man dressed in a black suit smiled when she approached. "Miss Selbryth? I hope you had a nice flight."

"Yes, thank you."

"Give me your baggage claim. I'll secure your suitcase."

The backseat of the black limousine looked like those she'd seen in movies: plush black leather seats for half a dozen people and a thick black carpet. The driver kept his focus on the roadway, so Marta sat in silence, feeling stiff as cardboard.

Philadelphia lay covered in clouds. Marta watched the dull afternoon light blend into a blur of skyscrapers much like Seattle. Within an hour's time they pulled into a curved driveway where the entrance sign read *Eaglecrest*. The elegant lines of the building and the boxwood bushes that flanked the driveway created the appearance of a private club. What was this place?

The driver opened the limousine's door for her. "Your things will be deposited in a room Mrs. Belfor-Timmons reserved for you. I'll return to drive you to the hotel when the receptionist calls me. Shall I escort you to the entrance?"

"No thanks. I'm fine alone." Marta walked to the double wide front doorway and pulled on the door handle. Locked. She heard a buzz and felt the handle release. A locked door? In a club? She walked inside.

The snap of the front door locking behind her startled her. A receptionist seated at a curved desk looked up from her typing and smiled. "May I help you?"

"Yes. I'm here to see Bartley Timmons."

"One moment." The receptionist turned away to use her phone, then turned back to Marta. "Someone will be with you shortly."

Marta sat on a couch by the window that overlooked the grounds. The lush manicured lawn edged with yellow and blue primroses sloped away from the building. Was this a club or something else?

The air in the reception area smelled of lilacs. The huge space had small conversational areas, each with four chairs. The coffee tables held the latest magazines, a bowl of fresh tulips mixed with lilacs, a cigarette lighter, and an ashtray. Marta looked through the latest *Seventeen* without seeing the photos or reading the words.

A tall blonde woman approached. "Miss Selbryth?"

Marta stood. The woman, an older version of Bartley, stepped closer. Her golden hair pulled into a sleek chignon made her look narrow. She wore a mauve suit with a tailored rose-colored blouse, a diamond bracelet, and gray leather pumps. She extended her hand. "I'm Bartley's mother, Alexandra Belford-Timmons. Thank you for coming. Let's talk a bit before you see Bartley."

They sat side by side. Marta waited for Mrs. Timmons to speak.

"I'm so glad you came, Marta."

"I'm glad I could come."

Mrs. Timmons played with her rings before she spoke with Marta. "Bartley is sick. According to her doctors, she's had a problem with diet pills for a long time. It's affected her heart and kidneys. We hadn't seen her since the end of summer when she moved to Billings. Had you noticed she'd lost weight since fall?"

"Yes," Marta said. "I thought she felt stressed like the rest of us from working long hours. Bartley is thin anyway."

Mrs. Timmons nodded. "Her doctors say her body is trying to shut down. She's trying to be a good patient, but it's hard when she's lonely and feeling like we're all against her. I called you because she's asked to see you."

"Why me?"

"She says you're her best friend."

Marta stared at Mrs. Timmons. Her best friend? How could that be with all her family contacts and the dancers she knows in San Francisco? "If she's sick, what can I do?"

"Encourage her to eat. She thinks she'll get fat if she eats all the food on her plate. As it is, she only eats a few bites then says she's full."

Why was this such news to her mother? Bartley always did that. Marta did it. Most dancers, except Lynne, watched their weight.

"If she continues to refuse to eat, the next step will be a feeding tube. That won't be pleasant."

Marta suppressed a shudder by squeezing her hands together.

"Can you talk with her, encourage her to eat?"

"I'll try. When can I see her?"

Mrs. Timmons stood. Marta stood as well. "She's in Suite 110. Stay as long as you wish. If you stay for dinner it may encourage her to eat. Just promise you will not help her procure diet pills."

Marta nodded. As she moved along the carpeted corridor, she pulled two diet pills from her dress pocket and slid them into the wallet in her purse, as if that would hide them any better.

All the doors were closed, but each had a wide window at eye level. Approaching Suite 110, Marta stopped and took a deep breath. Through the window in the door she saw Bartley seated in a swivel rocker reading a magazine. A young woman in a blue-gray dress sat at a desk to one side. When Marta knocked, the woman unlocked the door and stepped aside so Marta could enter.

"Hi, Bartley," Marta said.

Bartley's face lit up. She dropped the magazine and hurried to grab Marta.

"I knew you'd come. I've missed you so much!"

Bartley wore a soft peach skirt with a matching sweater set that hung off her bony frame. Her face looked skeletal. Her honey blonde hair that Marta had envied last August hung in dull strings around her face. Marta stared, unable to speak, so she encircled Bartley's shoulders, feeling her shoulder blades beneath her fingers.

"Marta. Say something."

"I've missed you so much. Why haven't you called or written? We've worried about you."

"I know, but this came up and I didn't know how to tell you I wasn't dancing right now."

They sat together on a leather sofa and talked until dinner. Outside, the small pond disappeared in the darkness. The young woman in the blue-gray dress remained seated nearby and only moved to let the server enter and set the table with two covered plates.

Both plates held small portions of chicken, green beans, a dinner roll, and a pat of butter. Marta laughed. "This looks like my hospital food, but I bet it tastes better."

"It's good, but it's hard to sit here and have someone watch me eat. They don't give me a napkin or a trash can so I can throw away food. Ana even checks my pockets to be certain I haven't shoved food in them. It's like I'm in food prison. Will you eat my roll for me? I hate bread these days."

"I can't eat all I have. The flight wore me out. I guess I lost my appetite." Marta shoved the food around her plate and noticed Bartley did the same.

When they set their plates back on the cart, Ana checked Bartley's almost full plate, made a note in a file, and rolled the food cart back to the hall. She returned to her seat at the nearby desk.

Marta watched the scene unfold. Her plate matched Bartley's. But she had an excuse, didn't she?

After they exhausted conversation about Marta's ankle, Lynne, Madame, their ballet companies, and Steve, Bartley stood and began to pace.

"I imagine my mother told you I have to stay here until I get stronger. They say I need to gain ten pounds before I'm released and can return to San Francisco. My mother's such a worry wart. I feel fine."

Marta reached for Bartley's hand. "What's happened to you?"

"What do you mean?"

"Bartley, you've lost a lot of weight."

"So have you."

"Me? I've gained weight from sitting around, waiting to get my casts off."

"I had the flu and then…" Bartley began crying. "They won't let me take diet pills. And the worst yet, that woman, Ana, sits and watches me all day long. She checks my room for diet pills and laxatives every day. Only my mother comes to visit me, and she's the one who put me in here. If you weren't here it would be worse. I'd have to go to see my shrink after dinner. I hate her. She thinks she knows me. She doesn't."

Marta forced a smile as she tightened her grip on Bartley's hand. "I'm going to see a psychiatrist. She's helping me sort through my jumbled feelings."

"Does she make you talk about everything?"

"Only what I want to discuss. It's helping me. Just try talking with her, Bartley. It might help."

"Maybe." Bartley picked at her stubby fingernails and bit her cuticles. "I'm sorry I've disappointed you by not being in San Francisco. I wanted you to be envious of my success. I was a bad friend. Then you got hurt, and it broke my heart."

"You've been a great friend. And I was jealous. The San Francisco Ballet is a wonderful place to dance. It certainly beats out the Intermountain Ballet Company."

Bartley smiled. "I guess it does. I'm sorry to have made you jealous."

"I'd have done the same if I'd gotten a position there. Right now you need to get well and invite me to San Francisco. You promised, remember?"

"I'm so glad you came." Bartley squeezed Marta's hands tightly. Tears slipped down her face. "I started auditioning for small solos, but when I got the flu I had fainting spells. They sent me to a doctor, and he called my parents." She scanned the suite, then moved close to Marta. "This looks like a nice place, but I can't leave. Do you know all the doors are locked? They force me to go to nutrition classes every day. They're all crazy. I'm no thinner than before. In fact, I'm fat."

Bartley's comments sounded like Marta's own just last week. The difference was that she actually had gained weight; her clothes were tighter than last fall. Bartley looked several sizes smaller since the end of the Nutcracker performances in December.

When Bartley's mother returned, the girls said their goodbyes wrapped in a snug embrace. As they parted, Bartley whispered, "When you come tomorrow, bring me diet pills; any kind you can find, okay? But don't let anyone know. It can be our tiny secret."

"I'll try," Marta said.

After a five-minute drive, Marta stepped into The Regents Inn. The reception area had overstuffed chairs arranged in conversational groups near a crackling fire in a metal faced fireplace. A uniformed maid tidied the side tables filled with silver trays of fruit and pastries, an assortment of juices in pitchers, and several wine decanters. Plates and glassware lay on a nearby table. Marta shuddered. More food. Why did everyone obsess over food?

Her room on the second floor was three times the size of her room in Billings. A cozy sofa and chair faced the picture window. The huge bed with a green silk spread and extra fluffy pillows looked small in the over-sized space. A fruit basket with her name on it sat on the corner of a massive desk.

Pale yellow marble covered the bathroom walls and floor. Even with a separate shower and tub, two sinks, and two toilets, the open space left ample room to practice a routine without any fear of bumping into fixtures.

She resisted the temptation to call Lynne or her mom and describe the hotel and her room. Keeping her promise kept her from sharing the luxury that surrounded her.

All night she tossed and turned, thinking of Bartley and how desperate she acted. The next morning she counted her stash of diet pills. Eight, plus the two in her purse. She had enough to share, but she'd promised Mrs. Timmons. She took two and locked the rest in her suitcase before she returned to Eaglecrest.

Bartley stood by the door, waiting for Marta. When she entered, Bartley hugged her. "Did you bring any?"

Marta mentally crossed her fingers. "I didn't know where to buy them. Besides, you need to do what the doctors say. Then you'll…"

Bartley shoved Marta with both hands. "You're like the others. I thought you were my best friend."

"I am, but they're right. You've lost too much weight."

"I hate you!" Bartley grabbed Marta's shoulders and shook her like a rag doll, then pushed her backward.

Marta screamed as she fell against a chair and landed on the floor, her legs tangled in the chair legs. Marta saw Ana rush to the door and hit a button. Then she stepped in to restrain Bartley, avoiding Bartley's flying arms, pushing her away from Marta.

"Marta, I need pills. You promised you'd bring them." Bartley twisted to free herself, but Ana held her tight. Two men unlocked the hall door and rushed past Marta to help restrain Bartley. When she relaxed, they led her into the bedroom and closed the door.

Marta lay on the floor feeling chained in place, watching the actions unfold like a violent movie scene. Another young woman entered the suite and helped her stand. "Are you okay?"

"I think so," Marta said. "Will Bartley be all right?"

"Perhaps. Please come with me." She led Marta back to the reception area and waited for her to sit down. "May I bring you something to drink?"

Marta shook her head.

"They'll let you return to visit with Bartley if she settles down."

Marta's whole body shook as she sat waiting for whatever might happen next. She rubbed her left thigh. Did she feel any new pain? No, but why did Bartley attack her? She acted possessed, like the woman in the scary movie *The Electric Monster* that she'd watched one night when she worked at the theater.

Suddenly, Marta felt her stomach roil. She raced down the hall to the public bathroom and threw up.

When she returned to the waiting area, she thumbed through magazines absentmindedly and watched the clock hands circle: thirty minutes, one hour, thirty more minutes. She replayed Bartley's reaction. Her eyes looked frightened when she grabbed Marta, like she might drown. But then she'd pushed Marta to the floor using super human strength.

Marta moved away from the receptionist, turned her back to the main room, and cried.

Two hours later, Marta sat beside Bartley in her suite, staring at a frightened, disheveled, red-eyed girl. Bartley stroked Marta's hands. "Did I hurt you, Marta? I'd never want to hurt you."

"No, I'm fine."

Bartley straightened and lifted her chin. "I told you I'd eat and gain back the weight, so why didn't you bring me pills?"

"I didn't have time. I'm only here for part of today. And I promised your mother."

Bartley let her body sag. Tears hung in her eyes. "She's wrong, you know. I can stop taking diet pills anytime I want."

Marta rubbed small circles on Bartley's shoulder. "Tell me about San Francisco and the big old house on Russian Hill. And all about dancing for a famous ballet company. I'm excited to come visit next summer."

In the late afternoon, Mrs. Timmons returned. "I hope you two had a good visit. It's time to get Marta to her plane."

Marta gripped Bartley's hands. "I promise to call you every week. Promise me you'll eat." Marta released Bartley's hands and backed away.

"I'll try, but I need..."

Marta shook her head. "Promise you'll eat."

Mrs. Timmons rode with Marta to the airport. They didn't speak for several minutes, giving Marta time to pull her thoughts together and try to make sense of what had happened.

"I'm sorry Bartley attacked you. Is your ankle okay?"

"I think so. I wish I'd known sooner that she was sick."

"So do I." Mrs. Timmons wiped her eyes and tucked her handkerchief in her sleeve. "It wasn't until she collapsed that we knew it was serious.

Looking back, she must have thought taking diet pills would be safe. I used them for years, to take off the winter weight, you know, before swim season."

"Bartley told me. She thought that if you took them they were safe for her to use as well."

Mrs. Timmons shook her head. "Ballet is so beautiful, but it demands so much from a dancer's body. Bartley always wanted to be perfect. She'll need to work hard to gain back her health. I should have paid more attention."

Marta didn't speak again until the limousine stopped at the airport terminal. "Thank you for inviting me to visit Bartley. She's a good friend. I know she'll get stronger now that she's getting help."

"Yes, she will. Thank you for coming, Marta. Your visit meant a lot to her."

The driver opened the car door for Marta. "I'll call her every Sunday."

30

Marta straightened her shoulders as she entered the dancers' door and walked to the dressing room. The flight home got her into Billings after eleven and in bed by twelve, but not to sleep. Starting her first rehearsal on three hours of sleep didn't bode well for her success. One pill would help her through the morning. As she swallowed it, she replayed Bartley's situation. She shuddered. After her audition she would start cutting back.

Several dancers said hello; most were surprised at seeing her return. She changed clothes, then joined Lynne to walk to the rehearsal.

"Where were you this weekend? I called but no one knew where you had gone. You missed a great last minute party at my place."

"A friend showed up unexpectedly."

"You could have brought her along."

Marta yawned.

Lynne studied Marta. "Looks like you two must have had a lot to talk about."

"We did." Marta shook out her hands and legs. The diet pill kicked in; she felt a surge of energy return. Now, if the knot in her stomach didn't interfere, she'd pick up the choreography with ease.

After struggling through warm-ups, Marta felt winded. The corps dancers standing around her looked ready to continue at a moment's notice. Her months without the rigor of rehearsals showed, even to herself.

"Let's talk before we begin the choreography." Damien smiled at the corps dancers. "Take a seat. I'd like to introduce you to our next program."

The dancers sat cross-legged on the floor, facing him.

"*Rhapsody in Blue* is an American piece written by Gershwin in the 1920s. We'll be using the symphony and two soloists: one on piano, the other on clarinet.

"Imagine a stage with a white backdrop covered with silvery stars and bold streaks of blue. You'll wear long, blue chiffon skirts and ballet slippers. The principals will wear silver costumes. Let me play the recording of the first section for you. I imagine most of you will recognize the opening clarinet slide."

Marta closed her eyes and pictured her father sitting in his rocking chair listening to the music. The tranquil introduction to the music pulled her along its graceful flow of notes. She swayed as she listened.

Damien lifted the needle off the record. "This is a change from our usual classical ballet that I hope will be well received. Your performance during the opening chords will set the mood for the entire work. I need you to be better than your best. Keep that in mind as you learn each dance."

The choreography required long slow moves as well as quick steps. Marta kept pace until her ankle tired, leaving her to walk through the steps rather than dance them. By the end of the hour her leotard was soaking wet, but she felt more alive than she had since her accident.

Every rehearsal during this last week in April resulted in the same situation: early on she danced as well as before the accident; midway her energy and ankle lagged. She iced her ankle before and after every practice. At least *pointe* shoes weren't required. That would have spelled disaster.

The first week of May raced forward. On the afternoons there were no corps rehearsals, Marta warmed up on her own until Damien was free to join her. Having the small practice room reserved for her lessons with Damien gave her ample space and a wall of mirrors to study her movements. And Madame couldn't chase her out.

The fact that Madame never spoke to her bothered Marta. It was as if they moved through the same building in separate worlds. Maybe she should make an appointment to talk with Madame. But what would she say? How are you today? I'm sorry I fell? Best to wait, do the audition, then speak with her.

Marta checked the clock: four o'clock. Damien should arrive soon. She needed every minute he could spare to perfect her audition. She restarted the record, posed, and stepped into the first *arabesque*. Damien stood in the doorway watching her practice. He nodded as he walked into the room. "Good. Your strength is returning. For the audition, you'll perform the first three minutes of the main theme. You've learned the steps, so let's refine your arm movements and your flow from one move to the next."

Marta used every ounce of energy and skill she could gather. Her ankle ached from the fall from when she visited Bartley a week ago; not the way she wanted to remember their visit. She shook her head to push the thoughts away. Damien stared at her, waiting for her full attention. She straightened and posed as he restarted the record.

Damien clapped the beat. "Reach further up and forward as you move. Stretch your back, elongate your entire body. Remember, you must think like a musical instrument being played by delicate hands."

ℐ

Each day after rehearsals two constants remained: sore muscles and ice packs. Each night she massaged her legs and soaked her tired feet before applying ice to her ankle. On the evenings Lynne came over, they exchanged back rubs and foot rubs.

"So, Marta, how is it to working with Damien?"

"It's great. He is patient and points out the details I need to show. I feel confident I can dance my audition so Madame will have to take me back."

"I'm glad to hear that. We need you; I need you. Can you imagine me facing Suzette and Marguerite alone? I don't think I can survive their whining and preening next fall without you pulling me back."

Marta laughed and pulled Lynne to her feet. "Come on. You need to keep me busy so I don't think about being alone so much. We can plan for the little girls, and you can help me bake for Damien's family."

"No thanks. I'm off to get a good night's sleep. We've got enough planned for the girls, and if I helped you bake, you'd need to toss it. You do remember I'm a disaster in the kitchen."

While Marta stirred the batter for two quick breads, she thought about Steve. His projects and tests kept him buried. They exchanged brief phone calls, but he seldom had time to stop in, and their trips around Billings had dropped away. He was closing in on his career much as she hoped she was closing in on her own.

Marta surprised herself by humming in the shower that evening. Everything was falling into place. Miss Wilson continued to treat her like an adult, so another visit with her sounded like a good idea. May's warm weather encouraged the flowers and her confidence to blossom. She continued to hum, content and hopeful that the pains she experienced every day would fade over the next three weeks, leaving her ready for the audition.

Sunday evening Steve broke away from his studies and work, and now he sat with Marta in the common room. He stretched. "I'm starting to understand how you feel when you have too much to do. I'm so tired from reworking my project and keeping up with other homework and tests, plus working at the paper."

"I thought you were enjoying your project."

"I am. But have you any idea of how much is written about the history of mining in the Billings area?"

Marta put her arm around his shoulder. "It will be over soon."

"Not really. I'll need to work through the summer session. Then I can walk through graduation after fall semester. Will you come to my graduation?"

"I'll try."

Steve stood and stretched again. "I'd better get back to work. I'll call you when I get a moment of free time. Think of me?"

"Always. And thanks for spending part of Mother's Day with me."

He hugged her close and spoke into her hair. "You sounded lonely. I knew you missed your mom, so…"

"So, thanks." Marta kissed him and walked him to his car. She watched him drive back toward the college. Miss Wilson was right. Other people felt the same tiredness she felt. Working through it must be part of being responsible for yourself.

The next morning Marta finished her exercises by eight-thirty and stood in the kitchen kneading dough, enjoying the twisting and folding and the smell of yeast. Early daisies swayed in the May breeze reminding her of the Gershwin choreography that swayed and blossomed as well. She enjoyed her private lessons with Damien, but not dancing with the rest of the corps. They either treated her like a bird with a broken wing or a mosquito to be brushed away. Once she mastered the audition selection, she'd be on her own and not have to face them again until next fall.

How would they treat her once she rejoined them for next season?

The past Sunday calls to Bartley lasted only a few minutes. She sounded tired even when Lynne entertained them both with stories of dancer flubs, arguments, and down right hissy fits. So far Lynne remained in the dark about Bartley's condition, just as Marta had promised Mrs. Timmons.

Marta rotated her bread dough in the greased bowl and covered it with a dishcloth. She grabbed an apple and headed to the common room.

The phone call came in at nine-thirty as Marta prepared to exercise.

"Marta? It's Lynne."

"You sound funny. Are you okay? Why aren't you in rehearsals?"

"I have bad news. Bartley died. Stay home. I'll be right ov—"

A shock wave traveled through Marta. She dropped the phone and crumbled to the floor. Tears flooded her eyes. Her body heaved, and her heart ached. How could this happen? Bartley said she felt stronger. Why weren't the doctors taking better care of her? Marta lay on the floor and cried.

Minutes ticked by. Marta washed her face, paced the common room, and checked the front window every few seconds. Where was Lynne? What could have possibly happened to Bartley? Maybe it was a belated April fool joke. No, Lynne would never joke about someone dying.

When Lynne drove up, Marta stood with the front door wide open. The minute she saw Lynne's face up close, her tears and the sag of her shoulders, Marta began to cry again. "What happened?"

Lynne wiped her face and shook her head. "She had a heart attack during the night. And this is even stranger. A nurse found her. A nurse? I didn't know she was sick, did you?"

Marta walked away from Lynne, then turned and swallowed. "I knew she was sick. Bartley's been in a clinic in Philadelphia. I visited her that weekend I said I had a friend in town."

"You saw her and you never mentioned it? What about our pact to have no secrets?"

"I promised her mother I wouldn't tell anyone."

Lynne stood and walked to the bay window. "So much for our pact. Why did they call you and not me?"

"I don't know. Maybe because you were busy with performances."

A quiet hung over the room as Marta explained her visit to Bartley. Her hand rested on Lynne's arm. "Let's go up to my room."

Lynne nodded and followed Marta upstairs. They sat cross-legged on the bed letting the silence spread.

"Tell me again about the diet pills, Marta."

"What do you mean?"

"I mean the part where Bartley asked you to share your diet pills with her."

Marta fidgeted and picked up her stuffed cat Bubbles. "What do you want to know."

"Everything."

Marta moved to her window and opened it before she sat in the rocking chair with her eyes closed. The fresh air carried the scent of lilacs.

"Marta? Spill it."

"I don't know when Bartley started taking pills for certain."

"What about you?"

"I started when we were on tour last December. They took the edge off my tiredness. Lots of people take them, Lynne."

Lynne stared at Marta. "Who takes diet pills? Name names, Marta."

Marta squirmed under Lynne's gaze. "I can't."

Lynne paced the room. "What if the pills caused her to die? You could be putting yourself in danger."

"I'm careful. I only take a few a week."

Lynne stopped pacing. "How few?"

Marta looked away and rocked.

"Marta?"

"One or two a day; sometimes three." Admitting this to Lynne felt right and wrong mixed together. At this moment, the no secrets pact loomed as a friendship breaker. If she understood the look on Lynne's face, she'd disappointed and deceived her best friend. They stared at each other. A silence hung in the room.

Lynne shook her head as she walked toward the bedroom door and placed her hand on the doorknob.

"Wait! Please. Let me explain."

Lynne turned and stared at Marta. "Okay. Try to make me understand why you'd take such stupid chances."

Marta closed her eyes. "It's hard to sit all the time and stay trim. My audition is less than two weeks away. I need the pills a little longer. I plan to quit."

"What if those pills killed Bartley?"

"That couldn't be the reason she died. She said she felt stronger."

"Stronger than what? Why didn't you trust me enough to tell me?"

"I promised Bartley and her mother."

Lynne resumed her pacing. "You said it yourself that she begged you for pills. If Bartley couldn't stop taking them, what makes you think you can?" Lynne skirted Marta and moved toward the bedroom door.

A surge of frustration gripped Marta. She stepped in front of her door and placed her palms against it. "You don't know how hard it is to come back and keep up with everyone, do you? You can't understand. You eat whatever you want while the rest of us struggle to stay slim. The pills help me keep up my energy when I'm wanting to eat your giant burger and your milk shakes. You don't get it, do you?"

Lynne reached around Marta for the door knob. "Who are you? You're scaring me, Marta."

They stood face-to-face in separate silences.

"I need to make a call," Lynne said.

Marta stepped aside, allowing Lynne to leave the room to use the hall phone. She turned her back toward Marta and spoke in whispers. Marta backed into her room listening to Lynne's voice, wanting yet not wanting to know who she spoke to and what she was being told.

When Lynne returned, she walked to the window and stood silent for a long minute. "Madame says the funeral is next Tuesday in Philadelphia. She's arranged for us to use the hotel meeting room that day for a local memorial."

Marta nodded and climbed onto her bed. She curled up and allowed fresh tears to stream down her face; she didn't wipe them away.

Lynne sat beside Marta.

"I miss her, Lynne. She was a special friend and a beautiful dancer. She loved the San Francisco Ballet. I'd never have had the confidence to go off by myself, would you?"

"We did, Marta. We came here. You were the one who took the biggest gamble. You didn't know anyone."

"Maybe you're right. But that was last fall." Marta looked around her room as if the answers were written on her wallpaper or her billowing curtains. She turned toward Lynne. "I don't want any more secrets between us. I want to tell you about the rest of my visit with her."

For half an hour Marta shared details and answered questions about her visit to Philadelphia. "She looked thin and acted like she'd explode if you made her sit still. She got so mad at me she shoved me to the floor."

"That's not the Bartley I know. She sounds crazy. And you're taking the same pills?"

Marta walked to the window. Outside, the street was empty. Marta tried to think of ways to explain the pills to Lynne. Her mind remained clouded. When she turned back toward Lynne, the door was open. She stood alone in her room.

Tears streamed down Marta's face. She'd never seen Lynne step away from any argument before this one. Was she mad or sad? Was she coming back, or was their friendship broken beyond repair?

Marta sat alone, paced, and waited. Lynne didn't return. Marta needed to do something to stop focusing on Bartley, so she went down to the kitchen. The dough she'd left on the work table oozed over the edge of the bowl and slid onto the counter. She buried her hands in the dough, pushing her fists into its yeasty stickiness. Tears streamed down her face as she scraped up the exhausted dough and dumped it into the garbage pail.

The hotel meeting room sign read *Timmons Memorial 1:00 - 2:00, Room A*. Marta and Lynne arrived fifteen minutes early. They turned on the lights, sat down without speaking, and waited.

A silver-framed photo of Bartley stood on the reception table beside a bouquet of white roses and a card addressed to Bartley's family. Marta touched the petals of the roses and shivered.

The conference table held a huge tray of quarter sandwiches, small white plates, a coffee urn, dozens of white cups, and a floral arrangement of wildflowers. Lynne picked up a note nestled in with the flowers and read aloud.

> *The Ladies Auxiliary of the Intermountain Ballet Company wish to express their condolences to the friends and family of Bartley Timmons. She was an extraordinary young woman.*

Marta sighed. "And an extraordinary friend."

Steve arrived. He sat quietly with Marta and Lynne in the circle of chairs they'd arranged. When dancers and townspeople arrived, the three acted as family, accepting cards and condolences, then inviting people to sit, eat, and talk.

At two o'clock Marta closed the door. "I don't think I could have done this much longer. I've never cried so much."

"It's probably the hardest thing I've done in my life," Lynne said as she wiped her eyes. "Were you surprised to see Karl here?"

"No," Marta said. "Karl's a nice guy when he's not forced to mop up our sweat. His mother is seriously ill. He said she'll be the next to go."

Lynne picked up Bartley's photo and placed it in her purse. "Damien came. I really like that guy. I didn't expect Madame to come, but she made an appearance, probably because it was expected of her."

Marta collected the cards from the small table and stuffed them into her bag. "Let's go, Lynne. I think we need to talk." She kissed Steve and gave him a hug. "Thanks for coming. I'll call you later."

Marta and Lynne drove to the neighborhood park near Marta's boarding house. The late afternoon sun soaked into their shoulders as they sat in the swings swaying back and forth without talking. How could the day be sunny and normal? Bartley was gone. Shouldn't the world look different?

Lynne stopped her swing and twisted to face Marta. "You need to stop taking those pills. Even if they didn't cause Bartley's death, they can't be good for you."

"I know."

"Is there anything I can do to help you? I mean, you have to stop."

Marta saw the serious look on Lynne's face. She couldn't afford to lose her last friend over diet pills. She nodded. "I know. I'll stop."

Over the next week Marta practiced until her body refused to move. She returned to her room each evening too exhausted to eat. Each day after breakfast she upped her diet pills, telling herself it was just until her audition on May 26. Then she'd quit.

On Saturday afternoon before her audition, Lynne dragged her for a drive to a four-building town called Molt. They split a sandwich at the lone cafe, then drove back roads trying to get lost for a few hours.

Marta stared out the front window of Lynne's wheezing car and swallowed down her sadness. "I might be gone by the little girls' recital. I'd be embarrassed to stay and be involved if I'm not part of the company."

"What? You want to leave me alone to prepare the little girls for their dances?"

Marta trailed her hand in the breeze as they drove back toward Billings. Her stomach ached and her voice caught in her throat as she answered. "Yep. I might. Better get all the work you can out of me before then."

"Hey, you'll make the company. I've watched you dance. You're a little stiff, but since you don't need *pointe* shoes at your audition, you'll do fine."

Marta wished she shared Lynne's certainty about the outcome. But every part of her body ached, especially her ankle. She'd practiced four hours each morning, then headed to the kitchen for an ice pack before taking a brief nap. Now she had one last day to prepare.

Sunday afternoon shadows crossed her window as Marta watched the street. Neighborhood children pedaled along the sidewalks with playing cards flapping against their tire spokes, laughing and racing to the tree at the end of the block. Younger children shouted "not it" and ran from one hiding place to another. Life was simple at six or eight or ten. Perhaps it could be simple at eighteen.

She splashed water on her face and went to practice one last time. Dancing would get her mind off everything beyond her control. Somehow it brought her closer to Bartley as well. They'd had their days together dancing, their trips, and their musketeer times. Marta needed to get stronger, to dance and to stay focused. She owed that to Bartley's memory.

The quiet in the basement usually comforted her. Today the silence hung like a heavy cloak. She sat a long while on her rickety chair trying to decide if she had the energy to stand and start. She took a diet pill from her pocket and swallowed it without water. It stuck in her throat. She swallowed harder.

After a dozen slow stretches, she sat on the chair massaging her calf. She held her breath as muscle spasms raced up her leg and tears blinded her. When she regained control, she forced herself to start the audition music.

The black disk spun, blurring the words on the label like a whirling pinwheel. The mournful clarinet and strings of the Gershwin music created an ache so deep her feet could not move. One sad crescendo after another tugged through her body. She swayed, imagining her feet moving to Damien's choreography. She loved Gershwin.

Marta shook out her arms and legs and restarted the record. She walked the steps, avoiding stress on her weak ankle, focusing attention on her arms and her location in the dance space. Again and again, she repeated the movements.

Sweat ran down her body. She used an old bath towel to wipe her arms and a mop to soak up the drips on the floor before she circled the room to cool down. She flopped down on the chair and sagged forward. The black, lifeless record had more energy than she could muster. Why did she feel so dizzy?

After a long series of deep breaths, she started the record to dance the selection one last time. Her hands, arms, and feet merged into the choreography. Her movements covered the entire basement as she forced her injured foot into proper positions. On and on she moved, dancing toward that special place where music and movement merged.

Everyday thoughts disappeared. Friends, family, and events vanished, replaced by Gershwin's melody. On and on, turning, lifting to *relevés*, and dipping to brush the floor. Over and over, working through her dizziness, perfecting her movements.

Until she felt something pop.

31

*M*arta's right ankle, her stronger one, popped. She felt a sharp pain like a bone sliding out of place.

A gasp escaped her lips as she pinwheeled her arms, trying to regain her balance. The fall off the porch at New Year's flashed through her brain. She stretched out her hands to break her fall, but it didn't help. She tumbled to the floor, bumping her head against the corner of the card table on the way down.

Marta lay sprawled on the cement floor, unwilling and unable to move, trying to make sense of what happened. She curled up to support her ankle with both hands. The record player needle circled the inner edge of the disk; its insistence matched the throbbing she felt beneath her fingers. Was her life circling back to her earlier fall? She crawled to the player and settled the needle on its bracket, then lay her head on the chair beside the table.

Her ankle lost its definition as her skin swelled. Her heartbeat pulsed through her ankle and her hands, as well as her chest. She needed ice and she needed to elevate her ankle. No one was home. She'd heard them share their plans to be out all Sunday afternoon. Could she crawl up the stairs? No. She felt so dizzy she thought she might vomit.

Marta lay back on the floor and put her injured foot on the chair. She replayed her moves before she heard the pop. She'd done two _balancés_ and a reach forward. Did the reach stress her ankle? It didn't matter now. Maybe she should try to crawl up the steps. She inhaled and started moving.

The cement floor made her bony knees ache, but she ignored the pain and managed to open the door. While she rested, she heard the front door open. She shouted, "Help! Help! I'm in the basement. Please! Help me!"

Shoes clomped down the stairs. Carol appeared. She bent down next to Marta, examining her like she might be a biology specimen stretched on the floor in front of her.

"What happened to you? Your face is white."

"My ankle. I need help getting up the steps."

Carol straightened. "Well, I can't lift you."

"I know. Could you go see if Mrs. B. is in her room or either of the men are home, please?"

Carol tromped up the stairs. When she returned minutes later she carried a tea towel filled with ice cubes. "No one's home. Put this on your ankle. I'll send someone down when they come in."

Marta sat alone on the floor icing her ankle after uttering a thank you to Carol, of all people.

The house remained so quiet Marta heard the sounds of cars passing on the street. When would everyone get back? It must be close to Sunday supper time. She leaned against the wall and closed her eyes. If they didn't return soon she'd try to climb the stairs. Could she still audition tomorrow, or should she cancel?

Within the next half hour James and Mrs. B. returned and helped Marta to the common room. She ate dinner off a tray with her foot elevated and thanked Mrs. B. for the steady stream of ice packs and for retrieving her crutches from her upstairs closet.

Mrs. B. accompanied Marta up stairs and turned back the bed covers for her. "It was a good thing Carol got back early. Starting the ice right away may be keeping the swelling down."

"Yes. I think it did. I'll need to thank her again for her help."

"Do you need anything else?"

"No. I'll just rest and call the doctor first thing in the morning."

"I'm sure you'll be fine, dear." Mrs. B. patted her shoulder and left.

Marta lay on her bed and replayed the move when she felt her ankle pop. Two *balancés,* just two; nothing dangerous or difficult.

By nine thirty the next morning, Marta sat in an examining room with her crutches tucked in beside her. Doctor Wycoff finished wrapping her ankle with an ace bandage and gave her pain pills. "This is just a strain, but since you are a dancer you'd best stay off it for a week; give your ankle a rest. Then we'll start a new therapy plan."

"What if I need to dance sooner than that?"

Dr. Wycoff shook his head. "With your history of anemia and now this, I'd wait a week. You need to ingest more calcium and strengthen your bones. Maybe I let you restart dancing too soon after your broken bone in January. We can't go back and re-examine that decision, so you'd best stay off your feet as much as possible over the next week."

"I'll try." That was a lie. Stay off her ankle for a week? She only had a few hours until her audition. There was no time to sit back and take pain pills. She shoved the bottle of pills into her purse, picked up her crutches, and hobbled out to the waiting room to call for a taxi to take her home.

Ten thirty. She sat in the common room staring at her right leg elevated and iced; the bandage lay in a heap next to her. Only a miracle would help now.

Minutes later Steve arrived and let himself in. "Hey, how are you? Mrs. B. called me at home. I just missed you at the doctor's office. Is there anything I can do for you?"

Marta shook her head. "Do you have time to sit with me?"

"Anything for you, Miss Fluff. Monday is my light day at school. I don't start until twelve. I could even make you lunch if you have Cheese Whiz and crackers."

Marta shook her head and couldn't find the smile needed to match Steve's little joke.

"Hey. It's going to be fine."

Marta drew up a stage smile buried inside her and plastered it on her face. There was no point in looking as sad as she felt. Maybe everything would be fine.

Steve massaged her calves as he talked about his upcoming newspaper assignments and shared funny stories he'd read off the news wire. Marta chuckled when he told her about a horse that followed a poodle all over downtown New York. They evaded capture until the horse stopped to snack on bushes in Central Park.

Steve pulled out the rough copy of his latest homework assignment: creating three unique pages: a front page, an editorial page, and a local news page. He spread them out on the coffee table beside Marta. "This professor likes us to think in new ways. We'll display our pages in the student union building so the students can vote on which ones appeal to them. My plan is to…"

Marta's focus drifted to the audition just hours away. She flexed her ankle and turned her attention back to Steve.

"These pages will be half our grade. I think I'm getting closer to a final idea. What do you think?"

"Guess you'd better stretch your imagination and outfox your fellow classmates." She knew he wanted to hear more praise, but for the life of her she'd not heard a word of what he'd said about his ideas.

Steve collected his pages and slid them into his briefcase. "The other half is my never-ending mining research. I'm so busy I can barely breathe." He stared at Marta. "Are you sure you're okay? Are you worried about your audition?"

She nodded. "I am. Sorry to be such poor company."

Steve checked his watch, ruffled her hair, and stood. "Sorry I have to go. Can't miss these next two classes. Each one is torture. Want me to fix you a quick lunch before I go?"

"No. I'm fine."

"Stay off that foot as long as you can. I know you'll have an amazing audition." He kissed her forehead, then her lips, and headed for the front door.

"Call me when you finish the audition, okay?"

"I will," she answered to an empty room.

After a long shower and an apple, she downed two diet pills. Then she sat watching the hour hand creep around the clock. Her ankle continued to throb. At four o'clock she use a shortened ace bandage to wrap her ankle, hobbled out, and checked the bike leaning against the back porch. Pedaling the bike would keep her muscles warm; she'd be ready to dance when she arrived.

She entered through the dancers' door and inhaled rosin and sweat. It hadn't been empty very long. She wiped her hands on her skirt, reliving her first day waiting on the steps. Maybe she should have called Lynne and asked her to stay after. No. Today she needed to be independent and do this on her own.

Numbness and butterflies crept through her body; her head spun. She shook out her hands and legs and touched the necklace Steve had given her at Christmastime. Today she broke the rule about no jewelry during practices. She needed a special bit of luck. She kissed it and tucked it inside her leotard.

Damien stood in the practice room, waiting for her. She straightened to walk as normal as possible toward him.

"Welcome back, Marta." He extended his hand.

She shook hands with him, then removed her layer of street clothes to reveal her leotard. Both her ankles were stiff; her right ankle remained slightly swollen as she pushed herself through a series of *pliés* at the *barre*. Maybe the bike ride hadn't been the greatest idea.

Perhaps she should ask Damien for extra time to recover from this latest setback. Lynne told her Madame was heading out to auditions over the weekend. If Marta delayed her audition, Madame might tell her she was too late. No, it was best to go ahead, take her chances, and dance today.

Marta stepped into a long chiffon practice skirt and hooked the waistband closed. A shyness enveloped her as she looked around the space where she'd been at home a few months earlier. Today it felt hollow and foreign.

At five o'clock sharp Madame thumped into the room and stood by the tall stool. She surveyed Marta from toe to head and nodded ever so slightly toward her. Marta curtsied.

Damien set the needle to the appropriate ring on the record. It scratched along the grooves, then slid onto the selection.

Marta rotated her ankles and stretched tall waiting for the Gershwin music to begin. On the opening clarinet slide she drifted into the music using exaggerated *developés* to match the long, lazy woodwind solo. Though both ankles ached, she kept dancing, ignoring the pain and the cramping, forcing her feet to point and *relevé* at the precise moments the music demanded.

On and on, she danced, alternately sweeping toward the floor and stretching toward the ceiling, transitioning from the adagio to the quick footwork. With the skirt caught up in her hands, Marta executed the series of *relevés* and turns, ignoring the throbbing in both ankles.

Damien lifted the needle off the record. The quiet in the room allowed Marta to hear the throbbing of her heartbeat in her ears. She slowed her breathing, curtsied to Madame and Damien, and straightened to stand in fifth position, fighting the tiredness that pressed through her body. Her audition was over.

"Thank you, Marta," said Damien. "We'll invite you back in a few minutes."

Marta sat on the hall floor too tired to pace or walk to the benches in the women's dressing room. Did they notice her struggles near the end of the selection, or had she shown enough strength and style to impress them?

How about her *relevés*? Her ankles weren't as strong as she needed them to be. Would her past strength and stamina be remembered today?

The practice room door opened. Damien approached her, smiled, and reached out a hand to help her to her feet. As they returned to the practice room, she studied his face but couldn't read his expression.

"Thank you for coming today, Marta," Damien said. "It's obvious that you understand the emotion of the music. I wish the others moved with your conviction. Throughout the season we've appreciated your ability to nuance each gesture. Your lines are strong and you've shown your ability to dance well within the corps."

Marta swallowed and nodded. Good. They'd noticed her efforts during the season.

Damien crossed his arms and tipped his head. "Here's our problem. Your feet still lack strength. It's been five months since your last performance. You've struggled with your endurance during recent practices with the company. It's probably too soon for you to return to the rigors of daily practices, let alone performances."

Madame leaned against the high stool with her head turned away from Marta. As she turned to face Marta, she lifted her chin, but then her expression softened. "Even if you take the summer and work out every day, there's no guarantee you'll regain your endurance or foot strength."

Marta swallowed hard and nodded. "I followed the doctor's orders and didn't practice until he gave me permission. Then I worked every day at home."

"We know. You've been a hard worker." Damien smiled. "Today you struggled. Did something happen recently?"

Madame nodded. "Today you moved like you were wearing over-sized rubber boots."

Marta looked away, unable to meet Damien's eyes until she swallowed down her tiredness. "I had a setback yesterday, but I still wanted to come and try. I knew you were heading out to auditions, and I hoped I could hold onto my position. I didn't mean to waste your time."

"You didn't waste our time," Damien said. "We know how much you want to dance. You're just not ready."

Madame leaned forward. "We've had our issues, but you've been dedicated to the company, and you have worked hard. Recovery from injuries takes more time than most of us are comfortable waiting through. If you rush your return, it may cause a life-changing injury. It has for many dancers."

"If I get stronger over the summer and the next year, may I audition again?"

Damien looked at Marta with the kind of smile that had encouraged her over the past few weeks. "We know you want to dance, but it's too risky for you to rush a return. Focus on getting stronger."

Madame's face wore a look of concern. "You need to heal and then rebuild your strength slowly." She paused. "This is a business. We can't wait on your recovery."

Marta felt the finality of Madame's comment. "I understand." Inside, she felt her heart shrink to the size of a walnut. Outside, she held herself tall. "Thank you for your time. I enjoyed being part of the company." She curtsied and walked from the room, holding onto the tattered remains of one last stage exit.

32

$\mathscr{A}$s Marta exited the front of the building, she slowed. Lynne sat on the steps and Steve leaned against his car parked at the curb. Marta forced a smile as Lynne stood and hurried toward her.

"Well? How did it go?"

Marta lifted her chin and pulled in her lips. She shook her head.

Lynne gasped. "Why? What happened?"

Marta wiped her eyes on the sleeve of her leotard. "Damien warned me that I might be rushing my return."

"You told him about yesterday, right?"

"No. I didn't want to sound like I was making excuses. He noticed my weakness today. It probably didn't matter anyway. I wasn't ready."

"I'm sorry, Marta. Did Madame say anything?"

"She shook her head. I saw her grimace as I finished my turns. She said she doubted I'd regain enough strength to dance by next fall."

"That ugly cow!"

"No, Lynne, she's right. I'm weak; I won't recover by August."

"What else did she say?" Lynne held Marta's hand, alternately squeezing and rubbing it.

"She kind of wished me well."

"Hm-m. The old girl has a bit of compassion after all."

Steve stayed by his car, only stepping forward after Lynne finished consoling Marta. He reached out for her hand, enclosing it in his own. "I'm sorry, Marta. I was sure you'd make it. Was it the injury yesterday?"

"Partly, but I wasn't ready."

"Want to go for a drive? Or I can take you home."

Marta shook her head. Tears rolled down her face. "I've got the bike. I'll get myself home. I need to be alone for a little while."

Steve kissed her cheek but said nothing more.

As she walked toward the bike stand, she stopped and turned to face her friends. They hadn't moved. Both looked concerned. "Thanks for being here. You are both important to me. I'll be fine."

That evening the only sound in Marta's room came from the rockers of her chair. She'd refused to see her friends or take their calls. She'd skipped dinner and sat with ice packs on both ankles, not feeling the icy coldness against her skin. By three a.m. all her tears were spent. One ache remained: to be gathered in her mom's arms.

At dawn, she stretched and walked to the window. When she pushed the curtains aside, she saw Steve's car parked at the curb. He stood leaning against his fender, arms crossed, staring up at her window. He waved when he saw her.

Marta opened the window and leaned out. "What are you doing?'

"Waiting to see if you needed anything."

"Have you been here all night?"

He walked closer to Marta's window. "Yeah. I thought if you looked out and saw me maybe you'd want to talk or go for a ride."

Marta wiped the new tears from her face. "You're too much. I don't know what to say."

"Say you'll come down, go for a ride, and get breakfast with me. I'm starving."

She laughed. "You're crazy. Give me a few minutes. I need a shower and clean clothes."

Marta rubbed her hair dry, ran a comb through it, and grabbed the first clothes her fingers touched. Did they match? Who cared? Nothing mattered anymore when she got down to it; except perhaps being with Steve.

Marta snagged two biscuits and two apples off the kitchen work table before she walked to Steve's car.

"Let's go to The Rims, okay?" Steve said.

"Sounds good."

They sat on the boulders, snacked, and watched sunlight skim the ridges to the east. A hot day looked to be on its way, the kind that made Marta nostalgic for the cool mornings back home.

Steve sat with his arm on the back of the boulder where Marta sat. He made no attempt to touch her. He gazed straight ahead with no emotion showing on his face. She sensed he didn't see the scenery.

She admired his profile. He gave off a comfortable manner, impetuous at times, but comfortable all the same. "Thanks for being there this morning."

"Where else would I be? I care about you. I know we've had a couple of rough spots, but I care; probably too much."

Marta half smiled and wiped her eyes. "It's been hard. I've been all mixed up. I didn't know how to be half of a couple."

Steve faced her and captured her hands. "Believe me, I know. I saw you struggle against my pushing. I'm sorry. I didn't want to lose you. Lynne told me you've been taking the same pills as Bartley. But you've stopped, right?"

"They're only to help me stay trim and to boost my energy."

"But Marta, you've stopped, haven't you?"

She didn't answer.

"Marta? Tell me."

"I plan to. Now that I'm not part of the company, I don't need them as much."

Steve shook his head; his hands tightened on hers. She pulled her hands free and tucked them under her bottom. An energy-charged silence hung between them.

"What are your plans, Miss Fluff?"

"Go home to Bremerton and figure out what to do with my life."

"Why can't you stay here and figure it out?"

That was a good question. Why couldn't she stay? She could find a job, pay off her doctor bills, and see Steve most every day. Could she be around Lynne, always talking about practices and performances? No. That would be torture.

"Marta? Why can't you stay?"

"There's not much left in Billings for me."

"Not even me?"

Marta shrugged. "I want there to be us, but you're busy starting a career and I'm...I don't know who I am. That's why I need to go home."

"You know how I feel about you, and now you're leaving?"

"Don't put it all on me. If I did stay, when would I see you?"

"As often as I could get away."

"If you are realistic, how often is that?

He hesitated. "I can't be certain. But... You might be right to leave. I want you to do what you need to help you recover."

They sat in silence watching the city below come to life. As the sun rose higher, it heated the air to a near stifling temperature. Steve stood and reached out his hand to Marta. "I'm still hungry. Will you go to breakfast with me?"

"Of course," she said as she accepted his hand.

They sat at a small table in The Granary. Marta kept her head down and pushed her scrambled eggs around on her plate. She nibbled on the toast but avoided the hash browns. Sitting here with Steve was harder than she expected. This might be their last meal together. She sighed and forked up a bite of her eggs.

"Eat. You might feel better."

Marta hesitated, swallowed, then pointed her fork at Steve. "I am eating." She laid the fork on the table. "These last two days have destroyed my appetite. I feel like I'm in mourning again, like when Bartley died. I can't really explain it."

Steve looked at her and nodded. He shoved his plate away and leaned his hands on the table as if he was waiting for her to continue.

Marta watched his eyes. He looked at her but said nothing. She fidgeted and bit off a small corner of toast. "I'm sorry." Tears slid down her face. She ignored them. "I can't handle anything right now. I need to get back and call my mom."

Steve gave her a brief nod, picked up the check, and followed her toward the exit. While he paid, she stepped out into the sunshine and looked at the traffic and the people walking along the sidewalk. She'd miss Billings and Steve and Lynne and Mrs. B., but not the heat. So much had happened in such a short time. Now it felt like she'd imagined all of it. Maybe she had.

On the boarding house porch, Steve took her hand loosely and rubbed his fingers across her knuckles. "I'm sorry things haven't gone as you'd hoped. If going home is what you need to do, I understand. Know that you'll always own a piece of my heart, Miss Fluff." He kissed her cheek and left.

Marta sat on the porch swing and let the waves of tears inside surge through her. There were no easy answers; something or someone had to change.

When she returned to her room, she alternately sat on the bed and paced. The pills kept coming up lately, first with Lynne and then with Steve. Was taking one or two a day, or maybe three a day, too many? Hardly. Plenty of people did that. Even Bartley's mom had taken them, and she was fine.

Bartley had been different. She skipped meals and took handfuls during the day. Marta only took them when she needed them, at first to boost her energy and then later to help control her weight while she wore the cast. Sometimes she did skip meals, but that was because Mrs. B.'s food was so rich. Since she started preparing for the audition, she'd only taken them when she became too tired to keep practicing. Plus, they didn't give her the jitters anymore. That was a good sign, wasn't it? Or did it mean she'd become dependent on them?

Marta stopped pacing and picked up a photo of Bartley. She traced her smile and remembered how much she'd admired Bartley's grace, her dancing style, and her thinness. When did Bartley's use of the pills get out of control? Was she dependent on them last Christmas, or did the pressure of moving and dancing in San Francisco make the difference? Did it matter when?

Marta stopped in front of her mirror and stared at the pale face looking back at her. Was she addicted to the diet pills like Bartley? No. She could stop whenever she didn't need them. Now that the audition was over, did she still need them? She resumed pacing. Her body trembled like she was freezing and her hands began to shake. What was happening to her?

She looked around her room, seeing nothing in particular. Suddenly, she opened drawers and rummaged through the pockets of her coats and sweaters, gathering pills, creating a small pile on her dresser. The small white ovals looked like polished aspirin waiting to soothe a headache or backache. Could she throw them away? Should she? Marta resumed her pacing. Each time she passed the dresser, she looked at the pills.

She gathered them up, set them in her sink, and turned on the warm water. Slowly they dissolved and disappeared down the drain. Instead of relief, Marta felt a hollowness in her chest, an emptiness, a loss. She exhaled a long, slow breath as the warm water continued to circle in the sink. As she turned off the water, she knew her next step.

Marta stretched the phone cord into her room and sat on her bed. While she waited for the call to go through, she relived her scrambled emotions. When she heard, "I'll accept the charges," she straightened.

"Mom," she said, steadying her voice, "I'm coming home."

33

"*Y*ou've made up your mind then?" Mrs. B. said.

"I have. It's hard to leave, but it's time." Marta sat with Mrs. B. in her private rooms drinking a cup of hot tea.

"You know you're welcome to stay here. I've enjoyed your company. You're like a daughter."

"I can't stay, Mrs. B. I need to go home and figure things out."

Mrs. B. nodded. "I understand. It's important to move forward, isn't it?"

"I've never considered being anything but a dancer. Now I need to find some way to support myself."

"You liked working with the little girls, didn't you? Perhaps you can teach ballet."

"Maybe. Once I mend. Or maybe I can get a job baking at McGavin's or start a sewing business."

They sat in silence, the only sound an occasional sip or cups resting back on their saucers. Marta took her final swallow, put her cup on the tray, and stood. "Thank you for the tea and everything else. I don't know what I'd have done without your help."

Mrs. B. stood and put her arms around Marta. "The pleasure has been mine, believe me."

Marta sat in her darkened room, listing all the things she'd miss: the rocking chair, the tall sash windows, the warm blast of heat when it finally reached her floor vent on cold mornings. But most of all, she'd miss time spent with Mrs. B. in the kitchen.

When she turned on her bedside lamp, the true nature of the room surprised her. She ran her hand over the scars on the rocker and the bed frame. She touched the spider cracks in the glass in the tall window facing the street. How had she not noticed them when she moved in? Perhaps this being her first place alone colored her view of the room. It *had* been comfy. It *had* looked fresh and crisp. Now, seeing its ordinariness made it easier to leave.

The following morning Marta called her mom with details. "You're sure it's okay if I stay with you until I can find work and set aside money to find my own place?"

"Of course, dear. When you left, the house became too quiet. I'll be glad you'll be here when I get up in the morning. And don't worry, your room is ready for you to come back and clean it."

Marta laughed. "Thanks a lot, Mom."

Lynne called later that night. "So it's for sure? You don't want to stay with me? We could terrorize Madame."

"I can't."

"I knew you'd say that. I'd probably do the same thing."

"Really?"

"Yep. Marta, you aren't the only one who misses home. I know I don't say it, but I miss my family, more now since Bartley died."

The phone line remained quiet for long seconds. "But, hey, Marta, we'll have a big party at my place. We can celebrate your escaping Billings."

"No, Lynne. It's...I don't want a party. I want get on the train and leave."

"But, Marta—"

"No, Lynne. Please?"

"Okay," Lynne said. "Whatever you want."

"That's what I want. Come over tomorrow afternoon. I have a few things to leave with you."

Marta arranged three boxes on her bed: one for home, one for Lynne, and one for giveaways. After sorting for an hour, she sat in the rocker going through her *pointe* shoe ribbon box. The satin ribbons felt silky as they dropped through her fingers. Should she count them, toss them, or keep them? She removed the last of the diet pills she'd hidden in the box, put them in her purse, and set the ribbon box next to her going home pile. She could always change her mind later.

When Lynne arrived, her aunt and the little girls came in as well with smiles and giggles.

"What's this?" Marta said. "It's not a dance day."

"We decided to have a little party in your honor," Mrs. Meadows said. "And the girls have something for you."

Lucy handed Marta a shoe box. "These are for you. Open them now."

Marta peeked inside. The box held a pile of cards. A laugh spread from her heart to her lips. One by one she looked at every card decorated with an assortment of little girl drawings: dancers, hearts, rainbows, sunshine, houses with smoking chimneys, flowers, horses, and cats. Each card said they'd miss her and hoped she'd be able to dance soon.

"Thanks, ladies. I'll keep these forever." Marta pressed them to her chest and allowed herself to cry.

"Will you come back for our recital?" Brenda asked.

"Not this year. Maybe next year."

"Where will be practice and learn to dance?" Carmen said.

"Mrs. B. might let you come here until you find another place. She loves to listen to your dance music playing."

Mrs. Meadows returned from her car carrying a pink cake with a ballerina on the top. "The girls picked this out for you."

"You're the ballerina on the top," Tracy said.

They took the cake to the basement to eat. Each girl danced for Marta, making up ideas on the spot. Lynne led them through their group dance, then their solos. All the while Marta smiled, feeling joy spread through her body.

After the little girls left, Marta took Lynne up to her room. She'd packed everything except her photos. Now she watched Lynne sift through the box intended for her use.

"Good grief!" Lynne said. "What did you leave me, all your dirty laundry?"

Marta laughed. "No, I left you the solo costumes for the little girls and plenty of odds and ends. Keep looking. You'll see."

Lynne pawed through the box, then dumped it on the floor. "You left a lot. You know I can't sew. How can I finish the costumes?"

"All you need to do is hem the sleeves and bottom edges and put on snaps and you'll be set," Marta said. "You can figure out a headpiece if you want."

"I guess I can handle that." Lynne held up a sweater. "Hey, isn't this mine? How did you get this?"

"You gave it to me after Christmas when you got a new one."

"Oh, that's right. Don't you want it? You can wear it and think of me." Marta took back the sweater.

They sat on the bed talking until Lynne checked the clock. "I've got to go. Got a late date tonight. Met him at the bookstore. He thinks I'm wonderful, especially since I told him I was a soloist. I might be next year; what's a little lie, huh?"

Marta shook her head. "You're so funny. He's lucky to know you regardless of whether you solo or not." Marta reached for Lynne's hands. "I'll miss all your crazy dating stories."

"I'll call you and bore you with them." Lynne piled things back into the box. "Oh! I have the latest on Madame and Herbert." Lynne sat down on the bed and leaned in close to Marta as if they might be overheard. "His wife is leaving him. And, get this, he's moving to New York. His company bought a plant back east that makes parts for his ah, that whatchamacallit, so he's out of here."

"Who's going to head up the patrons?"

Lynne cleared her throat as if to make a speech. "His wife. Diana had the money all this time. Isn't that a hoot? Her grandmother was Arinna Darvinilla, the ballerina.

"More news. There's a rumor that the Intermountain Ballet Company will start a ballet school in the near future. Diana insisted the new ballet academy be named for her grandmother. Madame had a fit. She thought it would be named for her. Who'd want to a member of the Cosper Ballet Academy?"

Marta closed her eyes and allowed herself a moment to feel sorry for Madame. What had happened to her to make her sour? It must have been very serious and heartbreaking.

Lynne stood and hoisted the box. "I'll see you tomorrow. I'm cooking for you, so get a bottle of Pepto and be ready at six thirty. And this time it's not a TV dinner. I'm fixing food that doesn't come in an aluminum tray!"

"Lynne?"

"Don't worry, it's not a party. I want you to have a good reason to leave town, and my cooking should do that."

☙

Late Wednesday morning, Marta entered the ballet company building through the front door. Karl sat in his usual place with the morning paper spread across his ample middle.

"Hi, Karl."

"Miss Marta. Nice to see you again. Ready to start dancing again, huh?"

"No, I'm leaving. My ankle hasn't healed enough for me to dance. Could I go up and see Damien?"

"Go on up. He's in all day now that rehearsals are winding down."

Karl stood and moved his chair aside. "Miss Marta? I'm sorry about your ankle. I have somethin' for you." He fumbled around in his desk, then handed her a photo. The inscription said, "Best Wishes, Maria Tallchief."

"Miss Tallchief danced here once. I managed the backstage crew. Such a beautiful dancer."

Marta looked at the photo. "I can't take this, Karl. It's yours."

"Naw. I'm retiring next spring. You take it. You've been a nice gal. I want you to have it."

"Thanks. May I give you a hug, Karl?"

Karl came out of his little room and the two hugged. "You be careful with that ankle, Marta. I'll miss you."

"I'll try, Karl. I'll miss you. Thanks for the photo."

Marta climbed the stairs and knocked on the office door. She heard, "Come in," and entered the room.

"Marta!" Damien stood, came around his desk, and greeted her with a hug.

"I wanted to thank you for helping me prepare for the audition."

"My pleasure. You tried your best. Be proud of that. What are you going to do now?"

"Go home. Keep working on my ankle. I want to dance again, if I can."

"And you might. Let me know if I can help in any way. You have lots of wonderful skills. It would be a shame for you to waste your talent."

"Thanks for your kindness." Marta looked to her feet. As she opened the door, she stopped. "Good luck with the tribute performances. The Gershwin evening should be a popular performance."

"I hope so. It's always a gamble to try something new and different."

Outside the office, she leaned against the wall until her breathing slowed and a calmness settled in. She had tried, done her best, but now it was time to step away, to create her own new and different.

With the rest of the day free, Marta strolled through town, picking up small gifts for the boarders, Mrs. B., and Lynne. Then she headed home to finish packing.

The dinner at Lynne's ended up being spaghetti with a jar of marinara sauce, a lettuce wedge salad with mayonnaise for dressing, and Coca Cola in wine glasses. They sat and laughed, talking about the drama at the company and their encounters with Madame and how they missed Bartley.

"Well, Marta, we had an exciting year, didn't we? I could have done without the sad parts."

"I agree." Marta fiddled with the edge of her place mat, then let her eyes wander around Lynne's apartment before she looked at Lynne. "I'll miss you so much. I promise to come back next year to see the little girls dance."

"I'll hold you to that." Lynne stood and collected their dishes as a knock sounded at the door. "Get that, will you?"

Marta opened the door. Steve was standing on the porch.

Marta's eyes widened. "Hi. How did you know...?" She turned and shouted, "Lynne?"

Steve touched Marta's hand. "Don't be mad. Lynne and I set this up. May I come in?" He handed her the largest bouquet of daisies she had ever seen. "I hope you like daisies."

Lynne joined them. "Of course she likes daisies. I thought you weren't going to make it."

"Had to raid my aunt's shop. Couldn't find enough wild ones."

Marta held the bouquet, enjoying the yellow and white daisy faces. There was no way she could stay upset with their tricking her. "Thanks, Steve."

"Are you ready to go, or should I wait in the car?"

Lynne put her arm around Marta. "If you don't take her soon I'll probably start to cry all over again, and that isn't a pretty scene."

Marta leaned her head against Lynne's shoulder. "I'll think of you every day, especially when I wear the blue sweater. Call me, write, and please come visit. I, I don't know what I am going to do without you." Marta began to cry.

"Now don't get me started again." Lynne wiped her eyes as she pushed Marta toward the door. "Get her out of here before the flood breaks. I'll see you tomorrow at the train."

"No, Lynne. Say good bye here. Please?"

Lynne grabbed Marta and hugged her tightly, crushing the flowers. "Whatever you want. You be happy and call me, hear?"

"I will." Marta headed out the door, then rushed back to hug Lynne. "Oh, Lynne, I'll miss you so, so much!"

"Go! Get out of here!"

Steve drove Marta to The Rims. The city lights sparkled in the warm evening. They wandered the edge, watching car lights below them move like grounded stars. He took Marta's hand and kissed her fingers.

She leaned against his chest. "Your being at Lynne's was a nice surprise."

"I'm glad you weren't mad." Steve put his arms around her shoulders. They stood quiet for long moments. "Marta, I want to tell you something important."

"What?"

"Okay. I've mentioned this several times, but you usually react so strongly I'm almost afraid to try again."

"What, Steve?"

He brushed aside her hair and traced the side of her face with his fingers. "From the first day I saw you, I knew you were special. I want you to know that I will always care about you."

Marta lay her head against his chest, listening to the loud thumping of his heart; it matched her own. "I care about you too, Steve."

"You do? For real?"

"Yes. I didn't want to, but I've always cared for you."

"Really? Then stay here. I'll work for the paper in town."

Marta shook her head. "I need to figure out who I am going to be since I'm not a dancer. I need time for everything to settle down. And you need space to think about where you want to work. I'd feel guilty if you settled for something less than what you dream about doing."

"So, you care about me, right?"

"Course I do. At first I needed to focus on my dance career. I didn't know how to handle being a girlfriend at the same time."

"Do you know how to handle it now?"

"Yes. When you're not around I feel like something, someone, is missing."

"You tell me this, and now you're leaving me?"

She nodded against his chest. "Can you understand? I have to leave to get back on track."

"Sure."

They stood in a knotted hug. Marta tried to absorb his presence, to save it for the times ahead when they'd not be together.

"Will you write to me in San Francisco or wherever I end up? You could come visit me or I could visit you. I don't want to lose you, Miss Fluff."

"You won't."

"I'll try to call you every Sunday. I promise I'll do a better job this time."

"I'll count on that."

Steve released his hold on her, moving her away so they could see each other's faces. "Can I entice you to wear the bracelet I gave you before I left for San Francisco?"

Marta studied his face. Was he serious? "You still want me to have it?"

"Of course. I hoped you'd agree to wear it one day." He pulled the box from his pocket, opened it, and held up the bracelet. The faint city lights made the diamonds sparkle like stars.

His fingers shook as he hooked the clasp. Marta touched his fingers and held them against the bracelet. "This is so beautiful. Are you sure you want me to have this, Steve?"

"Positive." He kissed her and let out a sigh. "Thank heavens you didn't say no this time."

Marta laughed. A tangled sensation grew inside her. "I've been so confused and moody and selfish. I'm trying to figure things out. One thing I do know is that I love you."

He kissed her again. "It's about time, Miss Fluff."

They stood wrapped together, alternately holding each other and kissing. When another car appeared on the side road, Steve released all but her hand. "We'd better go."

An hour later he backed down the boarding house porch steps, pulling Marta's hands along. "Tomorrow's a big day."

"I wouldn't call it that. But remember, you promised not come to the train. I can't stand saying good bye again. Promise?"

"I promise." He smiled and blew a kiss. "I love you, Miss Fluff."

"I love you too, ink boy."

Marta stood on the porch until Steve's car disappeared. Then she sat back in the swing. In a few hours she'd be on her way home, stepping into a life that wouldn't be choreographed until she set it in motion.

34

*S*unrise. Pale gray clouds covered the sky as Marta stood on The Rims one last time. The bike ride and the walk up the long hill wore her out, but she had been determined to make the trek on her own.

After nine short months she could pick out numerous landmarks: her boarding house street, the highway cutting east to west through the valley, the Beartooth Mountains, the Yellowstone River. She'd grown to love these open spaces, the cottonwoods, the big sky of Montana. But being a sea level, Puget Sound girl, she missed a cool edge in morning weather. Not long now until she'd be back home, for better or worse.

Late in the afternoon, Marta said her goodbyes on the boarding house porch. James hugged her. "You're a nice person. I hope you find what you're looking for."

Marta cried and hugged him tightly.

Shorty cleared his throat. "I hope when you dance in your old garage studio, you'll remember us. I listened to your music every time I heard you in the basement. It made me feel like I helped you in some tiny way. Did you get those eighty-four ribbons?"

"I came close, Shorty. I'm taking eighty-three ribbons home." Marta patted his slumped shoulders, then pulled him into a hug. "Thanks for remembering my ribbons."

That left Carol. Did she want or need to say goodbye to her? As Marta considered her options, Carol stepped out. "You're leaving? Well, good-bye." Carol walked to sit in the porch swing, set it in motion, and watched Marta with disinterest, as if she were a passerby, not someone she'd shared a house, meals, and a bathroom with over the last nine months.

Marta took Mrs. B.'s hand and gave her a small ballerina figurine she'd found in the second hand store. "I hope you'll come for a visit. My mom and I would both love it."

Mrs. B. hugged Marta. "You take care of yourself. You're talented in many ways. You'll find a way to dance again or something else to wrap your heart around."

A cab pulled up in front of the boarding house. Marta climbed in and waved until it turned the corner. Her head and her heart ached as she headed to the train.

The early evening train vibrated in readiness to depart. Passengers boarded, dragging luggage and children through the aisles. Marta sat in a window seat looking out at the depot, thinking about her life heading in an unknown direction. Her years of dancing and dreaming swirled around like dust. She fidgeted with the bracelet from Steve and touched the Christmas necklace tucked inside her blouse. She smiled, thinking of these tokens of their future together. Would that piece of her future hold together across so many miles and unknowns? She hoped so.

Marta caught a movement along the platform. She leaned forward to look out the window. Lynne and Steve smiled and waved as they opened a long, hand printed banner that read, "We love you, Miss Fluff." Lynne shrugged as if to say "how could we not come to say goodbye?"

Laughter filled Marta's heart as tears filled her eyes. Inside she broke apart, but she stifled a hysterical sob inching up her throat. She wiped her eyes and raced to the stairway and leaned out. She waved and waved shouting, "I love you both!"

The train lurched. The clatter of its circling wheels began. Her friends ran beside the train until they reached the end of the platform.

Marta stood in the stairway watching Lynne and Steve grow smaller and smaller. Within a short time, the entire city of Billings shrank away. Even The Rims dissolved into the prairie countryside. She returned to her seat and took a deep breath. She closed her eyes as the train rocked from side to side heading west.

"Miss? Miss?"

Marta awoke with a start, trying to remember where she was. On the train. A porter stood next to her seat, waiting for her to come fully awake.

"Excuse me, miss, but your friend handed me this package and asked me to give it to you when we'd left Billings." He handed her a small wrapped box.

"Thank you," she said.

Marta untied the ribbon, undid the wrapping, and lifted off the lid. A envelope inside said "Read this first." She opened the envelope and read:

> Marta, you left me more than your dirty clothes and the little
> girl costumes in that box. I thought you'd want to take this home
> with you as well.
>
> Lynne

Under the card she found another wrapping; so like Lynne to make things complicated. Inside that wrapping she found one pink ribbon with a tiny note attached that read:

> Found this tucked in the pocket of a blouse you stuffed in my take-
> away box. Best of luck on collecting your next eighty-four ribbons.

Tears streamed down Marta's face as she ran her fingers along the silky pink ribbon. She'd gotten her eighty-four ribbons after all. Did it matter anymore? Yes, it still mattered a lot.

She sat back, fingering the ribbon and watching the small mountain towns pass by as if playing on a large movie screen. Soon they'd start the climb into the Beartooth Mountains, leaving the prairie, Billings, and her career with the Intermountain Ballet Company behind.

Marta opened the pouch of stones she carried in her pocket, coiled up the ribbon, and dropped it inside. Dad wouldn't mind her sharing space in the pouch for a new treasure. Would he have agreed with her decision to return home? She hoped so. She missed him every day. Now she'd add Steve, Lynne, and Mrs. B. as people she'd also miss.

As she slid the pouch back into her pocket, a small kernel of expectation settled inside her, pushing away the sadness she'd been holding onto so tightly. She'd lived her dream of becoming a professional dancer and reached one goal. Now it was time to reach for a new one.

Marta curled her legs up under her skirt and turned to watch the scenery. The gentle rocking of the train, like the motion of a rocking chair, soothed her.

Next stop, home.

Author Notes

A book is like a ballet. I took the lessons and practiced over several years before I was ready to audition and actually write the book.

My mentors provided ongoing inspiration like a ballet summer camp, building up my skills. Lauraine Snelling invited me to join her intensive workshop. She stressed the importance of stepping into the characters' lives to understand what they were thinking and why. The Snoopy Dancers, the writers I met there, became my first cadre of support. Thanks, Ceil, Nancy Jo, and Eileen.

My second mentor, Kirby Larson, asked probing questions which highlighted my strengths and what I needed to continue to practice.

Like ballet, I had numerous practice sessions, sharing my interpretations in an effort to receive honest, useful feedback. Thanks, critique groups: Karen, Dusty, Dick, Sue, Gail, and Bill and Gretchen, Maureen, Nicki, and Emily. I appreciate your acting as my corps de ballet and supporting my debut novel.

Special thanks go out to my parents for providing me the opportunity to dance and to my dance teacher, Margie Speck, who taught me to love ballet. My first editors Ceil, Gretchen, and Nancy Jo and my early readers, Linda, Marilyn, and my husband trusted me to follow my dancing spirit through to the final bow.

My developmental editor, Sarah Overturf, acted like a ballet master in a dress rehearsal. Together we smoothed out the movement of the story.

Lastly, my publisher and creative designer, Karin Hoffman of Tendril Press, choreographed my performance. She brought the story to life as a completed work. Now, I'm waiting in the wings, hoping the audience, my readers, enjoy all the acts of the performance.

Thanks also to my husband, Rich, and my family for supporting me as I created Marta's ballet world.

Chat, Comment, and Connect with the Author

Book clubs and schools are invited to participate in FREE virtual discussions with Paddy Eger.

Chat:
Invite Paddy to chat with your group via the web or phone.

Comment:
Ask thought-provoking questions or give Paddy feedback.

Connect:
Find Paddy at a local book talk or meet and greet. Visit her blog and website for dates, times, and locations or to set up your group's virtual discussion. For more excerpts, backstory chapters not found in the book, author interviews, free books, news on latest releases and more visit PaddyEger.com/84Ribbons

About the Author

Paddy Eger's debut YA novel, 84 Ribbons, springs from her years of dance lessons. Between age three and twenty she performed ballet, character, and tap routines for local recitals, hospitals, area musicals, and for a World's Fair.

Although she never became a professional dancer, she is an avid supporter of dance and the arts. 84 Ribbons explores how one young dancer handles such stresses as overwork, eating disorders, depression, and competition. In the 1950s setting of the book, some of these health issues were nameless, but they did exist.

The world of ballet is a wonderful, graceful place peopled by extraordinary dancers, musicians, directors, and choreographers. Through her creative imagination, Paddy constructs a controversial ballet company where the director has little respect for new dancers. Fortunately, most directors value their dancers.

Paddy's love of story, coupled with her years as an educator, encourage her to write for young readers, giving them glimpses of reality through a fictional world.

General Reader's Guide

All of us lead complex and multi-faceted lives.

What are Marta's strengths? Her deficits?

What factors contribute to Marta's reluctance to begin a personal life?

What advice would you have given her during her recovery?

Marta is seventeen when the story begins and eighteen when its end.

What growth do you see in her over the ten months she dances with the Intermountain Dance Company?

What do you imagine happens over the next ten months?

The world of ballet and American society have made major changes since the late 1950s.

What changes have you noticed or heard mentioned?

How have those changes affected your life?

Check out additional information on paddyeger.com/84 Ribbons. You will find articles, information on ballets, Marta's blog, contests to name future characters, and much more as this ballet trilogy continues.

School Reader's Guide

For an extensive guide that follows the Common Core State Standards for ELA 6-12, download the guide file from paddyeger.com/84Ribbons The guide covers:

Key Discussion Questions
Post Reading
Creative Writing Prompt
Internet Resources
Related Readings
Select Interdisciplinary Activities

Coming Soon from Paddy Eger

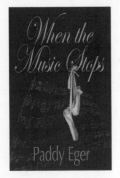

When the Music Stops

Marta's life: Part Two. Marta struggles to regain her ability to dance. As she finds a job to support herself, her dance and her personal life take several unexpected and harrowing turns. Will she be able to find a deeper well of strength to meet these new challenges head-on?

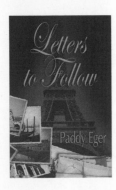

Letters to Follow

Marta's best friend Lynne begins a grand adventure when she travels to Paris on a dancer exchange. Her move to a wacky boarding house is not a good fit for an outspoken American dancer but it creates humorous encounters with the tenants. At the end of the exchange, Lynne becomes the travel companion for her harebrained Uncle Leo. She sends postcards and letters to Marta to retell her madcap adventures.

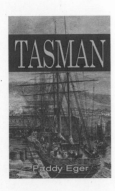

Tasman

In 1850, sixteen year-old Irish lad, Ean McCloud, steps off the boat, his legs in iron shackles, and steps into serving a three-year sentence at the Port Arthur Penal Colony in Tasmania. Falsely convicted, he must now survive the brutal conditions, the backbreaking labor, and time in the silent prison—a place that breaks men's souls. Follow Ean's adventures as he seeks not only to survive but to escape!